Homecoming

HOMECOMING

THE SCOTTISH YEARS OF
MARY, QUEEN OF SCOTS

ROSEMARY GORING

BIRLINN

First published in 2022 by
Birlinn Limited
West Newington House
10 Newington Road
Edinburgh
EH9 1QS

www.birlinn.co.uk

ISBN: 978 1 78027 723 3

British Library Cataloguing-in-Publication Data
A catalogue record for this book is available from the British Library.

Papers used by Birlinn are from well-managed forests and other responsible sources.

Designed and typeset by Hewer Text UK Ltd, Edinburgh
Printed and bound by Clays Ltd, Elcograf S.p.A.

FSC
www.fsc.org
MIX
Paper from
responsible sources
FSC® C018072

Contents

Author's note

The spelling of Stewart and Stuart was often interchangeable well into the sixteenth century, creating endless inconsistency and confusion. Mary's father James V was a Stewart, as were his predecessors, but her husband Henry, Lord Darnley was a Stuart (usually). However, even before her marriage to Darnley, Mary had been designated a Stuart by her French relatives, and by herself. For simplicity, I have used Stuart for her throughout. To emphasise her mother's French background and outlook, and to avoid the repetitive use of Mary, the dowager queen of Scotland, widow of James V and sometime Regent, is referred to as Marie de Guise.

Acknowledgements

This book was written, if not in the worst of times then surely in the strangest for many years. Libraries were shuttered, and the gates of castles, abbeys and ruins padlocked. Throughout it, the staff at Birlinn remained calm and upbeat. My thanks to all who were involved in bringing *Homecoming* safely into port, but especially to Andrew Simmons, whose good sense and shrewd editorial judgement can always be relied upon, and copy-editor Anita Joseph, for her forensic eye. Grateful thanks also to Professor Elizabeth Ewan, of the University of Guelph, who, when gaining access to a library was harder than breaching the walls of Edinburgh Castle, sent me her illuminating essay on the sights, sounds and smells people experienced in a medieval Scottish town.

Sally Craighead enthusiastically acted as chauffeur through the Highlands, which, despite suicidal pheasants determined to drive us over hairpin bends, allowed me to enjoy the scenery. Allan Hunter was untiring in urging me onwards when he sensed I was flagging, often asking, 'How's Mary?' On the home front, my husband Alan Taylor was admirably patient and forbearing, even though he had to tolerate the presence of Mary at breakfast, lunch and dinner. His commentary during jaunts to castles, museums and battlefields certainly enlivened the experience. As if that weren't enough, he made invaluable comments on the text and offered to build the index. My heart-felt thanks.

STEWART/STUART, HAMILTON and LENNOX

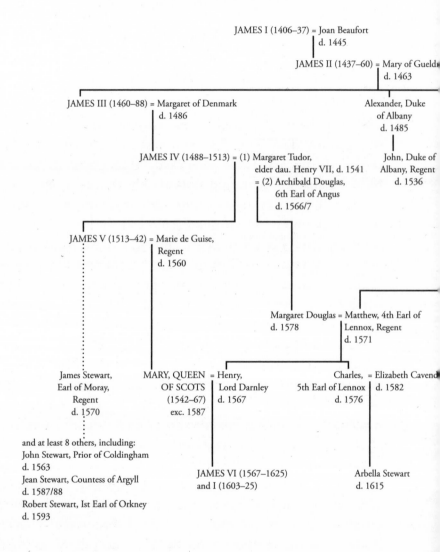

JAMES I (1406–37) = Joan Beaufort
d. 1445

JAMES II (1437–60) = Mary of Gueld•
d. 1463

JAMES III (1460–88) = Margaret of Denmark
d. 1486

Alexander, Duke
of Albany
d. 1485

JAMES IV (1488–1513) = (1) Margaret Tudor,
elder dau. Henry VII, d. 1541
= (2) Archibald Douglas,
6th Earl of Angus
d. 1566/7

John, Duke of
Albany, Regent
d. 1536

JAMES V (1513–42) = Marie de Guise,
Regent
d. 1560

Margaret Douglas = Matthew, 4th Earl of
d. 1578   Lennox, Regent
d. 1571

James Stewart,
Earl of Moray,
Regent
d. 1570

MARY, QUEEN = Henry,
OF SCOTS   Lord Darnley
(1542–67)   d. 1567
exc. 1587

Charles, = Elizabeth Cavend•
5th Earl of Lennox   d. 1582
d. 1576

and at least 8 others, including:
John Stewart, Prior of Coldingham
d. 1563
Jean Stewart, Countess of Argyll
d. 1587/88
Robert Stewart, 1st Earl of Orkney
d. 1593

JAMES VI (1567–1625)
and I (1603–25)

Arbella Stewart
d. 1615

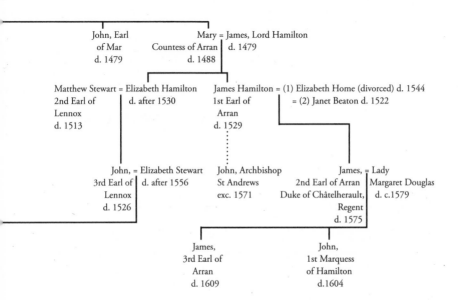

John, Earl
of Mar
d. 1479

Mary = James, Lord Hamilton
Countess of Arran | d. 1479
d. 1488

Matthew Stewart = Elizabeth Hamilton
2nd Earl of   d. after 1530
Lennox
d. 1513

James Hamilton = (1) Elizabeth Home (divorced) d. 1544
1st Earl of   = (2) Janet Beaton d. 1522
Arran
d. 1529

John, = Elizabeth Stewart
3rd Earl of   d. after 1556
Lennox
d. 1526

John, Archbishop
St Andrews
exc. 1571

James, = Lady
2nd Earl of Arran   Margaret Douglas
Duke of Châtelherault,   d. c.1579
Regent
d. 1575

James,
3rd Earl of
Arran
d. 1609

John,
1st Marquess
of Hamilton
d.1604

⋮ illegitimate descent

= married
exc. executed
d. died

GUISE

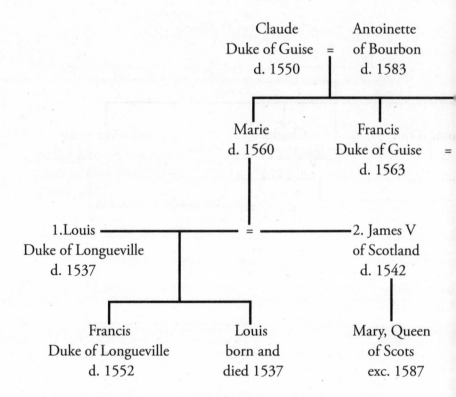

Claude
Duke of Guise = Antoinette
d. 1550   of Bourbon
d. 1583

Marie   Francis
d. 1560   Duke of Guise   =
d. 1563

1.Louis ——————— = ——————— 2. James V
Duke of Longueville   of Scotland
d. 1537   d. 1542

Francis   Louis   Mary, Queen
Duke of Longueville   born and   of Scots
d. 1552   died 1537   exc. 1587

nne d'Este   Charles   and seven more
d. 1607   Cardinal of Lorraine   who lived beyond infancy
                        d. 1574

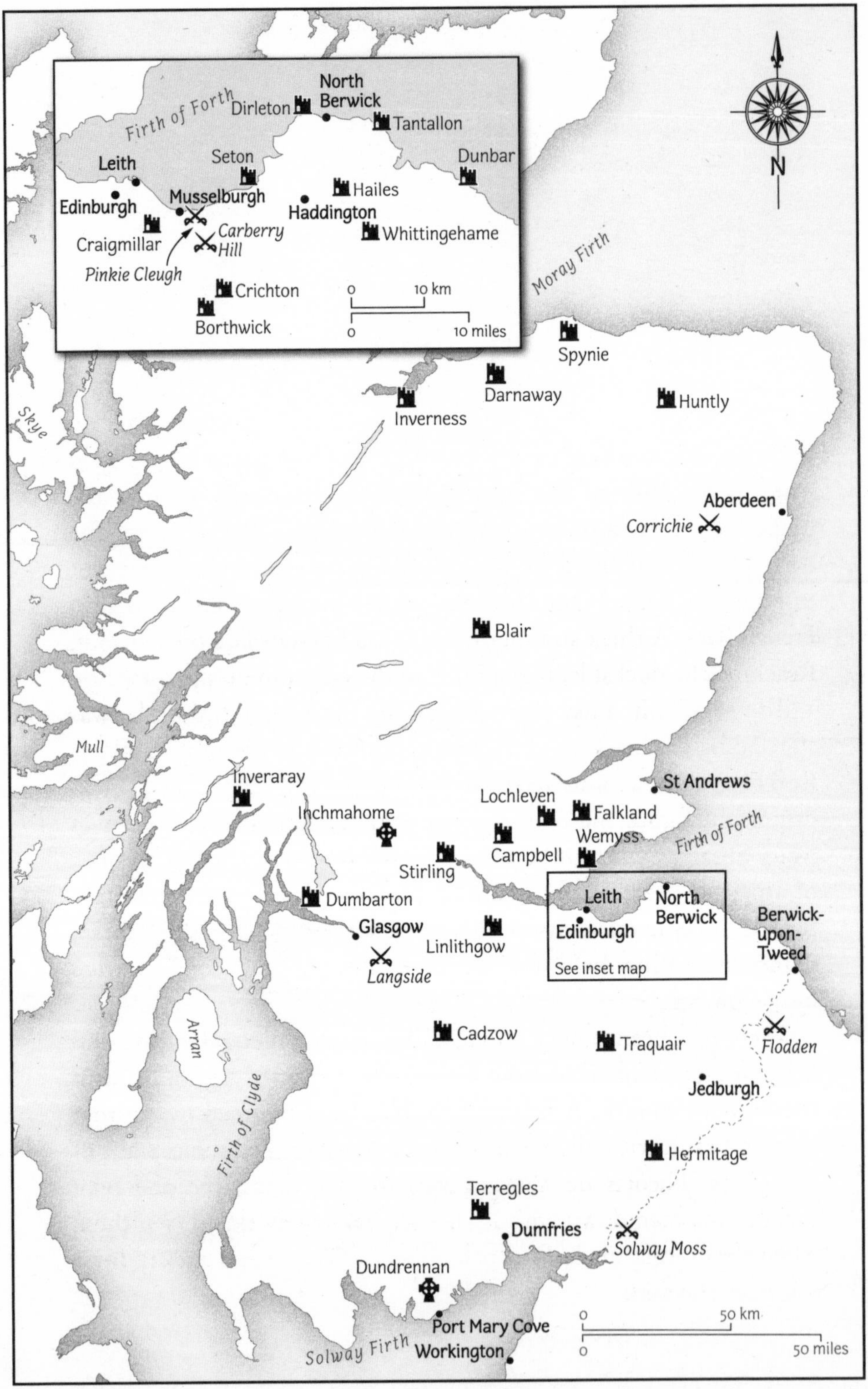

N
Firth of Forth
Dirleton
North Berwick
Tantallon
Leith
Seton
Dunbar
Edinburgh
Musselburgh
Hailes
Haddington
Craigmillar
Carberry Hill
Whittingehame
Pinkie Cleugh
Crichton
Borthwick
0 10 km
0 10 miles
Moray Firth
Spynie
Darnaway
Inverness
Huntly
Skye
Aberdeen
Corrichie
Blair
Mull
Inveraray
St Andrews
Lochleven
Falkland
Inchmahome
Wemyss
Firth of Forth
Campbell
Stirling
Leith
North Berwick
Dumbarton
Edinburgh
Berwick-upon-Tweed
Glasgow
Linlithgow
See inset map
Langside
Arran
Cadzow
Traquair
Flodden
Jedburgh
Firth of Clyde
Hermitage
Terregles
Dumfries
Solway Moss
Dundrennan
Port Mary Cove
Solway Firth
Workington
0 50 km
0 50 miles

Introduction

Early on the morning of 19 August 1561, two galley ships sailed beneath the cliffs of the Berwickshire coastline and, skirting the islands of the Firth of Forth, turned towards the Port of Leith. The oars dipped and lifted in unison, the crew sweating as they cut through the water. One ship was white, the other red; both flew French flags. A thick summer haar, or sea fog, cloaked the harbour. Reaching the dockside, they pulled in the oars and dropped anchor.

The small but busy port, which lay close to Edinburgh, was startled by the blasting of the ships' cannons. It was not a declaration of war but a salute to the woman on board, arguably the most important figure the country had ever welcomed back. She was Mary Stuart, Queen of Scotland, finally returned after an absence of thirteen years. Before setting foot on shore, she must have peered into the mist, wondering what sort of message this murky, damp beginning held for her long-awaited and long-overdue homecoming.

There had been omens enough. Five days earlier, when she and her entourage embarked from Calais, she witnessed a grim scene at the harbour mouth. A fishing boat had been rammed by another ship and sank with all crew on board. Mary begged the captain of her galley, Nicolas de Villegagnon, to save them, but the boat dragged the men down with it. The sea had barely closed over them when her flotilla made for open waters. 'What a sad augury for a journey!' she said.

This distressing episode cannot have eased her feelings of loss and sorrow as her vessel made its way into the Channel and the golden beaches of Calais slowly receded from sight. As the young, newly widowed queen stood at the rail, watching the coast of France disappear, she was tearful: 'Adieu, France, adieu my beloved France, I think I will never see your shores again.' That night, too melancholy to confine herself below deck, she asked her maidservants to bring bedding to the ship's poop. There she slept, as if the sea air would bring her comfort.

It is no wonder she felt forlorn. Mary Stuart had lived at the French court since she was five, having been sent there for safety. Now eighteen, she was in many respects more French than Scottish, although she still spoke Scots. Her English was not so fluent. She had been raised by the French elite, as well as a household of Scottish companions, attendants and servants. In the absence of her mother, her grandmother, Antoinette of Bourbon, and the Duke of Guise's wife, Anne d'Este, took particularly good care of her. Married at fifteen to the king's son Francis, at sixteen she became Queen of France. It would be only a year and a half before her husband died. Until that terrible event occurred, it is hard to imagine the splendour and the atmosphere of sycophancy in which she and the young king lived; or the isolation, since Francis was too feeble to be more than the puppet of powerful figures at court.

Scotland and France were separated by more than language or religion. The code of the court, and its unabashed opulence, were a world away from the mood and manners of Mary's homeland. She had been Queen of Scotland since she was six days old, but despite her country now being in the hands of a Protestant clique, which had ushered in the Reformation and deposed her mother Marie de Guise as Regent, the decision to return had been neither easy nor automatic. For some historians, knowing she swithered for even a day before agreeing to take up her throne is among the first of many indictments that could be made of her. The moment her husband was buried she should have made for Edinburgh.

Instead, Mary weighed up her options. Widowed in December 1560, not long after her mother's death, she spent the next few months doggedly trying to negotiate marriage with Don Carlos, the disabled and mentally unstable son of the King of Spain. This would have made her one of the most powerful royals in Europe. Around the same time, emissaries from the Scottish Parliament were followed by her older half-brother, James Stewart, illegitimate son of James V, who paid a visit to the French court. He was one of the Protestant reformers who had toppled her mother; his mission was not to cause dread but to assure her that she would be welcomed in Scotland. He promised that although the country was now Protestant she would be allowed to continue to practise her Catholic faith without interference.

Don Carlos was alarmingly underweight and had so many disabilities he made the puny and sickly Francis, King of France, look robust. Yet only when all hope of this union was quashed did Mary turn her face north. Rather than remain in France as dowager queen, where she would have lived in luxury on the income from her extensive estates, she decided to leave. It was the most important decision of her life thus far, and she knew it might not end well. As she told the English ambassador, she had resolved to 'hazard all she had' and return to rule her people.

It was a serious gamble, but, as an inveterate card and games player who had inherited her father James V's impetuosity, taking risks was in Mary's blood. Her mind made up, she announced her imminent departure and spent the summer touring her estates and visiting her Guise relatives. It was a protracted business, taking her from Fontainebleau to Nancy, Rheims and Joinville among other of the Guise properties. And it was not uneventful. As so often before and later, Mary fell seriously ill and was bed-bound and frail for weeks. The emotional strain of the past eighteen months, in which she had lost her father-in-law, her mother and her husband, had caught up with her.

Yet poor health conveniently allowed her to deflect political pressure. Mary's party would require safe conduct through England on their way to Scotland in case their ships were obliged to put into port before they reached the border, but her cousin Elizabeth I insisted

Mary must first ratify the controversial Treaty of Edinburgh. Its terms obliged her to renounce all claim to the English throne. Mary prevaricated, saying she was too unwell to take such a serious decision and needed to consult with Parliament when she reached Holyrood.

The young widow's farewell tour culminated in St Germain in Paris, where a spectacular four-day fête was held in her honour. After this she left for Calais, although the details of her journey were kept secret for fear of an English ambush. On the quayside, her uncle, the Cardinal of Lorraine, had last-minute qualms about her hoard of jewels going on board with her. Perhaps, he suggested, she should hand them to him for safekeeping. If she did not laugh outright, Mary surely smiled as she reminded him that if he was happy to trust her to the ship, then her jewellery would be no less safe.

Once underway, with France behind her and Scotland far off, Mary's spirits dipped. She knew far too little of the country she was intending to govern. The optimism of youth carried her only so far; the prospect of leaving everything familiar behind her, of picking up the reins in an alien place, with no mother to guide her, must have been daunting. Perhaps the haar that hid the galleys' entrance to the Port of Leith suited her mood that August morning, blurring the edges of what she would quickly learn was a calloused and critical nation.

Nevertheless, as she stepped onto the flagstones of the dockside, she appeared invigorated by the adventure that lay ahead of her. Always in times of crisis or drama, Mary rose to the occasion. She liked nothing better than a challenge. She looked magnificent too. Her arrival, days earlier than expected, meant nobody was prepared for her. But at the roar of the cannons, word raced through the fog-bound port and a crowd gathered. Onlookers were rewarded with a sight they would never forget. Although dressed in mourning black, with a white veil, the queen radiated glamour and regal assurance. People's response was so warm that she was soon smiling, immediately winning hearts. Surrounding her was a posse of attendants and relatives. Her Guise uncles led the way – not the cardinal or the duke, who remained in France to further their own interests – followed by Mary's closest companions. The famous four Maries had been her friends since childhood, and the richness of their clothes, and their ornate head-dresses, would have made people gape.

* * *

Homecoming is an account of Mary's time in Scotland, and the buildings and places where she made history. More of her life was spent out of the country than within, but most of the pivotal choices and life-changing events that shaped her destiny happened in her homeland. Had she opted never to return, she would have been a distant, shadowy, romantic figure, dislocated from her roots. If she had enjoyed a long and happy life in France or elsewhere, she would never have been the woman she was born to be. Whatever else can be said about her short and ultimately pitiful reign, and the anguish of the years that followed, it was better for her, and for Scotland, that she took up her throne. That she failed to control the competing factions at her own court and the political machinations in Elizabethan England was not necessarily her fault. Could Scotland, in those remorseless times, have been as culpable for her downfall as either her enemies or her unwise decisions?

Mary was five when she left Scotland, but those early years in the care of her shrewd French mother were crucial in forming her sense of herself and her inheritance. This book covers the period of her childhood before her departure in 1548 and picks up once more when she returns in 1561. Although a great deal happened in the time she spent out of the country, especially during almost nineteen years of captivity in England before her death in 1587, Scotland was the crucible in which her fortunes were forged. She was here, as an adult, for a mere seven years, from August 1561 to May 1568, but she left an indelible impression. While her own tragedy is evergreen, the subject of endless speculation, there is no question that her impact on the affairs of people and parliament, and ultimately upon the country's historical trajectory, has been incalculable.

It is not only Mary's political stamp that can still be detected. Many of the places where her story unfolded remain largely intact, whether castles, houses, palaces or battlefields. Those that have disappeared beneath towns and development or which now lie in ruins, are not so much forgotten as laid to rest. But the surviving buildings where she lived and the still recognisable landscapes she knew well add a physical, material dimension to history. The events that took shape around Mary, Queen of Scots grow deeper and darker when you can touch the walls she touched, or take the narrow winding stairs she climbed in her heels and rustling skirts. The same applies to the unimaginable clash of armies, at locations such as Langside or Carberry Hill. Here, even the most vivid imagination struggles to bridge the gulf between modern rural tranquillity or suburban streets, and an era of swords, daggers and shotguns. Tracing Mary's steps puts past events on a human scale, shrinking the distance between then and now. It also reinforces the stark difference between her world and our own.

In *Homecoming*, the question of who is to blame for Mary's misfortunes, and what sort of Scotland she returned to, is explored around the locations that feature most prominently in her career. During the open-ended years of imprisonment in England she must have run their names through her mind – Holyroodhouse, Stirling Castle, Seton Palace, Kirk o' Field, Dundrennan Abbey – as if she were fingering beads on a rosary. By this point, languishing as she was in varying degrees of comfort in castles and stately homes, she was left with nothing but memories, grudges and dreams.

From Inverness to Galloway, Langside to Dunbar, the key moments of Mary's life gradually came together to form a pattern. A design that had begun with great promise and goodwill on her return to Scotland as its eighteen-year-old queen was to end on the executioner's block. Nobody, of course, knew that at the time. Place by place, mile by mile, history was made: her birth at Linlithgow Palace, as her father lay dying in Falkland Palace; her mother's cleverly calculated flight to the safety of Stirling Castle, where her infant could not be snatched; the imposing fortress of Dumbarton Castle, from where the child queen sailed for France, her ship under the same captain who later brought her home; Holyrood Palace, where she encountered her Parliament, and allies and foes alike, culminating in the murder of her dear friend David Rizzio . . . On and on the drama goes, unfolding in palatial homes such as Huntly Castle, or hunting lodges such as Traquair House, or fortresses like Hermitage Castle, or the island prison of Lochleven, where it seemed she might just manage to reverse all her misfortunes. And, of course, on the field of battle the enduring medieval nature of royal rule was laid bare. Leading her troops was a role well suited to Mary's courageous temperament, which faltered only at the very end, before she fled.

Standing at the entrance to some of these buildings, the enormity of the young queen's task can be felt. The minatory appearance of defensive structures such as Edinburgh or Hermitage castles highlights the constant threat Mary faced. Scorch marks on the cobbles in St Andrews were a reminder of martyrs burned at the stake, the stains as black as if their boiling blood had been tar. Heads of criminals and traitors were stuck on spikes outside towns or on castle walls, as both warning and spectacle. There would be frequent days when, from Holyrood Palace or Stirling Castle, Mary heard carpenters preparing the gallows for another man to swing.

Despite the cultural advances of the Renaissance, which was evident in many of the finest palaces and castles, these were harsh times. Refinements in debate and philosophy, in art and music, were not matched by an end to brutal retribution. The composure Mary showed on the day of her execution, at Fotheringhay Castle on 8 February 1587, suggests that royals in this century, as in all those before it, always knew their death might be violent and public. In a sense they were almost bred to prepare for it. And they knew that, in those circumstances, dignity would be as important as bravery, the final verdict on their legacy.

All of this can be intuited in the places Mary visited or lived, as can intimations of the luxury with which she was surrounded. But no matter the extravagant Flemish tapestries or the procession of rich courses at her dining table, the comforts even the least privileged Scots take for granted today were unheard of then: clean drinking water from a tap, central heating, bathroom plumbing, light in the dead of night at the flick of a switch.

By comparison, the queen and her lowest subjects drank beer rather than water, which was less likely to cause illness. Sanitation, even for the rich, was primitive. Over time, the middens outside a castle's walls would grow so foul no window could be opened. The streets of towns and cities reeked of ordure, gutted fish, offal, and the unburied corpses not just of animals but of people.

Seeing where and how Mary lived adds a third dimension to understanding her and her era. Her mind was filled with matters elevated and basic. Medical knowledge was rudimentary, although many understood the beneficial properties of plants. Frequently unwell, the queen often had recourse to such knowledge. The distances travelled on horseback or by litter, as she visited her realm, show the importance of horses to the work of royalty. When Mary's ship and its partner set sail from Calais, it was accompanied by at least twelve others, conveying vast quantities of furniture, clothes, bed linens, tapestries, candlesticks and paintings. Also on board were over a hundred horses and mules.

Elizabeth had, finally, granted a safe passage, but the courier dispatched to hand it to Mary before she left France did not reach her in time, in part because her whereabouts were unknown. As the royal galleys sailed up the North Sea, an English fleet was close behind. It did not engage but loomed in the near distance, a decidedly ominous presence. Eventually, Elizabeth's men boarded one of the baggage ships, which was carrying Mary's horses, on the pretext of searching for pirates. The horses were detained for a month at Tynemouth before being ridden north. This was nothing more than sabre-rattling, but in the meantime Mary was without her favourite palfrey, which she rode on formal occasions. For such a horse-lover and first-class rider, this was a serious irritation.

Such small, seemingly trivial details broaden our view of the past, emphasising the gulf between Mary's life and that of ordinary citizens in her own era and in ours. *Homecoming* is an attempt to capture the essence and feel of her everyday affairs, as well as the spectacular events that occurred while she was in Scotland. Pegged on the buildings and places where many of these events occurred, this retelling is, in a sense, a travelogue or guide to Mary's Scotland, shadowing her footsteps from birth until her final departure.

Homecoming ends on the coast of the Solway Firth, after the queen's horse had splashed through the burn towards the boat that was to carry her to England. Despite assuring her followers that she would be back by the end of August, she would never return. She was to spend nearly twenty years as a prisoner, in increasingly fragile health. That life sentence appears so never-ending, filled with abortive attempts to free her and too many months of excruciating boredom, it can come as a surprise to remember that when eventually she died she was only forty-four. That was not young in 1587, but Mary had aged far more than her years, even by contemporary standards. The effects of incarceration, too little exercise, mental torment and damp, cold apartments took their toll. For such an active, sporting woman, confinement was especially cruel. Worse was her cousin Elizabeth's refusal ever to meet her. It must have been an exceptionally dark day when Mary discovered that her faith in Elizabeth helping her regain her throne was misplaced, and that her advisors, who had begged her to stay in Scotland, had been right all along.

Between 1568 and her death in 1587, Mary was moved between locations and captors. She began her life as a prisoner in Carlisle Castle, then Bolton Castle, followed by a series of well-guarded residences, such as Tutbury Castle and Chartley Hall, under the guard of gaolers as decent as Sir Ralph Sadler and the Earl of Shrewsbury, and as harsh as her final keeper, Sir Amyas Paulet. Her last days were spent in Fotheringhay Castle.

These dragging years saw an inquiry by the English court into Mary's role in Darnley's murder. She was not allowed to testify, but despite the best efforts of George Buchanan and the Earl of Moray to besmirch Mary, using the infamous Casket Letters, they failed to persuade the commissioners of her hand in her husband's death. A later attempt to marry the Duke of Norfolk backfired by rousing Elizabeth's wrath. When Norfolk was subsequently found plotting Elizabeth's removal with the help of Spain, he was executed. This dastardly scheme dramatically turned English public opinion against Mary, who was seen as a 'monstrous dragon' aiming to restore Catholic rule to the country by killing their sovereign.

Worse was to follow. Late in her captivity there were attempts to negotiate Mary's release and permit her to return as joint ruler to Scotland. According to a recently discovered letter from Elizabeth to Mary's current captor, Sir Ralph Sadler, in 1584, the Queen of England was prepared to consider such a momentous step. She asked Sadler to discover Mary's terms should her liberation be agreed. Mary's reply stressed that, once freed, she would renounce all claim to the English throne and never plot against Elizabeth. She would uphold the Protestant Reformation and rule Scotland jointly, with her son James, who was by now eighteen years old, and allow Elizabeth to vet whomever James wished to marry.

For a brief spell, Mary seemed poised to be restored to Scotland. What might then have happened is the stuff of fiction. With the Catholic Mary and Protestant James ruling the country between them, things would certainly have been interesting. But it was only at this late stage in her life that Mary discovered how wholly her son had been turned against her while she had been absent. He was not the doting child of her deluded imagination, whom she hoped would one day rescue her. James would have nothing to do with this proposal, insisting he alone was Scotland's monarch. Instead, he made a separate arrangement with Elizabeth, thereby leaving his mother to her fate. Perhaps feeling all other avenues had been exhausted now that even her own son had abandoned her, Mary became embroiled in the so-called Babington Plot to dispose of Elizabeth and put her on the throne.

Although the instigator of the plot, young Sir Anthony Babington, was an ardent supporter of Mary, whom he saw as a Catholic martyr, his scheme played into the hands of Elizabeth's foremost agent, Sir Francis Walsingham. Walsingham's goal was to engineer Mary's end and, with a network of spies to rival George Smiley's, he slowly closed the trap around her. Mary had already been told by the English Parliament that any plot that was discovered which intended to help her, even if she was entirely unaware of it, would lead to her death. Yet, far from distancing herself from Babington's proposals, she eagerly replied. When this incriminating letter was intercepted, Elizabeth was left with little option but to put Parliament's injunction into practice.

Previously, despite the urging of her advisors, Elizabeth had been unable to contemplate having a crowned queen executed, since the implications for her own safety were unthinkable. Now that Mary had been found actively scheming against her, she was forced to act. Even so, Elizabeth vacillated, finding this final decision almost beyond her. But once she had issued the command, the Scottish queen was dead within days. In the early hours of the morning of her execution, Mary wrote movingly to her brother-in-law, Henri III of France. A sonnet, thought to have been included with that letter and recently discovered in the Bodleian Library, shows Mary's state of mind. Describing herself as 'lacking health and heart and peace', she continues, 'Ask only that my misery should cease.'

The composure with which Mary faced the axeman, and the horror of his misplaced blows, has fascinated every generation since. Whatever one thinks of her as a ruler, no one can question her courage and nerve. In this, as in so many other facets of her life, she was truly queenly.

Mary's reputation has been barnacled down the centuries by layer upon layer of supposition, misinformation and opinion. It is hard to remember she was once a proud, vivacious young woman with hopes and aspirations like any other royal of her era. By following her trail through the Scottish countryside, and the various houses and castles where she visited and lived, it is possible to catch a fleeting glimpse of her and remember she was as full of vigour and plans as anyone who ever lived.

Buildings speak loudly about the society for which they were designed. Despite their sumptuous furnishings, all of Mary's haunts were heavily defended, ready at a moment's notice to fend off assault.

Some, like Holyrood Palace, had a drawbridge that could be raised to seal it off. Others had ramparts, from which guards could rain arrows and shot on besiegers, as at Hermitage or Crichton castles. Not a few, such as Stirling and Edinburgh, had rows of cannons, with which to send armies running. Even the most decorative and graceful, like Falkland and Seton palaces, had walls too thick for gunpowder or siege engines to breach.

These fortifications continued indoors. Quite apart from gun-loops, arrow slits and portcullises, whose purpose was to deter those outside, most of the residences where Mary stayed came furnished with their personal prisons. Some were windowless pits in which enemies or criminals were left to starve to death, out of earshot. Others were blessed with a latrine and barred windows that let in fresh air. Upstairs there were furnished rooms with thick wooden doors, fitted with bolts and locks, which could be pressed into service as temporary prisons. Wherever she went, Mary's miserable future was prefigured in the rooms and dungeons around her. Familiar with the history of the wives of Henry VIII, or the fate of Lady Jane Grey, or the princes in the towers, she would not have been unaware of the implications for her own safety in these menacing provisions.

Early in her captivity in England, while still in Carlisle, Mary was visited by the Puritan Sir Francis Knollys, who was impressed by her. 'She showeth a readiness to expose herself to all perils in hope of victory,' he reported. 'The thing that most she thirsteth after is victory.' Mary never disguised the ends to which she was prepared to go to save herself, telling Knollys, 'being a desperate person, I will use any attempts that may serve my purpose, either by myself or my friends'. It was the same fighting spirit in which she had returned to Scotland.

Homecoming does not follow Mary into England, yet the decisions she took while in Scotland, and the depth of enmity she inspired in her Protestant foes, laid the foundation for her tragic end. We could view each of these steps, which ultimately led her across the border, as a line of gunpowder whose fuse took nineteen years to ignite. Her captivity was a terrible ordeal, but it was the manner in which she negotiated her reign that brought her there. Her attitude to her homeland, and the country's response to its new ruler, decided her future. Like her grandfather and father before her, Mary, Queen of Scots was a consummate risk-taker. Like them, hazarding everything she had led ultimately to her death.

Chapter 1

'As goodly a child as I have seen'

LINLITHGOW PALACE

The room where Mary Stuart probably was born lies open to the sky. In the north-west corner of Linlithgow Palace, it has no floor, and its deeply recessed window, looking north across the loch, appears to hover in the middle of a wall. Visitors can stand in what was once the king's sumptuous bedroom suite and, craning their necks, try to picture the lying-in chamber two storeys overhead, in the small room above the queen's bedchamber. It was here that, on either Thursday 7 or Friday 8 December 1542, the infant who was to become one of the most famous – and infamous – European rulers made her first appearance. Outside, the country was in the grip of a ferocious winter. Inside, fires blazed, sending plumes of smoke over the market town of Linlithgow below.

Even though today Linlithgow Palace is in ruins, verdigrised by moss and damp, its scale and grandeur are striking. Sandstone walls glow pink and rose depending on the light. Had Mary spent her childhood here, she would have soaked up a sense of entitlement and privilege. Set above a loch on which swans regally glide, and surrounded by grass and trees, for a small, impoverished and, in some minds, primitive country, it was a magnificently sophisticated royal dwelling. Mary's mother, Marie de Guise, brought up close to the wealth and splendour of the French court, considered it as fine as any French chateau. As the backdrop for the opening act of Mary's life, it could not have been better designed. The timing, however, was dreadful.

Since the baby princess arrived with greater haste than expected, Marie de Guise was unprepared. It is thought that the stress of her husband's illness contributed to Mary's sudden birth, and it's little wonder if this was the case. James V was perilously ill when Marie went into labour. After a shocking military defeat by the English at the Battle of Solway Moss two weeks earlier, he had made a fleeting visit to see his heavily pregnant wife in Linlithgow. James then retreated to the royal hunting lodge of Falkland Palace, where he took to his bed. What should have been a happy, hopeful time for the king and queen, whose first two children had died in infancy, was instead fraught with worry and fear. Informed of his daughter's birth – messages travelled slowly across ice- and snow-bound roads – James is said to have turned his face to the wall in despair, saying, 'It came with a lass and it will go with a lass.' Six days of delirium followed, and then he died.

It is not impossible that the cause of his death was a broken heart, as some contemporaries believed, but it is more likely he had contracted a disease during the campaign, perhaps dysentery from contaminated water, or cholera. His cryptic words about lasses referred to the House of Stewart. The throne had passed to the Stewarts when Marjorie Bruce, ill-fated daughter of Robert the Bruce, married Walter Stewart, the High Steward of Scotland in 1314. James doubtless presumed the family name would pass to another dynasty on his daughter's own marriage in years to come. Like everyone else, he could not have predicted Mary's tumultuous career, nor the eventual triumph of his grandson James VI who, in 1603, took the throne of England as well as Scotland. In so doing he perpetuated the Stuart hold on power and united both countries in a manner unthinkable a century earlier.

While James had retreated to his bed in Falkland, his wife, gripped by contractions, was in her lying-in room. Normally women went into confinement some weeks before their baby was due, to prepare themselves. Marie de Guise, however, was taken by surprise.

Unless in exceptional circumstances when a doctor was required, a birth was an exclusively female event. As with other royals, Marie de Guise had a midwife in attendance, a luxury poorer women could not afford. As the room was hastily made ready, tapestries were hung over the window to keep out the light and protect the pregnant woman's eyes. The fire was stoked, heating the cold stone walls. Herbs might have been thrown onto the flames or strewn among the rushes on the floor to scent the air and soothe the mother-to-be.

There was much superstition and dread around childbirth; in this period one in three women did not survive their child-bearing years. Rank played a part in protecting the well-off from some of the dangers, since a midwife was skilled in delivery. She could intervene to turn a breech position, and if the mother had died in labour, could perform a caesarean in the hope of saving the baby. If it looked as if the infant would not survive to be baptised formally, a midwife had the right to conduct this ceremony, although she had to make sure she pronounced the liturgy correctly. There was a case in France where the midwife muddled her words and was ordered to leave the profession.

As soon as Mary was born, she was taken by the midwife to be bathed, swaddled and suckled by a wet nurse. Wet nurses were carefully vetted for character, since they would be feeding the baby for the next eighteen months and more. In this respect, aristocratic women were less fortunate than commoners. Breastfeeding reduces fertility, meaning that everyday mothers often had a couple of years' grace between children. Noble women, in contrast, were frequently in a state of almost permanent pregnancy. There could be no mistaking the role they were intended to perform in producing sufficient heirs for the safe succession of title and wealth.

Once the infant Mary had been fed, she was then returned to her mother and placed in a cradle by her bed. All midwives had to take an oath to promise they would not remove anything that could later be used by witches, such as the placenta, umbilical cord or cowl. With so many hazards surrounding a birth, it is not surprising that fear of supernatural malice was rife. Even if Marie's attendants gave her talismans or holy artefacts to help her through the ordeal, she would have been praying. Afterwards too. Reports that the premature infant was weak and unlikely to survive spread fast, but whether or not they had any basis in truth – it was also said that Marie de Guise was at death's door – she would have been asking God to protect her child at every turn.

Oblivious to the treacherous political landscape into which she had been born, at six days old, on 14 December 1542, Mary Stuart became Queen of Scotland. She was not the first royal to inherit the throne so prematurely, and while living in these quarters. Thirty years earlier, in April 1512, her father had been born in the same room. As one of the family's favourite homes, the palace's comfort and quiet made it appealing as a royal nursery. Eighteen months after James's grand baptism in the palace chapel on Easter Sunday, he became king when, on 9 September 1513, his father James IV was killed on the battlefield at Flodden in Northumberland on the border between England and Scotland.

James's mother, Margaret Tudor, sister of Henry VIII, had also given birth prematurely, and was obliged to send out hastily for provisions. At this point, Margaret Tudor's future looked bright, and widowhood was the last thing on her mind. At the time of her son James's arrival, life was good. Her husband, James IV, was in the political ascendant, leading Scotland into the Renaissance age and forging influential links with European monarchy, notably King Louis XII of France, a liaison that was to prove disastrous. He had also, seemingly, set aside the country's long and bitter hostility with England, although the agreement of peace, signed by James IV and Henry VII in 1502, was dangerously close to buckling.

An intellectual, artistic and exceptionally pious man (despite his many marital infidelities), James IV had remodelled much of the palace. The site of a royal manor house since the twelfth century, it was built by David I, who also founded the burgh of Linlithgow. Much of the original residence was destroyed by fire in 1424, but the following year James I began to rebuild it, and James III further extended it. With an even grander vision in mind, James IV made major renovations and updates as a gift for Margaret, ahead of their marriage in 1503. Rising over Linlithgow, twenty miles west of Edinburgh, this soaring fortress was as loud a statement of confidence and regal ambition as Versailles or the Schönbrunn Palace would be. Its towering influence over this unassuming town must have been considerable. Even now the palace dominates the skyline, though it no longer shines at night with braziers and candles, or torchlit processions of visitors and tradesfolk arriving at the gate.

Marie de Guise's delight in her daughter must have been mingled with concern. Losing children was a common occurrence, even for the richest and most pampered. It was a sorrow little spoken of, but the fate of the young sons who had succumbed to illness so recently must have been at the front of her mind. And initially, Mary did not appear to be thriving.

Rumours that she was sickly spread as fast as the frozen roads permitted. One informant reported to Henry VIII that she had died, telling him what he wanted to hear. Others were unimpressed that James V's heir was not a son. The religious reformer John Knox, in his unashamedly biased history of these times, recalled that 'all men lamented that the realm was left without a male to succeed'. It is possibly his only utterance with which the dead king would have agreed. There was no altering the baby's gender, but Marie was keen to dispel the notion of Mary's precarious health. When the English envoy, Sir Ralph Sadler, paid a visit three months later, Marie ordered her nurse to unwind the infant's swaddling, to show how fine and fit she was. Sadler was duly impressed, informing Henry VIII, 'it is as goodly a child as I have seen of her age, and as like to live, with the grace of God'.

Within a few days of birth, Mary had been baptised in St Michael's Church outside the palace's southern gate. The Treasurer's Accounts record 54 shillings for white taffeta purchased for the occasion. Since 8 December was celebrated as the Virgin Mary's birthday, Mary was named in her honour. Yet Mary's ambassador and later historian, John Leslie, having had special access to the royal records, claimed in his *Historie of Scotland* (1578) that she was born on 7 December. At this distance, as with so many details of the queen's life, it is impossible to know with certainty what is true. She, for one, always believed it was the 8th.

A feature of the town since the fifteenth century, St Michael's now has a spiky aluminium spire, designed in the 1960s by Sir Basil Spence. On sunny days, this eye-catching feature, representing Jesus Christ's crown of thorns, draws the attention of travellers on the train between Edinburgh and Glasgow, but in Mary's lifetime it had a spire more like that of St Giles' Cathedral in Edinburgh.

Sadler and other guests eager to see the infant queen would have been received in her mother's apartments, on the second floor of the north-west tower, above the king's quarters. The walls were hung with tapestries for warmth and colour, and in the great freeze of 1542, even though the windows were glazed, there would have been furs in abundance to cocoon the royal widow and her child's cradle from draughts.

They say it takes a village to raise a child, and Linlithgow Palace was several villages rolled into one. The king's servants were dressed in scarlet and yellow, the queen's French retinue in black. Hundreds were employed here, some living under the same roof as the royals, often sleeping on the floor, as skivvies, cooks, maidservants, wet nurses, seamstresses, butlers, porters, nursemaids, ladies-in-waiting, grooms, pages and guards – to mention but a few. A woman was employed simply to rock the baby's cradle, and others to unswaddle and change her. An evil-looking oversized toasting fork in the palace museum is in fact a spear for catching eels, known as a leister. It is proof that, along with an abundance of fish, the loch was rich in food to be roasted, stewed, griddled or pickled. The household employed experts to bring in a daily catch, whenever the ice permitted. From 1424 to James V's era there would also have been a perpetual soundtrack to palace life of hammering and the chink of chisels, as successive kings added their stamp to the palace.

James V's mainly cosmetic additions include the jewel-like entrance archway, embossed with heraldic motifs, and an ornate painted stone fountain in the courtyard. This flowed with water, brought by lead pipes from a spring in the town. On special occasions it splashed with wine, easily supplied from the cavernous cellars conveniently located close to the king's rooms, and connected by one of the palace's many turnpike stairs. The fountain has been substantially renovated, and on arriving in the French-style courtyard, it is the first thing to catch the eye. If it is impressive today, what must it have been like when it was brightly painted, mirroring the rich clothes and jewels of the nobles at court? Sculpted with a profusion of figures, among them lion, griffin, unicorns, mermaid, drummer and cherubs, it is laden with symbolic meaning, some of it sadly lost down the years.

Nothing prepares the visitor for the beauty and magnificence of this, the favourite royal residence of many kings. Although the town is attractive, the palace is spectacular. In 1542, the contrast must have been even more striking, and deliberately so, as the Stewarts, with their love of theatre, did all in their power to reinforce their image.

Built in four wings around a central courtyard, its northern wing is just possibly where James and Mary were born. This part of the palace collapsed in 1607 and was rebuilt by James VI. Compared with the north-west tower, it offered an abundance of space for the king's consort, in keeping with her status. Yet if this had been the case, as the palace guidebook suggests, surely these living quarters would have been replicated in the updated design?

There is great charm, and an echo of bygone pride and pomp, in this extraordinary place, whose gaping windows and tumbledown ramparts are home to crows and rooks. While they patrol the walls, chattering and cawing and unconcerned by the click and flash of cameras, it is also the haunt of pigeons. Launching themselves off its parapets, they float like paragliders over the loch hundreds of feet below. Five centuries ago, they would not have been so carefree. Birds and fowl of every kind lived in danger of being served up in pies by an army of cooks and servants in the vast kitchens downstairs, where the fireplaces were big enough to stand in.

While I was strolling through the open-air rooms, a class of primary-school pupils was being coached by their teacher ahead of a performance in the Great Hall. It brought a welcome touch of life into a space once filled with voices and laughter. Following a warren of passageways and narrow stone stairs up and down all four wings, the profusion of rooms is disorientating: among them the chapel, banqueting hall, presence chamber, bedrooms, cellars, kitchens, privies. There is even, on the rooftop, a small turret, like the crow's nest on a ship. It is said that from here Margaret Tudor scanned the horizon, waiting in vain for her husband to return from Flodden.

From such a vantage point, the view across the rolling fields and hills of West Lothian is spectacular. In 1542 it needed to be. The single good thing to come from James V's untimely death was Henry VIII's pause in hostilities, an unusually chivalrous move for such a warmonger. The general of his army had persuaded him to hold fire, urging that it 'should not be to Your Majesty's honour that we, your soldiers, should make war or invade upon a dead body or upon a widow or on a young suckling, his daughter, and specially upon the time of the funerals of the said King, at which time all his realm must lament'.

* * *

Since 1513, when James IV had led an army into England, the two countries had been intermittently but incessantly at war. The disaster of Flodden, in which Scotland lost about 10,000 men, many from the ruling class, was still raw. By the time James V was old enough to rule, there was trouble domestically among his nobles, and internationally as the main European powers – France, Spain, Germany, the Netherlands and the Hapsburg empire – vied for pre-eminence. England, meanwhile, was desperate to assert its claim to be Scotland's overlord. This was a state of mind that, since Edward I's reign and the Wars of Independence led by Robert the Bruce, had often flared into conflict.

Flodden saw an end to the Treaty of Perpetual Peace, and Henry VIII, who was James V's uncle, and had once plotted to kidnap him, took every opportunity to remind him that he considered

Scotland his. The calamitous Battle of Solway Moss was the result of James refusing to meet Henry in York, where he feared for his safety. James led a reluctant army into the north-west of England, where his forces were either slaughtered or, when retreating, floundered and drowned in the oncoming tide of the Solway estuary. Twelve hundred of his men were taken prisoner, among them one of his closest courtiers, Oliver Sinclair, leader of his troops.

James was one of a succession of child kings, and his realm was ruled by a regent until he came of age. The long line of regents since 1424 (five minorities and regents) has been seen by some historians as diminishing the royal family's status and authority. Jenny Wormald argues the opposite. She offers evidence to suggest that Scottish nobles helped kings eject troublesome factions in order to maintain a strong Crown, which was very much to their advantage. Even so, by the time James died, competing noble families were circling the crown like jackals around a carcass. These were powerful individuals, many of them related to the king and the infant queen, such as the earls of Arran, Huntly and Argyll. As Antonia Fraser writes in her unsurpassed biography of Mary: 'Kinship as a concept was all-important in Scotland of the period: unfortunately kinship to the monarchy was universally held to strengthen the position of the family concerned, rather than add to the resources of the monarchy.' However it is viewed, the country into which Mary was born was balanced on a knife edge.

The tight-knit kin system, however, did have great benefits in helping to keep law and order throughout a far-flung, often inaccessible country. Mary's story has sometimes been written as if Scotland was outrageously ungovernable and treacherous, a precursor of Sicily in its deadly mafia-like anarchy. This is unhelpful, suggesting as it does that the elements of the tragedy that were to unfold can be blamed largely on a barbarous nation compared to its more enlightened English and European neighbours. Instead of proving vengeful and tyrannical, the Crown had shown remarkable restraint in dealing with those who stepped over the line. The phrase *primus inter pares* – first among equals – describes the position of the Scottish monarch in these times. It was a double-edged sword that, when Mary fell heir, made the country vulnerable to outside interference.

There was no question in 1542 of Marie de Guise, a foreigner and a woman, stepping into the dead king's shoes as Regent. It was bad enough that the heir was female. The family next in line to the throne was the Hamiltons, whose head was James Hamilton, Earl of Arran. He was extraordinarily indecisive and wavering in his loyalties and beliefs, switching sides so often he could never be relied upon. His claim was contested by the Lennox Stewarts (from which family Lord Darnley came), but Arran would have immediately assumed the role had he not been challenged by the wily churchman, Cardinal David Beaton. Beaton produced a will reputedly made by James V in which he split the governance of the country between him, Arran, and three others – Huntly, Moray and Argyll. According to this document, Beaton was given pre-eminence, including oversight of Mary.

Since the will was palpably a forgery, the cardinal's claims were rejected, and he was arrested. Meanwhile, those nobles taken prisoner at the Battle of Solway Moss, who had come under Henry VIII's influence, were allowed to return home in exchange for hostages and on one condition: that they pressed Henry's case for Mary to marry his five-year-old son Edward, the Prince of Wales.

Nearly forty years earlier, when James IV married Henry VII's young daughter Margaret Tudor, the union had signalled his intention of keeping the peace with his neighbour. Eventually, at Flodden, that accord came to a brutal end, nearly destroying Scotland in the process. James V had married two French aristocrats, with the aim of strengthening the auld alliance between their countries, but his death presented Henry VIII with an opportunity to improve his position. A marriage between his son Edward and the infant Scottish queen would give him a direct hand in ruling Scotland. At the same time it closed a dangerous back door from which France, Scotland's long-time ally, could attack England from the north.

Arran became Lord Governor in January 1543, and immediately

the mood changed. Internal jostling for supremacy was paused, in light of Henry's demands. Marie de Guise was a wise mother and dowager queen, and did not openly dismiss the idea of this alliance. In such a turbulent age, it might even have proved advantageous for her daughter. A portrait of Edward from around this time, attributed to William Scrots, shows a pale-skinned, russet-haired boy, already dressed with imperial grandeur. He wears a feathered black chapeau, yellow silk doublet and hose, slashed embroidered sleeves, and a leather short-sleeved cloak lined with white fur. He is holding a short sword, and staring at the viewer with a disconcertingly hard gaze.

A marriage contract, named after Greenwich Palace on the Thames, was duly drawn up. Along with the agreement of peace between both countries during Henry's and Mary's reigns, it stipulated that until she was eleven, Mary would have English companions living with her to oversee her education and welfare. After this, she would be married by proxy and move to the English court. Also emphasised was that at all times before and after the marriage, Scotland would remain an independent nation.

Rulers in early modern Europe were no more trustworthy than some political leaders today, and probably far less so since they had no ballot box to hold them in check. Before the treaties could be ratified, the English envoy Sadler was involved in a near miss by arrow. The public were in uproar at the prospect of being bound hand and foot to England. When Henry attacked Scottish ships in the Firth of Forth, Marie de Guise began to fear her daughter might be abducted and taken prisoner to England. She would not have been the first Scottish royal to spend their childhood in such a way.

The guards' room and underground prison at Linlithgow, and the remains of the barbican wall constructed by James IV, give an impression of strength, but the palace could not resist sustained attack. Marie de Guise needed an impregnable fortress within which to protect her child, a place where no enemy could reach her. So, after spending her first seven months in a fairytale palace, on 27 July

1543 Mary was carried off northwards. She never again spent long in Linlithgow Palace, and would remember nothing of her cloistered infancy here other than through her mother's reminiscences. Yet the day she rode away from it for the last time, in April 1567, was to become one of the most significant in her reign.

Chapter 2

'Not as clean as they might be'

SIXTEENTH-CENTURY SCOTS

For as long as she was in her mother's care, young Mary had nothing to fear. Marie de Guise was a remarkable woman: stoical, far-sighted and shrewd. Mary's father, on the other hand, while charismatic and politically hard-headed, could be impulsive and self-gratifying. Mary was his only legitimate child to survive, but he had fathered at least nine illegitimate offspring, some of whom were to play a significant, and in one instance profoundly malign, role in her life.

It is arguably the greatest of Mary's misfortunes that she was to spend fewer than six years with her mother before being packed off to France. Thereafter, apart from one visit, their contact was entirely by letter. Mary was seventeen when Marie de Guise died. Although they had been apart for years, she was said to have mourned deeply. Throughout her years of captivity in England, until the day of her execution, she kept a portrait of her mother close.

In appearance, Marie de Guise looks keen-eyed and intelligent. She has widely spaced blue-green eyes, finely arched eyebrows, a neat mouth, auburn hair, and a composure that seems to go beyond the stillness required by the portrait painter. She was famously tall and well built, leading to one of the best-known quips of the Tudor age. When Henry VIII offered for her hand – after banishing his first wife, beheading the second and his third dying in childbirth – she is said to have joked that while she was a large woman, her neck was small. It was a nod to Anne Boleyn's gallows humour; she said that her executioner would have an easy job since her neck was small.

A portrait of Marie attributed to the Dutch artist Corneille de Lyon was painted shortly before her marriage to James V. Held in the Scottish National Portrait Gallery, it shows her in a chic black headdress and gown, their severity offset by an elegant cut and glimpses of white gauze. It was a style that her daughter was later to emulate. Whereas Marie's second husband, James V, was a typical Stewart, with vulpine features dominated by a long nose, rich red hair and a hint of scrawniness in his physique, Marie de Guise was, writes historian John Guy, 'one of the most beautiful women in Scotland'. It was Mary's luck to inherit her looks from her mother, but to what degree she was like her in character is debatable.

Marie de Guise was recently widowed when James V, whose spouse had also just died, formally asked to marry her. His first wife, Madeleine de Valois, daughter of the French King Francis I, fell fatally ill within a few months of reaching Scotland. Her father had feared the cold climate would kill her. Even when courting Madeleine, James's eye had fallen on Marie, then married to Louis d'Orléans, Duke of Longueville, and she had made an impression on the Scottish king.

Leaving behind her three-year-old boy Francis, and an infant son newly in his grave, Marie accepted this marriage of dynastic convenience with a courage befitting her distinguished name. She had dearly loved her first husband – '*mon bon mari et ami*' – and kept his last letter to her for the rest of her days (it can be found in the National Library of Scotland's archives). But, born into the circles revolving around the volatile French court, she was a pragmatist. When she and James were married, she was wise enough to understand that she had a very simple role to play. It was her responsibility to produce an heir, accept with grace her husband's flagrant womanising and act as a diplomatic bridgehead with France. Effectively, as with so many political marriages, she was an embedded agent whose duty it was to remind James of his obligations to her homeland.

Those who portray the Scottish court in this period as a snake pit would not be wrong, but it was trumped in venom, as in much else, by the French. Marie de Guise was no Machiavelli, but her relatives, parents and some of her siblings were exceptionally cunning and self-serving. When necessary, they could be ruthless. Opportunists who kept their eye firmly on the main chance for themselves, they were willing to sacrifice any who threatened their position. At a future date, this would include Mary.

Marie was the daughter of the formidable Antoinette of Bourbon and Claude, Duke of Guise. One of ten surviving and high-flying children, she was soon obliged to entrust Mary to the care of her own mother and the tutelage and guidance of her two most power-ful brothers. Claude was a leading figure in the Church as Cardinal of Lorraine, and Francis was his father's heir as Duke of Guise. Closely allied to the king, by the time Marie and James married they had ensured the Guises were among the leading families in France.

As queen consort, Marie de Guise was widely liked, and even loved, especially by her French retinue, whom she paid well. She made every effort to settle in Scotland, praising the country fulsomely to her husband. Some of her compliments hint at surprise, reflecting what she had previously heard of it. While the French were willing to send their daughters off to marry the Scottish king, they had a low view of a country they considered bleak, cold and appallingly backward.

This attitude arose partly from a miserable description by the fourteenth-century chronicler Jean Froissart, on a military campaign with the French army in Scotland around 1365, whose impressions were never shaken off: 'When these barons and knights of France, who had been used to handsome hotels, ornamented apartments, and castles with good soft beds to repose on, saw themselves in such poverty, they began to laugh, and to say before the admiral, "What could have brought us hither? We have never known till now what was meant by poverty and hard living."'

For the soldiers, the auld alliance was a matter of regret: 'They said they had never suffered so much in any expedition, and wished the King of France would make a truce with the English for two or three years, and then march to Scotland and utterly destroy it: for never had they seen such wicked nor such ignorant hypocrites and traitors.'

If hypocrisy was another word for hygiene, then they had a point. Even 200 years later, visitors to Scotland were appalled at the filth of the accommodation on offer, especially in hostels and inns. Sheets were grimed, crockery crusted, and chamber pots either emptied out of a window endangering passers-by or added to the midden that grew near the back door, fragrancing the air like a farmyard. Even Mary, Queen of Scots' entourage, when it arrived at the French court in 1548, was found wanting. Mary's grandmother Antoinette of Bourbon considered them 'not as clean as they might be'.

The accusations of treachery and double-dealing that the French threw at the Scots could have equally been levelled at them, while sneering at the condition of the country was rank prejudice. The state of the ordinary people in Mary's era was not markedly less comfortable than that of the rest of Europe. Citizens of cities and towns (which were not large) and the fertile Lowlands were probably better off than those living off the rugged land in the north; in what was still an overwhelmingly rural population life might be far from luxurious, but only in times of famine or plague was it desperate.

The mercantile class was prosperous, as were many of the clergy. In 1498, the Spanish ambassador, Don Pedro de Ayala, painted a rather glowing (and partial) picture: 'The towns and villages are populous. The houses are good, all built of hewn stone, and provided with excellent doors, glass windows, and a great number of chimneys. All the furniture that is used in Italy, Spain and France is to be found in their dwellings. It has not been bought in modern times only, but inherited from preceding ages.'

This overlooked the fact that ordinary people's existence could be spartan. Even though they generally ate as well as and possibly more healthily than their social superiors, commoners' houses were poorly made, damp and draughty. There was so little in the way of beds or chairs we would today consider them unfurnished. There might be a table with benches or stools, but only the head of the house could hope for a chair. Margaret Sanderson's work on living conditions of the period shows that if people could afford a candlestick, it would be taken from room to room as required.

In the relatively affluent farming land around Melrose, during Mary's reign, Sanderson found records indicating that low one- and two-room cottages were made with tree trunks forming an apex for the thatched roof. Windows would be unglazed, and the doorway often covered by skins. There were no fireplaces, and smoke from a central fire in the main or single room found its way out through the thatch or the cracks in the walls. Animals slept under the same roof, sometimes partitioned off, and their ordure drained away by a gutter. Chickens occupied the rafters at night. The few remaining black-houses and longhouses in the Highlands and Islands give a vivid idea of medieval conditions.

Diet, other than for the well off, was plain but plentiful, with fish, meat and oatmeal forming the basis. In 1435, an Italian visitor who would one day become Pope Pius II, remarked that 'even the common people eat flesh and fish to repletion'. The rich preferred white wheaten bread to the rougher, healthier fare. Dairy products were widely available. Vegetables and fruit, by comparison, were less so, although according to Don Pedro de Ayala, in the late fifteenth century there was an abundance of berries.

Fish was salted, dried or smoked for consumption in winter, as was meat. Ale was drunk by all who could afford it, as it was safer than water. Alcohol was popular across the classes, and those who had deep pockets did not stint. A record of festive purchases by the wealthy people of Dunfermline at Christmas in 1503 shows that considerably more than half their money was spent on beer, a third on wine, a tiny fraction on ale and the rest on bread and coal.

At home, beds were a luxury, as were blankets. Some household-ers had bedframes, but many slept either on straw-filled pallets or on the earthen floor in their cloaks or plaids. As for the food offered to a foreign army, the French soldiers' disdain sounds more like racism than a justifiable complaint. Since the Scottish aristocracy had its roots in medieval French society, upper-class cuisine would have been familiar to anyone from western Europe.

Similarly, those with ample money enjoyed the same delicacies as their European counterparts. Fine wines, spices, cloths and silks, paintings and furniture were imported from overseas, and artisans from all over Europe were employed to work on buildings and their interiors. Daughters of aristocrats played musical instruments, and sons were sent to university on the Continent.

* * *

Material possessions are one thing, but the overall mood of a society is another, and while they ate fairly well, most sixteenth-century Scots lived hand to mouth, with little buffer between them and hardship. Perhaps to provide solace in a strange and lonely land, Marie established a Little France wherever she went. (In this too her daughter would copy her.) In time – especially when she finally gained control of the country as Regent in 1554 – this irked the Scots, who in some districts felt besieged and intimidated by the number of French troops brought in to bolster Marie de Guise's position. Not recognising the impact of this on the body politic was one of the weaknesses in Marie's generally astute governance. At one point, in 1559, the Port of Leith was so heavily garrisoned with French soldiers against impending English attack that Leithers were close to revolt. Given the choice between their long-held desire to declare independence from Edinburgh, and being rid of the French, they did not hesitate. Expelling the 'auld ally' was paramount.

The tension the presence of the French military in Scotland created is indicative of shifting alliances in this slippery era. Half a century earlier, Europe had been unthinkingly and unswervingly Catholic. The gradual appearance of reformist religious belief was to change all that, and with unimaginable speed. Several currents fed into what was to become a tidal surge. On the Continent, the Protestant Reformation, sparked by Martin Luther's *Ninety-five Theses* in 1517, laid the basis for a powerful theology that challenged the papacy's dominance. This invigoratingly democratic creed was to be ably and devoutly promoted in Scotland by John Knox. To read his comments about those who stayed true to Rome – he condemned the sacrament of Mass as 'idolatry' – it is hard to believe that Knox had started out as a Catholic priest. No one better exemplifies the excessive zeal of the converted. Or the fact that, when on the attack, Christians of all stripes could be merciless and cruel despite the New Testament's emphasis on charity and love.

From the 1520s, as the Reformation began to take hold, old certainties withered and allegiances shifted. At the time of his death in 1542, James V was astutely attempting to reform the Catholic Church from within. Had he lived to be successful in reshaping the Church, thereby preventing the Protestants gaining the upper hand at home, how different Mary's prospects might have been.

When the infant queen was being rocked in her cradle in Linlithgow, the Pope still had a firm grip on Scotland and France. England, by this time, was almost a decade into its Reformation, following Henry VIII's break with the Catholic Church, engineered to allow him to marry Anne Boleyn. By 1561, when Mary returned after a thirteen-year absence to take up her throne, Scotland had turned Protestant almost overnight. France, by contrast, was about to be plunged into the Wars of Religion, pitting the Protestant Huguenots against Catholics, which would be bloody and trau-matic. Already, Protestant conspirators and martyrs were being tortured and hanged. This was a dreadful sight that young Mary and her husband, the Dauphin, were obliged to witness. On one occa-sion she was reported to have fainted.

As religious affiliations splintered, major political allegiances were no longer determined strictly along religious lines. That the Catholic Spaniard Philip II could consider marrying the English Protestant Queen Elizabeth I to cement the bond between their two countries and the Netherlands shows how the playing board had altered. When decades later Spain was intent on invading England, it was France who became Elizabeth's ally, a collaboration that defied centuries of antagonism.

As the Reformation took hold, England began to take on a new

meaning for many Scots. Before successfully overthrowing the established religion, reformers like Knox found a safe haven, and like-
minded thinkers, south of the border. They had allies also in
Scandinavia, the Netherlands and Germany. Previously, Scots who
dared to put so much as a toe into England would have received a
chillier welcome than if they carried the plague, and been in as great
danger. Now, the possibility of convoluted liaisons and destabilising
treacheries multiplied. In due course, Mary would discover that the
Reformation had turned a difficult situation in Scotland into something altogether more challenging.

* * *

The dramatis personae in the story of Mary Stuart could be viewed
as a Greek chorus, the backdrop to her tragedy, had they not each at
some point taken a lead role on the stage. As events unfolded, the
courtiers and cousins, friends and family who formed her inner
circle and sat on the Privy Council and in Parliament were decisive
in influencing her decisions. Some were impressive figures, putting
the interests of the country as high as their own. Others were weasels.
One such was the vacillating James Hamilton, Earl of Arran, who
acted as Regent when James V died, despite his obvious unsuitabil-
ity for the role.

The Hamiltons were a powerful family, with land near Edinburgh
and in the west. They had a network of connections that, when
called upon, made them formidable. James Hamilton's grandmother
Mary, Countess of Arran, was James II's eldest daughter, and sister
of James III. After the Battle of Flodden, the countess's nephew John
Stewart, Duke of Albany, was appointed Regent, even though he
had spent most of his life in France. When he died in 1536, James
Hamilton, Earl of Arran, was next in line to the throne after
James V's heirs. Vexingly for the earl, there was some doubt over
whether his father had been properly divorced before he married his
mother, thereby potentially rendering him a bastard. This shady area
allowed the Lennox Stewarts to press their claim. They too were
descended through James II's daughter Mary, by her marriage to

Lord Hamilton, but this time through her daughter Elizabeth. Their sense of entitlement as successors to the royal line was therefore entirely legitimate. Despite this, the Hamiltons remained in pole position as next in line after royal heirs until the reign of Mary's son, James VI and I.

The Earl of Arran's main residence was Kinneil House, near Bo'ness in Midlothian. Within easy reach of Linlithgow Palace, this old family home was refashioned into a grand mansion during Arran's years as Regent. That alone suggests how lucrative the role was, with all Crown income and properties in his hands.

A portrait by the Dutch artist Cornelis Ketel of the Earl of Arran, later to become Duke of Châtelherault for services rendered to the French Crown, is held in the Duke of Hamilton's collection. It shows a stout man with cropped auburn hair, bushy grey beard, puffy eyes and a self-satisfied expression. Fat fingers move towards the magnificent jewelled chain around his neck, while the other hand clutches a leather glove. Compared with many of the leading players at court, he looks avuncular, even amiable. Out of a line-up you would pick him as trustworthy, but you would be wrong. Marie de Guise, who got to know him well, described him as 'simple and the most inconstant man in the world, for whatsoever he determineth today, he changeth tomorrow'. Like many ditherers, he was more dangerous than he appeared. Since he could change tack without obvious reason, there was no second-guessing him. All that was certain was that whatever course he followed would be to his own advantage.

Chapter 3

'What snatching and catching, what bruising and broostling'

STIRLING CASTLE

A kestrel hovering over the Lowlands in the summer of 1543 would have witnessed something out of the ordinary. Over the space of several days, a procession of servants and carriage horses filed like ants from Linlithgow Palace to the ancient fortress of Stirling Castle. Closer inspection would have revealed the horses' panniers and crates stuffed with clothes and bedding, cooking utensils, silver plate and portraits. Twenty-four horses carried the dowager queen's enormous, dismantled bed, as well as those of her entourage, with one man charged with taking care of the princess's cradle. The royal household was about to flit. But as yet, there was no sign of the royal party on the road.

Shortly after Mary's birth, negotiations began on behalf of Henry VIII for the marriage of his son with Mary. Initially, these were conducted by the English diplomat Sir Ralph Sadler. His first encounter with the infant Mary, when he reported her excellent health to Henry, was the start of protracted discussions in which he, and others, put Henry's proposal to Marie de Guise and the Regent Arran.

Marie was not alone in seeing benefits in this liaison, or in at least appearing to give it serious consideration. After enquiring about his own reward for his part in making it happen, Arran too was in favour. He saw that allying himself with England could be advantageous. Parliament agreed to contracts being drawn up, and in July the Treaties of Greenwich were produced. They included so many caveats that they stood little chance of ever being put into practice. Even Arran saw how badly they would be received: 'every man, woman and child in Scotland would liever [rather] die in one day than accept them', he complained. Henry VIII doubtless realised that what he could not achieve by diplomacy or law could be won by brute force. But for the moment, legal documents that would seemingly offer Scotland a less disputatious future lay awaiting signatures.

In the meantime, Marie de Guise plotted on behalf of her daughter. The Regent Arran had placed Marie under a form of house arrest, preventing contact with her relatives in France. He seems to have been unaware that she had half-emptied Linlithgow Palace despite infiltrating her household with spies. They must have been extraordinarily dim-witted if they did not spot the disappearance of domestic goods and the contents of the kitchens in cumbersome and noisy carts. The only advantage Marie de Guise had over the Regent was that she retained custody of her child. Even so, she needed his permission to take the queen from the palace. Cleverly, she gained Sadler's agreement to her relocating to Stirling, without explaining her real reason, which was the risk of Mary's abduction by the English. After this, Arran, who wanted to keep Henry VIII on his side, could hardly have said no.

On 27 July, accompanied by 2,500 cavalry and 1,000 infantry, the dowager queen and her baby headed north. It would have been an imposing spectacle. The baggage train stretched for a mile, but since Mary was teething it might not have been the easiest of journeys.

By this time, Marie de Guise's supporter Cardinal Beaton had escaped from prison, and one of the most important figures in Mary's story had returned from exile. Matthew Stuart, Earl of Lennox – later to become father of Mary's future husband Henry Stuart, Lord Darnley – had been in the French king's Scottish guard. A natural ally of Marie de Guise, he rallied to her cause, thereby helping to bolster the pro-French clique at court. He was also Arran's worst enemy. In part this was because of his claim to the Regent's role, but his strongest grievance was that Arran's close relative, Sir James Hamilton of Finnart, had killed his father at the Battle of Linlithgow Bridge. This contest, between Hamiltons and Lennoxes, prefigured the intensity of this pair's rivalry and loathing, which was indelibly to colour events over the next two decades.

In appearance, the 26-year-old Matthew Stuart was the epitome of an aristocrat: a tall, lithe and good-looking military man. Born in 1516, and raised in France since the age of ten, he was a naturalised French subject. His manners were polished, as the court of Francis I required, and he had a natural charm that drew people, especially women, to him. Attractive though he undoubtedly was, he was steely at heart. Intent on ousting Arran from the Regency, he hoped gradually to worm his way into the dowager queen's affections, and marry her. Yet within weeks of his return, he had already switched to the pro-English league. These courtiers were like adders, forever shedding their skins.

* * *

The complexity of events surrounding the Treaties of Greenwich demonstrate, in miniature, the deadly three-way tussle between England, Scotland and France into which Mary was born. They also show the equally complicated and even more unpredictable wrangling around the Scottish crown. Scotland's nobles were divided between pro-English and pro-French camps, but those allegiances could change overnight. Associations between noble families were dictated by strong codes of loyalty whose fault lines shifted according to circumstances. To the outsider, they looked unfathomable. From the inside, they demanded constant alertness. It was not only convention that dictated noblemen slept with a sword by their bedside. The combined elements of international and domestic agendas and personal ambitions made the middle years of the sixteenth century the very definition of interesting times.

For many months, Arran was hand in glove with Henry VIII. The king had promised to install him as King of Scotland by force, if popular resistance to Mary marrying Edward proved too strong. In response to this, two critically important bonds were drawn up by the two opposing parties at court. The first, made in June, supported Arran, and pledged to send hostages to England as surety for the marriage treaty between their countries. It was signed by sixteen influential nobles, including the earls of Angus and Argyll, and the Earl of Glencairn, son of one of the original Protestant reformers. It was Glencairn who had delivered the letter to Marie de Guise, demanding the Reformation, and who years later would sack the chapel at Holyrood Palace when Mary, Queen of Scots was in captivity. The second, more considered, political statement was composed at Linlithgow Palace in late July, presumably with the Queen Mother's knowledge and approval. Headed by Cardinal Beaton, it was signed by the earls of Lennox, Argyll (he had changed his mind within a few weeks), Huntly, Bothwell (recently returned from exile), Menteith and Sutherland, four bishops and almost forty other lords and landowners. Lambasting the personal greed of those, principally Arran, running the country, it promised to resist all English attempts to subsume Scotland.

Removing Mary from Linlithgow to Stirling was a tangible expression of affairs of state. Peasants harvesting the fields would have understood, as they watched the royal procession pass, what was happening. Imposing though it was, Linlithgow was not well placed to withstand sustained attack or siege. Whereas castles such as Dunbar or Dumbarton could be provisioned under cover of darkness by sea or underground tunnels, Linlithgow could be encircled by the enemy and cut off from all avenues of help.

Stirling Castle was a different matter. Spread broodingly over a massive rock, it has been described as the brooch that pins the Lowlands and Highlands together. The view from the ramparts stretches for miles over lush fields, woodland and purpling hills, all deceptively peaceful. In 1543, the wind-bitten town of Stirling huddled beneath its walls. To the south lay Edinburgh. Sixty miles further on was the border with England. To the east was the River Forth and the North Sea, by which route Marie de Guise could contact her French family. To the west was the Gaelic-speaking kingdom of Argyll and the Western Isles, which the Stewart kings had tried, with mixed success, to bring into the fold. The region was under the control of the immensely powerful Archibald Campbell. It was his son, the fifth Earl, who, with his brother-in-law Lord James Stewart, headed the Lords of the Congregation – the Scottish Protestant lords – who took on Marie de Guise, and later Mary Stuart herself. And to the north was the Highlands: rugged, mountainous and almost as resistant to being tamed as the west.

Stirling Castle gives a strong flavour of the world into which Mary had arrived. Home to Scottish royalty since the twelfth century, it had been at the centre of some of the most crucial conflicts in the country's history. The Battle of Bannockburn in 1314 took place a few miles beyond its gates, leaving hundreds dead and wounded. The English friar and poet Robert Baston was brought along with the English army, to chronicle what Edward II assumed would be a triumph. Instead, he fell prisoner to the Scots who, in return for his freedom, demanded that he write about what he had seen.

Edwin Morgan's translation of the original Latin offers a glimpse of that day: 'What snatching and catching, what bruising and broostling, what grief! . . . What slashing and slaughtering, what wounding and wailing, what a rout!' One of the most famous and celebrated encounters between the English and the Scots, it was led by Robert the Bruce. In seeing off the ferociously predatory Edward, Bruce's army affirmed Scotland's nascent sense of itself as an independent nation, ruled from within its own borders.

A sense of danger still permeates Stirling Castle. The massive towered entrance which Marie de Guise and Mary would have reached by a narrow and craggy path was intended to convey the monarchy's absolute power. Built by James IV, this five-storey forework would have looked like something from *Les Très Riches Heures du Duc de Berry*: simple, louring and impregnable. Arrow-slit windows on the lower floors were a reminder of its primary function as a fortress.

At such a distance, and with Mary's story so familiar, it is difficult to remember that for Marie de Guise every day was new and uncertain. Nothing more powerfully evokes the physical brutality of that era, and the ends to which enemies were prepared to go, than the forbidding walls of this most medieval of castles.

Yet from its windows Marie could enjoy a less threatening scene. The terraced slopes and plains beneath the castle had been turned into an enclosed deer park by James IV. When Marie and her little daughter arrived, these grounds held not only deer and wild boar but also white cattle, horses and the oxen that were used to pull the royal artillery. Fields growing crops to feed the animals, as well as the royal household, would have been well on the way to ripening, turning to gold under the summer sun. Within these boundaries was an orchard planted with 1,500 plum trees, which would soon be temptingly ripe. Among them were specimens of plum and pear that Marie de Guise had brought from France. There were also avenues of mature trees, and large kitchen-garden plots. All this, and more, had turned the castle into a model of domestic foresight and self-sufficiency. To add to the abundance, the moat was brimming with pike.

Once over the threshold, the dowager queen would have felt safer than she had in months. As a result, it was to become her main residence until the early 1550s, when she relocated to Holyroodhouse. Stirling Castle was her property, a gift from her husband when they married. It was a well-judged gesture, showing that, like earlier kings, James V understood the risks the royal family ran. It had been his intention to turn his kingdom into a peaceful and prosperous realm, but, as he was all too aware by the end of his life, dreams are one thing, reality another.

In 1304, Stirling Castle had withstood a three-month siege by Edward I. Not even his War Wolf, a fearsome trebuchet, could batter it into submission. This must have comforted Marie de Guise when picturing Henry VIII's fury at discovering the infant queen had been taken north, beyond easy reach. Even so, her nerves were obviously still on edge, since at some point in the following few years she had a battery of guns built. These cannons were trained on the approach to the castle and on Stirling Bridge on the plain below, which in 1297 was the site of the first battle in Scotland's Wars of Independence.

Previous monarchs had helped shape the fortress, but James IV and his son made the most enduring impression. Quite apart from the park and orchards, Mary's grandfather's hand was evident throughout, from the defensive entrance and the King's Old Building, to the Great Hall, under whose vaulting hammer-beam ceiling 300 could gather for state occasions and grand dinners. The building that houses the Great Hall is painted today in much the same shade of tinned salmon as in 1503, when it was completed. It sits like a jewel within the defensive walls, a luminous symbol from half a millennium ago when most people believed that kings were divine, and some still thought that dragons dwelled under the mountains.

The most impressive and largest surviving medieval structure in the country, it required five fireplaces to heat it in winter. Even now, you can almost hear heralds trumpeting the monarch's approach. Although James IV had embarked on a political and aesthetic project to bring his people into the modern age, this hall is a mirror of the late Middle Ages and its flamboyant grandeur.

But it was James's son who transformed Stirling Castle. Accounts show that when James V came to the throne, the country was all but bankrupt. It says much for his vision that, despite this, his greatest expenditure was on building: Falkland Palace, Holyroodhouse and Stirling, where he began a superb Renaissance palace that he was unlikely to have seen completed.

It is thought that the arrival of Marie de Guise and Mary hastened the building works. While it was being finished, they would have occupied the King's Inner Hall, which was no great hardship. Once it was ready, they would have lived in the height of luxury, because James's plan was to create an eye-wateringly contemporary statement about royal status and dignity. He intended for his subjects to live in a cultured, sophisticated country, and to put the barbarism of the past behind them.

Rectangular in shape, the dark stone palace is built around an even darker courtyard. This is known as the lion's den, after the beast bought in Flanders in 1537 that was once enclosed there. Unluckily for them, lions were prized accessories for royals, often given as diplomatic gifts. As far back as David II they had been shown off in captivity at court, much as mafia dons today keep panthers or alligators as pets.

The royal apartments on the first floor are splendid. The ceiling in the King's Inner Hall was originally decorated with the famous Stirling Heads, a collection of forty or so carved wooden cameos. Representing some of the most notable names of the day, and those from the Stewart past, they include James V, in his wedding outfit, sewn with 50,000 pearls, and his father and Margaret Tudor. There are Henry VII and Henry VIII, James V's first wife Madeleine de Valois, and an assortment of anonymous aristocratic or court figures, whose names are not recorded. Vivid replicas are now in their place, but as with all of this beautifully restored palace, it is not difficult to imagine it as it might have been when Mary was a child and she was finding her feet in the first place she would ever properly remember as home.

In this impressive space, James V once held court, giving audiences in a capacious hall dominated by the Scottish Royal Arms painted above the fireplace. Through another door is the king's bedchamber. It has been left unfurnished, as it would have been after he died. All it contains today is an undressed four-poster bed beside which, when I visited, a lutenist in red stockings and mob cap, pewter-buttoned breeches and waistcoat sat quietly strumming. As throughout the palace, the walls are magnificently painted, with another version of the Royal Arms of Scotland above the fireplace, this time featuring a resplendent unicorn.

In almost every corner is a castle guide, the men in doublets and hose, the women in the black pinafore dresses and caps of middle-ranking domestic staff. They add a touch of authenticity to the scene, and their animation, and music, are a reminder that the people of Mary's day were essentially much the same as we are. The conditions they lived under might have been more as it is for those in war-torn areas today, where the next attack could be around the corner, but this did not make violence less frightening. In so many respects, their existences were perilous: execution was the sentence for even minor offences; people were burned at the stake for heresy, or hanged for theft. An incautious word spoken against the monarch, or merely contemplating what would happen when he or she died, was treason, and ferociously punished.

It is in the queen's chambers that the past comes alive. Her rooms are fully decorated, the walls hung with brocaded cloth of gold, the four-poster state bed a profusion of puce velvet and turquoise silk. The sight of the bed alone would have reduced most ordinary folk to silence. It was only for show, since the queen would have slept in a more private small room off the bedchamber. This, presumably, is where the bed from Linlithgow, dragged in pieces up the castle rock by coach horses, was placed. Though more humble than the state bed, it too would have been a four-poster. It was either in this bed, or one very similar, that years later, on her first royal procession through the country, Mary nearly died when a candle set fire to the drapes, and she was stifled by smoke. There is a reminder of this perpetual danger for all householders, rich or poor, in the guard-rooms of the castle. Enormously long poles with a hook at the end are hung on the walls between prison cells. Known as cleiks, these were used by teams of men to pull down burning rafters or thatch to prevent fire spreading.

One of the great delights of this palace is that it combines fabulous ostentation with human-scale comfort. Unlike Buckingham Palace or Fontainebleau, it is designed not just for pomp but for the owners' pleasure. To this end, the walls would have been hung with tapestries, partly for warmth, but mainly, you suspect, for decoration. Mention is made of unicorn tapestries owned by James IV and his wife, though these have never been found. Instead, a sumptuous replica set of seven tapestries adorns the Queen's Inner Hall, where Marie de Guise would have received her most favoured guests.

The long-lost tapestry set, which would have taken a couple of years to weave, cost James IV as much as a warship, another of his many indulgences. The richly decorative modern pieces on the queen's walls depict the chase, capture, killing and resurrection of the unicorn, a beast famed for the magical power of its horn. The allure of this mythical creature seems never to fade. It is the centre-piece of a magnificent series of Flemish tapestries called *The Lady and the Unicorn*, made from a Parisian design, from wool and silk, around the year 1500. Considered one of the greatest artworks from the Middle Ages, these are held in the Musée de Cluny in Paris. In a small room, where visitors talk in whispers, it is possible to view them closely and absorb the atmosphere of a chamber filled with hangings similar to those that once graced James IV's quarters. These rose-coloured, intricately woven hangings lay neglected in a French chateau for centuries, at the mercy of mould, mice and owners who would cut them up for footstool covers. Even though they are a little faded and threadbare, they are enchanting. Hence the number of cushion covers and Christmas cards their image adorns.

James V's intention was to inspire awe in visitors, from the classi-cal and biblical statues placed in niches on the palace walls – includ-ing one of himself scowling as sternly as John Knox from behind an Old Testament beard – to the ceilings painted in gold leaf. Architecturally, the palace was one of the most inventive Renaissance structures in Britain at the time. But there was also a practical purpose behind its design.

Its construction has been described as marking the end of the Middle Ages. This transition was aesthetic but also psychological. After the turmoil of his grandfather's and father's reigns, James was determined to put the monarch at a distance from his court. The arrangement of the king's and queen's rooms was like a maze, each guarded door leading to a place of greater safety for the king and his family. This allowed him to retreat from public, obliging petitioners or courtiers to wait in outer rooms until he was in the mood to see them. It was a paradigm shift in the way the king was viewed, and would prove a mixed blessing.

Chapter 4

'Put all to fyre and swoorde'

HENRY VIII'S ROUGH WOOING

Little more than a month after Mary arrived at Stirling Castle, she was crowned Queen of Scotland. This ancient ceremony took place in the old Chapel Royal, which has long since been demolished. The date was hardly auspicious: 9 September 1543 was the thirtieth anniversary of the Battle of Flodden. Some see this as a dreadful oversight or misstep; John Guy calls it a 'delicious irony'; others believe it shows the country's refusal to be dogged by superstition or defined by the past. In reality, though, as the Regent Albany and James V had learned to their cost, Flodden was still fresh in the memory whenever the king's troops were mustered.

Whether Marie de Guise took any of this into consideration is unknown. Possibly she had more important things on her mind. Cardinal Beaton, the Archbishop of St Andrews, conducted the coronation service, and the heavy crown was held above Mary's head by the Regent Arran. The sight of him with the crown in his hands must have set minds racing. At this moment, a nine-month-old baby was all that stood between him and the throne. Yet while he was venal, he was neither depraved nor stupid. In recent weeks, he had made a U-turn that became the talk of Europe. He switched sides from supporting Henry VIII's aims to ally himself with Cardinal Beaton and his followers. The day before Mary's coronation he had officially renounced Protestantism and returned to the Catholic Church. In so doing he was throwing in his lot with the pro-French party, and ending any hope of a future in league with Henry VIII.

The ceremony would have been as splendid as Marie de Guise could arrange at short notice, but nothing would have outshone the Honours of Scotland. This is the first occasion on which the regalia are recorded as being used together, and Mary grew up knowing that hers had been one of the most impressive coronations ever. The Honours comprised a sceptre and sword gifted by the Pope and, most exquisite of all, the crown, remodelled by James V. Crimson-capped, it is set with oriental and Scottish pearls, white topazes, amethysts, jacinths, rock crystal and diamonds. Made from gold mined in Scotland, possibly at Crawford Moor, it sits on a bed of ermine. If the sight of its twinkling jewels did not make Mary cease crying for a moment, then as an adult with a love of finery she must have recognised their distinction.

Now housed in the Crown Room at Edinburgh Castle, and having survived war, occupation and a century-long interment in an old oak chest, the Honours of Scotland still sparkle. Their refined splendour is evidence that those who wear and bear them are very different from the rest of us. It is arguably as difficult for us to understand the psyche of the present members of the House of Windsor as to fathom Mary, Queen of Scots. When it comes to royalty, the gulf is measured less in centuries than in attitude, outlook, breeding and upbringing.

In her mother's arms, Mary cried her way through the proceedings. One can either interpret that as an ill omen or as sore gums. The King's Inner Hall would have been lavishly decorated as the court gathered for this momentous event. While Mary bawled, each of the lords and bishops knelt before her to pledge their allegiance. Two months later, in November, there was another celebration, as Marie de Guise expressed her relief at her daughter's coronation by throwing an extravagant party for her own twenty-eighth birthday.

Stirling Castle was to feature often in Mary's life when she returned to Scotland. No time spent there was more significant, however, than these formative years when, until she left the country for

France, Stirling was her home. It is bitterly ironic that this was where she last saw her infant son James, in 1567, before events overtook her. She had placed him there for his safety, but before long he would be brought up to believe his mother was the source of danger. While she languished in captivity in England, he was being raised by her enemies who, if they mentioned her at all, took every opportunity to defame her.

In the autumn of 1543, all this was far off. Much more pressing was the question of Mary's future. In December, Parliament roundly refuted the Treaties of Greenwich. In response the English lion roared. As soon as winter ended, Henry VIII sent his troops north, slashing and burning, raping and killing in the towns and villages along the border and deep into the Lothians. This psychopathically murderous campaign of terror was dubbed the Rough Wooing. The object of Henry's policy – wholly to destroy those who stood between him and his prize – was made clear in an order he gave to the Earl of Hertford in April 1544. Warden of the Scottish Marches and Henry's brother-in-law by his third wife Jane Seymour, Hertford was left in no doubt of what he had to do:

Put all to fyre and swoorde, burne Edinborough towne, so rased and defaced when you have sacked and gotten what ye can of it, as there may remayn forever a perpetuel memory of the vengeaunce of God lightened upon [them] for their faulsehode and disloyailtye. Do what ye can out of hande, and without long tarying, to beate down and over throwe the castle, sack Holyrod house, and as many townes and villaiges about Edinborough as ye may conveniently, sack Lythe and burne and subverte it and all the rest, putting man, woman and childe to fyre and swoorde without exception where any resistence shal be made agaynst you, and this done, passe over to the Fyfelande and extende like extremityes and destructions in all townes and villaiges wherunto ye may reche convenyently, not forgetting among all the rest so to spoyle and turne upset downe the Cardinalles town of St Andrews, as thupper stone may be the nether, and not one stick stande by an other, sparing no creature alyve within the same, specially such as either in frendeship or blood be alyed to the Cardinall.

Immediately in the English army's path lay Melrose, a morning's ride from the border and an easy target on the soldiers' way to the capital. With its wealthy abbey and monastic orchards and fields, it was a plum ripe for crushing. Historian Margaret Sanderson estimates that not just Melrose was destroyed but in the area around it '192 settlements, towers, farmsteads, fortified houses, and the protective walls within which people and stock had taken refuge, 243 larger villages, and seven monasteries and friaries'. In this period, she writes, there were times when settlements 'must temporarily have looked like refugee camps'.

Forty miles east, the fishing town of Dunbar also suffered appallingly. It was torched, with the townsfolk mercilessly trapped. The footprints of Mary's history are trampled all across the country, but nowhere more deeply than in the Lowlands and the Borders. All of us who live in these parts are, knowingly or not, treading over the chessboard on which her reign was played out.

The situation remained hazardous for the next few years. Unaware of the trouble brewing, Mary grew into an energetic child who loved music and dancing, horses and dogs, and inherited her mother's fondness for card games and fun. Life at this point would not have been taxing. While ordinary children might be expected to help with domestic or agricultural chores by the time they were five or six, Mary's hands would have remained soft and white, used only to draw, or to learn to write or, as she grew older, to hold a needle. Yet though she was pampered and privileged, her mother would have been reasonably strict, disciplining her when needed. In this respect, the influence down the centuries of the saintly Queen Margaret had not been to a Scottish child's benefit. As the stern medieval queen's friend and biographer, the chronicler Turgot of Durham recorded, Margaret believed in whipping a child when required.

If any such treatment was meted out to Mary, it would surely only have been by her mother. Whether Marie was in favour of smacking or hitting children to teach them to behave, as was most of the country, is not recorded. Since Mary was a lively child, with a sense of humour, she must occasionally, or frequently, have stepped out of line. What happened next, we will never know, but it is hard to imagine Marie de Guise wielding a switch or cane. Given the closeness of mother and daughter, it seems probable that Mary's upbringing was as carefree and loving as it was possible to be in a society where children had to grow up quickly.

Although the Queen Mother's retinue was from France, since Mary was Queen of Scotland, and would one day rule her country, she was raised to speak in Scots, not French. Yet there was discussion as early as 1544 about turning to the King of France for help, and binding Mary to her mother's land in some immediately advantageous way.

Henry VIII died in January 1547, but the impasse continued. Under Hertford (now Duke of Somerset), who had been appointed Lord Protector until Prince Edward came of age, reprisals became even more relentless. The turning point, for Mary, was a dreadful military defeat at Musselburgh, a few miles down the coast from Edinburgh, in September that year. The Battle of Pinkie Cleugh, which some claim was even more disastrous than Flodden, left thousands of commanders and nobles dead in a matter of hours. The English official William Patten, who accompanied the army, later described the scene: 'a pitiful sight of the dead corpses lying dispersed abroad, some their legs off, some but houghed [their hamstrings cut], and left lying half-dead, some thrust quite through the body, others the arms cut off, diverse their necks half asunder, many their heads cloven, of sundry the brains pasht out, some others again their heads quite off, with other many kinds of killing'.

Learning of the calamity at Pinkie, Marie de Guise hurried Mary from Stirling to Inchmahome Priory. It was like retreating to a panic room. For three weeks the child queen and her servants took refuge on this tiny, heart-shaped island in the Lake of Menteith, west of Stirling. While four-year-old Mary allegedly and improbably learned Greek and planted trees, the Scottish court was forced to recognise that without outside help England would soon over-run them. After the Battle of Pinkie, they had dug themselves in across much of southern Scotland. Somerset had established his headquarters in Haddington, from where the Lothians could be controlled and Edinburgh kept in a state of permanent anxiety. Under these conditions peace was impossible. Even worse, if the English succeeded in carrying off their queen then with her would go the country's hopes of independence.

All Parliament could do was call on help from France. There was considerable public and political resistance to cementing the old ties with this supercilious and unreliable ally which, it was (rightly) feared, wanted to turn Scotland into a vassal state. In that respect it was no different to England. An additional consideration, as Protestantism began to gain ground, was the French monarchy, which would bolster the Catholic cause at home. Unappealing as England's bullying tactics were, its spiritual direction chimed with a growing number of Scots.

Into this arena stepped the self-seeking Arran. Promising the French king Henri II he would lay his offer of marrying Mary to his son the Dauphin before Parliament, Arran was as good as his word. Henri's timing was excellent. He proposed that when they were of an age, Mary would marry his son Francis. In due course the Dauphin would inherit the French throne, making Mary queen of one of the most powerful countries in Europe. Added to this, he promised to protect Scotland against 'our old enemies of England' as if it were his own country he was safe-guarding. It was an inviting proposition. For Marie de Guise, a formal alliance with her home-land was just what she had always wanted. In not pressing this issue earlier, she had played her cards cleverly.

Yet the minute this agreement, known as the Treaty of Haddington, was signed, Mary's life was in greater danger than ever. When England learned of the deal, it was feared that Somerset's men would try to snatch her and forcibly marry her to the Prince of Wales. The Queen Mother had scored a political coup, but one for which she personally would suffer. It would not be possible to keep her daughter safe in

Scotland until she was old enough to marry Francis, the Dauphin. She would have to be brought up in France, among Marie de Guise's own family. Partly for reasons of security, but also in anticipation of Mary being dispatched to France, in February 1548 she was escorted to Dumbarton Castle, on the west coast, from where she would sail to safety.

Chapter 5

Treaties and Treason

DUMBARTON CASTLE

Carried by litter, accompanied by a small army and a large entourage, but without her mother, Mary reached Dumbarton Castle on 22 February 1548. One of the most atmospheric, history-soaked locations in the country, the castle's position on the Firth of Clyde was so spectacularly well defended it barely needed walls or guns. A massive volcanic plug, cleaved in the middle to produce the effect of two basalt sponge puddings, Dumbarton Rock had been used as a fortress since the Romans abandoned the Antonine Wall.

The oldest recorded fortified base in the country, the location has served as the stronghold of Britons, Vikings and Scots. Once the heart of the kingdom of Strathclyde, its past is eventful. It was here, for instance, that William Wallace was imprisoned, before transportation to London for his execution as a traitor, when he was hanged, drawn and quartered. Years later, after his glory days, Robert the Bruce built a manor house nearby across the River Leven, which snakes past the rock before joining the Firth of Clyde.

If five-year-old Mary parted the drapes on her litter as the journey neared its end, Dumbarton Rock would have appeared gigantic and grim, louring over the visitors as they approached its cliffs. Even a young child would have realised that this was no happy playground where she and her companions could roam free. With sheer rock faces plunging to sea firth on one side and river on the other, it was a mother and nanny's nightmare. It is safe to assume that during her months here much of Mary's time was spent indoors, or within the yards of the battle-worn castle. As for exploring the countryside, this was strictly forbidden, for fear of her abduction.

Unaware of the dangers of the long and uncomfortable journey she had just made, Mary's immediate consideration would have been settling into her new home without her mother. Given her sociable and confident temperament, and the friends and relatives surrounding her, she was less likely to have felt apprehensive or mournful than excited. It might even have seemed like an adventure, especially with the winter sea beyond the windows and gulls screaming overhead.

Today, the first impression on climbing to the castle esplanade, where a cannon points downriver, is of landing in a military base. Most of the rock's buildings date from the eighteenth century, when it survived the twin threats of the Jacobites and Napoleon. Sadly, there are scant remains from the mid sixteenth century. The most notable feature from Mary's time is the fourteenth-century Portcullis Arch, a pointed stone doorway reached by steep steps through a gully of rock, green with moss and running with rain. On one side rises White Tower Crag, on the other the Beak. The arch forms a forbidding narrow passageway, shaped like the eye of a needle, and carrying an echo of the Crusades. When Mary was in residence, it would have been closely patrolled, with armed guards at the top of the steps and midway down. Below it, the guardhouse from 1548 is also still intact, lodged between Dumbarton Rock's forbidding cliffs. Should any attackers get this far, they would find themselves trapped like rats in a pipe.

Beyond the Portcullis Arch, at the head of the gully, lies a battery of old cannons pointing eastwards and a neat Georgian prison, built for French prisoners during the Napoleonic Wars. Nothing better illustrates the inconstancy of European allegiances. In Mary's reign, France was Scotland's staunchest ally. In the late eighteenth century, by which time England and Scotland had set aside centuries of rancour with the Union of Crowns and Parliaments, it had become Britain's number-one enemy.

Hundreds of shallow steps lead up the rock face to a narrow bridge which, to the fanciful, bears a resemblance to Durin's Bridge in *The Lord of the Rings*, though thankfully with handrails. Beyond lies the summit of White Tower Crag. It catches the breath to see all points of the compass spread out beneath and beyond, and it is this prospect, rather than the architectural remains, that best illuminates this part of Mary's story. Two hundred and forty feet high, the crag looks north to Ben Lomond and the distant Cairngorms. The vista is a haze of watercolour blue, scudded by clouds and darkening showers. On the Dumbarton side lies the River Leven, and a sheltered, deep harbour. South-west is an eagle's view over the steel grey water past Argyll and Bute, to open sea and the passage to France.

Few fortresses have been more secure or forbidding. To ensure the young queen did not feel her confinement as imprisonment, she was accompanied by her quartet of maids, or 'Maries', who would play a central role in the following years. This posse were girls of her own age from noble families, whose parents saw the benefits they would reap by close association with the queen. There was Mary Fleming, whose widowed mother Lady Fleming (James V's illegitimate half-sister) was Mary's aunt and had been appointed to act as her niece's governess in France. Her father, once Lord Chamberlain of Scotland, had recently been killed at the Battle of Pinkie Cleugh. Little Mary Fleming would come to be known as 'the flower of the flock' for her beauty. While in France, her mother was nicknamed *La Belle Écossaise*.

Then there was Mary Beaton, distantly related to Cardinal Beaton, whose mother had been one of Marie de Guise's ladies-in-waiting. She would one day, as Muriel Spark might have said, be famous for sex. Her affair with the English ambassador, Sir Thomas Randolph, was no secret.

Mary Livingston was the daughter of Lord Livingston, one of Mary's two guardians while in France. The first of the Maries to marry, she was famous for fun. Nicknamed 'Lusty' for her vivacity and love of dancing, she attracted the defamatory scorn of John Knox. He claimed she married in haste because she was already pregnant, but there is no evidence to support this accusation. Livingston might have been lively, but she was also a faithful servant and was entrusted to make an inventory of Mary's jewellery for the will she composed shortly before giving birth.

Finally, and most enduringly, there was Mary Seton, daughter of the austere George, fourth Lord Seton. He was one of the few lords to remain unswervingly loyal to Marie de Guise, as his son, the fifth lord – another George – would later be to Mary, Queen of Scots. The elder Seton's wife was another of Marie de Guise's ladies-in-waiting. Any romantic hopes Mary Seton had for herself were dashed as a young woman, and she was to remain Mary's companion long into her captivity in England. She did not leave her until 1583, four years before her execution, and only because of ill health. Her most remarked-upon skill as attendant, other than devotion, was as a hair-dresser. While the queen was imprisoned, the English courtier, Sir Francis Knollys, described Seton's talent, writing that she 'did set such a curled hair upon the Queen . . . every other day she hath a new device of head dressing, without any cost, and yet setteth forth a woman gaily well'.

While at Dumbarton, young Mary's hair would have been tended to with great care by her nurses, who would assist her to dress each morning. Despite the novelty of her situation, these months must have dragged. Her mother visited only briefly in May, and again in July when Mary was about to leave for France. Not long after her arrival, however, the child had worse to contend with than boredom or sadness. In March she came down with measles and became so ill that rumours spread of her death.

As an adult, Mary Stuart would frequently fall seriously ill at moments of high emotional pressure. It might be taking too big a leap to wonder if this was one such occasion, since children are regularly unwell, and in this century often did not survive. Yet for Mary this was a momentous and possibly unnerving period. She was faced with the imminent prospect of permanently leaving her mother, to be taken in by strangers in a foreign land, whose language she did not speak. Whether or not there was an underlying psychological trigger, this anxious episode was a precursor of what would become a familiar and worrying pattern.

Several of the palaces and castles where Mary lived as a child played a part in her later life, but she returned only once to Dumbarton. This was in July 1563, when she was on a royal progression in the west. The castle accounts record the preparations made for her arrival: 144 loaves, 150 eggs, 47 trout, 16 pounds of butter and almost 16 gallons of white wine.

One of the most important royal castles, Dumbarton had a series of governors, who included the fickle and self-aggrandising Matthew, Earl of Lennox, who held it in the early 1540s. When Marie de Guise made it clear she would not marry him, he retreated here to nurse his resentment. Shortly thereafter, he switched to Henry VIII's side. When the French sent financial and military aid to Marie de Guise, their ships sailing into the Clyde in 1543, Lennox confiscated the ambassadors' money and guns. This was a step too far. Since he was a naturalised French citizen, this rendered him open to charges of treason. When this was pointed out, he withdrew. Shortly afterwards he left for England.

Part of Lennox's agreement with Henry was that, if he were ever to become Regent – to which end he required Henry's aid – he would rule Scotland entirely under his guidance. Until that happy day, he would not want for comfort. On his marriage to Margaret Douglas, daughter of Margaret Tudor by her second husband, Archibald Angus, Earl of Douglas, he took possession of considerable estates in Yorkshire, which were Margaret's dowry from the king. Nicely settled, it would be twenty years before he returned to Scotland, to foment further trouble.

When Mary returned from France to take up her throne, Dumbarton Castle was being held by the former Regent Arran, the Duke of Châtelherault. To his chagrin, and at the urging of Lord James Stewart, Mary's half-brother, he was forced to surrender it to her in April 1562. He did so in tears, after being accused of helping to hatch a plan to abduct Mary to the castle, even though it was his mentally ill son who had been privy to the plot. That poor fellow, who cherished a lifelong adoration of the queen, was kept in genteel captivity from then until his death in 1609.

* * *

Back in 1548, and before any formal agreement was made, a French fleet was sighted off Dunbar, just north of the border, in June. Sailing on past the Bass Rock, these 130 ships, carrying 5,500 infantry and 1,000 cavalry, must have made a cheering sight for a beleaguered nation who dreaded what was heading their way from the south. Doubtless, the news made a shiver run down the spines of Somerset's men.

On landing, the French made immediately for Haddington to rid it of the English, and it was there, in a nunnery outside the town where John Knox had been born, that a binding matrimonial and political contract between both countries was signed. For his part in making the Treaty of Haddington happen, Arran was awarded the duchy of Châtelherault by the French king. He must have savoured the title of duke, not least because it came with an annual revenue of £1,000.

The date of the treaty was 7 July 1548, and as the ink dried, Mary's royal career began to take shape. Shortly afterwards, the French sailed up the east coast of Scotland, out of English reach, across the hazardous seas north of Scotland, past Orkney. Skirting the Hebrides, they continued down the west coast to Dumbarton. In command of this perilous voyage was Vice-Admiral Nicolas Durand de Villegagnon, a brilliant French soldier and adventurer who later established a French colony in Brazil.

In the middle of July, the Queen Mother visited Dumbarton Castle, to be with her daughter before she left the country. Time was short, but one can imagine how happy, yet wistful, she would have been in Mary's company. This was also an opportunity to instruct her child on the behaviour and the duties expected of her when she reached the care of her French relatives; perhaps also on what she could hope to find.

As a signal of how well Mary would be treated, the king had sent his own ship to carry her to France. So it was that on 29 July Marie de Guise watched her five-year-old daughter walk calmly along the stone pier and board the royal ship, heading for a new life. They would meet only once again.

Mary was not the only young royal to set sail from Dumbarton to France. Robert the Bruce's nine-year-old heir David II was given refuge in the castle when the King of England was dangerously eager to oust the Bruces and put a Balliol on the throne. After his army's defeat in 1333 at the Battle of Halidon Hill, David was hurried off to France along with his wife Joan, daughter of Edward II, whom he had married when David was four and Joan was seven. A century later, in 1436, Margaret, the eldest daughter of James I, sailed from the castle aged eleven to marry Louis, the future French king. Her father was wretched at letting her go, and reportedly her marriage was a most unhappy pairing. Margaret was more in sympathy with her father-in-law Charles VII than with her husband.

These examples, and there are many others, are a reminder of how the marriage market for young royals operated. Alliances were ruthlessly political and dynastic. Nuptial ties were the strongest assurance of ongoing cooperation and friendship between great houses and thrones. In general, boys were considered old enough to marry at fourteen, girls at twelve, but exceptions allowing younger liaisons could be made. Considerations of love or romance for the couple were irrelevant, as they had assiduously been taught.

Marie de Guise had already been obliged to relinquish one child when she left France to marry James V. Now history was being repeated. Had she wished, she could have put her own maternal needs ahead of political concerns, but the Queen Mother was doing the more difficult thing: protecting her daughter's inheritance in Scotland and keeping it safe until she could reclaim it.

When Mary embarked, she had no fear of being lonely. Apart from the Maries, there was a large entourage to keep her company and remind her of home. It included her nurse, Jean (or Janet) Sinclair, and her guardians lords Erskine and Livingston. Livingston, who had led the Scots against the English in 1522, would stay with her in France until his death. For a short period at least, three of her half-brothers, with whom she had been brought up at Stirling, would also be with her. Her younger brothers were John Stewart and Robert Stewart. The eldest, Lord James Stewart, who was seventeen, was to play a pivotal role in her future life, but at this point was soon to leave the French court for the University of Paris. What he was like as a youth is uncertain, but he was later described as an imposing figure of a man, with an equally substantial sense of royal entitlement.

The group settled into their quarters on board, in expectation of sailing with the tide. Instead they found themselves becalmed. Confined to dock for ten days until the weather turned, they did not weigh anchor until 7 August. When finally they departed, it was a rough journey. Mary was noted as mocking her companions for being seasick, a rather heartless response to their distress. From this it may be assumed she was in high spirits.

Chapter 6

Mary and le petit roi

THE YEARS IN FRANCE

The years Mary spent in France have often been described as the happiest of her life, even though separation from her mother casts doubt on this claim. Once in France, she came under the care of her grandmother, Antoinette of Bourbon. A petite and lively woman with a sharp sense of humour and a commanding presence, her soldier grandfather Claude, Duke of Guise, presided over one of the most powerful and ambitious clans in the country. The main family base was in Joinville, in the north-east of the country, close to their original home of Lorraine. They not only had the ear of the king, but poured much advice into it.

Henri II took to Mary immediately. He was impressed by her maturity and understanding, though appalled that she could not speak French. His wife Catherine de' Medici was a Florentine, daughter of Lorenzo de' Medici, Duke of Urbino. She was to play a large part in Mary's life at court, especially as she grew older. Portraits show a round-faced woman with the prominent eyes for which the Medici were renowned. Long after Mary had departed, in 1572 Catherine became infamous for her part in the St Bartholomew's Day Massacre, in which around 2,000 Huguenots were murdered for their Protestant beliefs. Whether she incited this is not clear, but the implication that she could be ruthless seems evident. Catherine gave birth to ten children; Francis, the Dauphin, was her first. He must have felt like a miracle, because she had spent years trying to conceive, eventually doing so with the help of medics and their potions. Catherine was kind enough to Mary when she was to become Francis's wife, and for the duration of their short marriage, but, while never actively unpleasant, as soon as Mary was widowed, Catherine cooled, casting her inconvenient and potentially troublesome daughter-in-law into social Siberia.

Several important personalities at court helped raise Mary in these years. Chief among them was her aunt Anne d'Esté, wife of her uncle Francis. Anne held her in genuine affection and was to be a second mother while Mary was in France. Another who figured prominently was Diane de Poitiers, a patron of the arts. The king's mistress, who was twenty years his senior, she appears to have been the love of his life. At the Palace of Fontainebleau, where Mary often visited, the monograms of Henri and Catherine are inscribed, but the initial D is also prominent.

Of those who exerted a profound and ongoing significance in Mary's political life, when she was preparing to take up her throne and during her reign, by far the most important figures were her uncles. Francis, the Duke of Guise's eldest son and heir, was a talented military strategist and courageous general. He was almost thirty when Mary arrived, the same year in which he married the Italian princess Anne d'Esté, daughter of the Duke of Ferrara. Portraits show him to be sharp-faced, with a thin gingery moustache and beard. In one of them he is in full armour, more armadillo than man. Unexpectedly for someone so martial, his eyes are gentle, as is his expression. This impression is misleading. Even so, he was Mary's favourite of her Guise uncles.

Charles, later Cardinal of Lorraine, had been appointed Archbishop of Rheims when he was fourteen, in order to retain the role within the Guise family. Five years younger than his brother Francis, he too was exceptionally clever, in his case in the field of statecraft rather than military conflict. When Henri II took the throne, it was Charles who handed him his crown. Like his brother, he had a wispy moustache and beard. In his pomp he was the scourge of the Huguenots, and as merciless in their persecution as any zealot. His is a strong, wilful face, and while not without humour, suggests someone not to be crossed. El Greco's portrait of him in full cardinal's outfit depicts an implacable nature, which events seem to have borne out. He inspired fear as well as respect, and did not enjoy the same public adulation as Francis, whose dashing exploits made him a national hero, in some quarters at least.

It was Charles with whom young Mary had most dealings, since he oversaw her education. Once she had been established in her own household, he began to instruct her on matters a monarch needed to understand. What she could not know was the extent to which the Guise brothers were prepared to use her as a pawn in their schemes, and the ways in which Scotland would suffer for this.

Mary's upbringing in France was a happy time. Although her mother visited only once, for a prolonged stay in 1550, she was surrounded by attentive guardians. In the case of her uncles, it was in their best interests that she flourished, since she was the key to France's ambitions to control England from the north, and to halt the spread of Protestantism.

Open, generous, and tender-hearted, Mary had a talent for friendship. From the moment she and her future husband met, they formed a lasting bond. Young Francis was almost five years old when Mary arrived at court. He was sickly, undersized and sullen. Both he and Mary recognised that they were meant to be close and affectionate, and in appearance at least they played their parts well. In this they were aided by courtiers who schooled them in flowery rhetoric and a child-like version of the gallantry and coquetry expected of future partners.

Nevertheless, despite all adult interference, they became genuinely fond of each other. As Mary grew into an exceptionally attractive and personable young woman, the discrepancy between her vigorous good health and the Dauphin's near invalid state could hardly have been more pronounced. Although Francis was euphemistically described as 'weak-minded', and was probably physically deformed, they were the best of friends. Not that it would have mattered had they disliked each other. Dynastic and political interests would be served, whatever their feelings.

So it was that on 24 April 1558, fifteen-year-old Mary and fourteen-year-old Francis married. The ceremony was conducted with eye-watering flamboyance at Notre Dame Cathedral in Paris. When coins were thrown into the crowd, there was such a scuffle that several people fainted, and others had the clothes torn from their backs. A student witnessed the clamour, and wrote a poem catching the scene: 'gentlemen lost / their cloaks, ladies their farthingales, / merchants their gowns, masters of arts their / hoods, students their cornered caps and clerics / had their scapularies violently torn from their / shoulders . . .'

The pandemonium suggests the need, and greed, of the people. In hindsight, the splendour of Mary's dress, and the sumptuous trappings of court as she processed around the city, look like a rehearsal for the grievances of the French Revolution, so wide was the gulf between the rulers and the ruled. Yet the Guise family was wise: the generosity shown to commoners that day was tacit acknowledgement that without public support, the whole Valois enterprise could be imperilled.

If Mary was aware of such undercurrents, she gave no sign. She had grown up in extreme luxury, in the Guise family's various chateaux and town houses, not to mention all the other royal castles and houses throughout France, such as Blois and Chambord, where she would have stayed over the years. Initially treated as the darling of the court, at the age of eleven, in 1554, she was set up with a household and budget of her own as befitted a queen in her own right.

In Scotland, her mother was almost literally holding the fort. She managed to gain the Regency from Arran in 1554, but her strongly pro-French policy, and the gifting of senior positions in her household to her fellow countrymen, caused resentment. The presence of the French in Scotland in large numbers turned

the fondly held dream of the auld alliance into a fractious reality. As Protestantism began to gain a foothold, Marie de Guise
was increasingly seen as an overbearingly Catholic ruler, whose
aim was not to protect Scotland's interests but to further those
of France. With the duke and cardinal in control there, and
their sister holding sway in Scotland, the Guises seemed alarmingly power-hungry. In a series of bonds, between 1557 and
1562, a handful of lords kicked against their unwanted Regent
and the country's bondage to France. At the same time, the
religious mood grew more tense. The anxiety all this created
was such that even the great switherer Arran, Duke of
Châtelherault, finally joined them in pledging to oust Marie de
Guise.

In 1558, the Dauphin Francis was granted the Scottish Crown
Matrimonial. This was a largely symbolic title, but not so mean-
ingless that it would not later be the issue over which Lord Darnley
would stake his reputation. Francis's elevation coincided with the
death of Mary Tudor and the ascendancy of the Protestant queen,
Elizabeth I. This sudden reversal of Catholicism in England threw
the pieces on Europe's chessboard into the air once more, and
strengthened the Scottish Protestant lords' hand. It also dramatically changed Mary's situation, and her aspirations. Until the
unmarried Elizabeth should bear children, Mary was next in line
to the English throne, through her great-grandfather Henry VII.
Since the legitimacy of Henry VIII's marriage to Elizabeth's mother
Anne Boleyn was contested because the divorce from his first wife
Catherine of Aragon was never recognised by Rome, arguably
Mary was in fact the immediate heir to the English crown. Henry
VIII had tried to pre-empt this possibility in his final will and
testament by excluding foreigners – which included Scots – from
inheriting his crown, but this could reasonably have been tested in
court.

Consequently, Henri II made a move that was to colour the rest
of Mary's life. On hearing of Mary Tudor's death, the king declared
her Queen of England, Ireland and Scotland. He had the English

royal arms added to her and Francis's insignia and to their house-hold silver and furniture. 'Make way for the Queen of England!' was the cry when Mary went into chapel. A spy for the English minister William Cecil – soon to be Elizabeth I's consigliere – reported this provocative claim to him. It was the hinge on which the next thirty years would swing, and the eventual cause of Mary's downfall.

A year later, in 1559, in something resembling a *coup d'état*, the Protestant lords, led by Lord James Stewart and the Earl of Argyll, deposed Marie de Guise from the Regency. They did this allegedly and ludicrously in the name of their young queen across the channel, claiming it was necessary for the health of the kingdom. A council of twenty-four nobles was placed in the Regent's stead.

From Mary's perspective, the timing could hardly have been worse. The Queen Mother had bolstered her own position in 1554 by bringing in French troops, but after her deposition, while the French occupied Leith, she retreated to the stronghold of Edinburgh Castle. There, on 11 June 1560, she died, dread-fully bloated and suffering, most probably, from congestive heart failure. The news was kept from Mary for ten days, but when it was broken to her by the cardinal, she was distraught. A Venetian ambassador described how she 'showed and still shows such signs of grief, that during the greater part of yesterday she passed from one agony to another'.

It was her second bereavement in a year, and another was to come. The previous summer, Henri II had been fatally wounded in a joust by a member of the Garde Écossaise. After his prolonged death, on 10 July 1559 his son, *le petit roi*, was crowned Francis II, and Mary became Queen of France. For the young and inexperienced couple, this exalted position, at the helm of one of the most powerful and wealthy countries in Europe, was not to last more than eighteen months. During that period it was the Guise brothers who took the decisions.

Shortly after Henri's death, Mary confided she was pregnant. Although nothing came of it, it is interesting that she considered it

a possibility. Since privacy and puritanism were for future centuries, it seems unlikely she would have been ignorant about sex.
That she would have lied about something so important to the
hopes of the Valois Crown seems hardly credible. Yet Antonia
Fraser believes there was no proper consummation: 'the king's
undeveloped and probably deformed physique and generally
infantile constitution make it extremely unlikely that anything
more than the most awkward embraces took place between them;
whether or not Mary was technically a virgin when she arrived in
Scotland, she was certainly mentally one, in that her physical rela-
tion with Francis can hardly have given her any real idea of the
meaning of physical love.' Fraser suggests Mary persuaded herself
she was with child because everyone was so eager that she produce
an heir.

Then, in November 1560, Francis fell dreadfully ill and on
5 December died in agony from what is thought to have been a
brain tumour. Although sudden, early and grisly death was common,
the distress Francis and his father endured in their final days, and
whose deathbeds Mary attended, must have been harrowing and
even traumatic. Add to this the recent death of her mother, and it
was a bleak time indeed.

Almost overnight, Mary Stuart's position changed. Summer
turned to winter, and her wardrobe with it. She was suddenly the
dowager queen, and marginalised in the affairs of the French
court. Dressed in the nun-like white deuil, a long veil signifying
mourning, she handed her jewels as Queen of France back to her
mother-in-law. Catherine de' Medici had a full inventory made,
in case the young widow had kept anything to which she was not
entitled.

Mary's value now lay in her role as queen of a distant, poor and
uncivilised country that was strategically useful for France. Equally,
if she became the wife of another major European player, she could
also act to the benefit of her dead husband's realm. At the same time
as she became effectively *persona non grata*, the star of the Guise
brothers had fallen. Catherine de' Medici did not want Mary to

marry her second son, Charles IX of France, while the Guise brothers pressed for her to marry Don Carlos, the son of Philip II of Spain. Philip, the widower of Mary Tudor, was soon to marry Catherine de' Medici's daughter Elizabeth. Whatever her private feelings, Mary was plainly open to the idea of taking a second, powerful husband. The effect this would have had on Scotland is hard to calculate. It might have left it rudderless, with its ruler absent for much of her reign, or with a foreigner taking possession of the Crown Matrimonial whose influence was not to the country's advantage.

While marriage prospects were being considered – and ruthlessly squashed by the shrewd Catherine de' Medici – Mary downsized her household. Gradually she realised she had run out of options. Enlisting advisors who were familiar with Scotland, she planned her return. It could have and should have been a brilliant fresh start. Yet the influence of her Guise uncles meant that, young though she was, she had already made bad decisions. By far the worst of these was the treaty she had signed ahead of her marriage with Francis, three years earlier.

The backdrop to this marriage contract, which was anything but a formality, was the exquisite Chateau de Fontainebleau, south of Paris in the Île-de-France. It seems sinister that this stunning location played a potentially ruinous role in Scotland's affairs. An hour's train journey from the Gare de Lyon, this chateau in the centre of the bustling market town of Fontainebleau was formerly the King of France's hunting lodge. Still surrounded by 130 acres of parkland and gardens, it was rebuilt initially by Francis I, thereby introducing the Renaissance to France. Catherine de' Medici influenced its renovation, hence the Italianate courtyard and gardens. When Mary visited as a child and young woman it would have been spectacularly sophisticated, but within seventy years it had changed beyond recognition into the highly formalised royal chateau tourists enjoy today.

The venerable real (royal) tennis court in the front courtyard of the chateau is a remnant of the early modern era. It would not have been around in Mary's day, but she would have been very familiar with the *jeu de paume*, a favourite aristocratic sport. It was a pastime which, on her return to Scotland, she could enjoy in Falkland Palace, where her father had built a real tennis court, the year before her birth. Falkland's court is the oldest surviving example in the world.

The game that was played at Fontainebleau on 4 April 1558, by contrast, was exceptionally serious. Mary was presented with three secret legally binding documents that related exclusively to Scotland and its relationship to France after she married the Dauphin. Although they were worded to imply that Scotland would remain an independent kingdom, the first ensured that if she died without issue, the King of France and his heirs were to inherit Scotland, including Mary's right to the throne of England. The second affirmed that if she died without an heir, the King of France was entitled to all the country's revenues until he had been reimbursed for Mary's upbringing and his military protection of Scotland with one million pieces of gold. Thirdly, in a letter signed by her and Francis, all these provisions were guaranteed to be wholly within the law, and would henceforth remain in place, no matter what future changes she wished to make or any contracts that the Scottish Parliament made following her recent meeting with its commissioners.

That this was unlawful under Scots law cannot, surely, have been pointed out to her. Or if it was, she was encouraged to downplay its significance. That is the most charitable interpretation that could be put on her knowingly agreeing to terms that effectively consigned her homeland to the position of a vassal state. It has even been suggested that Mary signed innocently, confused by the documents' overblown language. Since she was no fool, and well educated, it is doubtful the opacity of the terms would have foxed her, had she actually read them. Instead it seems she was either complicit in conspiring to perpetrate a terrible injustice on her own people or, having been duped by her uncles, entirely unaware of the signifi-cance of what she had agreed to. For a future leading figure in European politics, it is hard to know which is worse. Historians such as Kate Williams believe she had little choice, while others, includ-ing Jenny Wormald, see it as a shocking dereliction of duty.

Whatever the truth behind these secret contracts, Mary would soon have reason to lose faith in the duke and cardinal. A year after she married Francis, the Lords of the Congregation managed to persuade Elizabeth I to support them, and Scotland, under their rule. (Sir William Cecil, Elizabeth's chief advisor, threatened to resign if she did not agree.) The long-term strategy, which was Cecil's dream, was to create a unified Protestant realm, in which Scotland was a useful but inferior annexe to the mighty England.

Seeing the threat this posed to Catholic France, the Guise brothers signed, on Mary's behalf but without her knowledge, an infamous agreement known as the Treaty of Edinburgh. A three-way bond, between Scotland's Protestant lords, England and France, as represented by the Guise brothers, its terms were as heinous as the secret deal signed at Fontainebleau. France ceded Mary's right to the English crown and endorsed Elizabeth's claim. Under its terms, the French were to withdraw from Scotland, thereby leaving Marie de Guise exposed. And if Scotland at any point in future did not hold the Protestant line, England would be within its rights to step in and get rid of troublesome Catholic and French influences. As John Guy writes of this astonishing document, 'It is almost impossible to exaggerate its significance.'

This was what you could call the Protestant plot. Mary got wind of a Catholic plot her uncles were trying to arrange, also without her say-so. This one proposed France allying with its long-time rival Spain to conquer Scotland before advancing on the coveted prize of England. On learning of this, Mary tearfully confronted the cardinal and the duke. She must have realised that these relatives, whose experience and support she had relied heavily upon to this point, were prepared to throw her, and her mother, to the wolves.

Recognising their covetousness must have come as a shock, and a humiliation. It has often been said that Mary placed inordinate importance on family ties and the loyalty these demanded. With her Stewart relatives, this idealistic principle was to prove as unfounded as with her French kin. Perhaps by the time she grew disillusioned with some of her Stewart family it came as less of a surprise, given the way her French relatives had treated her. Discovering she was in the hands of puppeteers highlighted her political and personal isolation. As would become apparent during her years in Scotland, an absence of trustworthy advisors was to contribute to her undoing.

Chapter 7

'The very face of heaven'

ARRIVAL IN LEITH

The galleys bringing Mary to Scotland sailed from Calais, with a flotilla of baggage ships in their wake. There were fears that the English might try to intercept and kidnap the queen, but while an English fleet followed close behind, there was no attempt, and never any intention, to capture her. Even the ships carrying 100 of the queen's horses, which were impounded for a month at Tynemouth, were finally released once the paperwork had been dealt with.

Mary was kept company on the trip, among others, by three uncles, her four Maries, the besotted chronicler Pierre de Brantôme, and the poet Pierre de Châtelard, whose story does not end well. He might have been half in love with Mary too, or he might, as some allege, have been a spy, intending to bring her down. Speeded by a favourable wind, the royal galley reached its destination far more swiftly than expected. Five days after departure, it glided into port in Leith around nine on the morning of 19 August 1561, followed by its companion. Onboard, cannons were fired to signal the queen's presence, and locals hurried to find out what was happening.

Thanks to John Knox, we know what the weather was like. Years later, when recalling Mary Stuart's arrival, he wrote: 'The very face of heaven the time of her arrival did manifestly speak what comfort was brought unto this country with her, to wit, sorrow, dolour, darkness and all impiety.'

Although it was summer, a thick haar wrapped itself over the town, dense as a London pea-souper. Scottish summers are brief and quixotic, but Mary was unfortunate in coming home to the dreichest possible day. While there would have been an abundance of hooded cloaks and furs in her luggage, not to mention warm bedding, she would have understood, from the first hour of her return, that this was almost a foreign country. The picture before her, as the ship berthed, would have had a Nordic air, pungently reinforced by the smell of fresh and salted fish being loaded and unpacked by the shore.

Leith was a tightly huddled port, where ships could drop anchor along the River of Leith within stepping distance of taverns and warehouses. The buildings were tall and steeply roofed, and the quayside broad. Drawings from the seventeenth century show rugged wooden piers, oil-streaked water, and a motley variety of boats and watermen. Even though Mary arrived early in the morning, the portside would have been bustling with merchants and horses, sailors and pedlars. One of the country's biggest ports, with markets in northern Europe and the Mediterranean and beyond, it did a roaring trade exporting hides, grain, timber, fish and coal, and importing delicacies such as wine, fruit and spices. Yet for all its international connections, it can rarely have seen someone as arrestingly glamorous as Mary. With seagulls skirling overhead and the eerie rattle of masts and rigging hidden in the fog, it would have been an unforgettable moment for the queen as she prepared to disembark.

In 1561, Leith was a fiercely independent community, bristling at any attempt by nearby Edinburgh to smother its identity. When Mary first saw it, the evidence of her mother's Regency was all around: massive earth ramparts thrown up by the English, military towers built by the French, and between these the unrepaired ravages of English attack in the 1540s.

The Siege of Leith, during the last months of Marie de Guise's life, was one of the defining moments in the town's history. When, in return for its loyalty, she offered to designate it a royal burgh, she had found the key to its heart. Although many Leithers were keen to see Protestantism prevail, the port's interests came first. As a result, French troops – around 3,000 or 4,000, some with their families – lived alongside Scots, lodging in their best rooms and getting thoroughly on their nerves. Problems with supplies on both sides meant the French and the besieging English army were equally unhappy. Taking advantage of the situation, Leithers charged soldiers, regardless of their nationality, as much as three days' wages for a hunk of bread. It was revenge, of a sort, for the disdain which both nations had always shown them.

These days, while there is still talk in some parts of 'the free state of Leith', it is an increasingly gentrified part of Edinburgh, having been officially engulfed by the city a century ago. Leith Walk, the wide, mile-long boulevard that leads from the centre of the port into the heart of the capital, is a barometer of change. When for several years I lived overlooking leafy Leith Links, where Mary reputedly once played golf, Leith Walk – and much of Leith itself – was drearily run-down. Shortly thereafter it became acclaimed as the seedy setting for Irvine Welsh's bestselling *Trainspotting*, a blackly comic novel, and later film, about the drugs culture in the town during the era in which Edinburgh gained an unenviable reputation as the Aids capital of Europe.

Today, the Walk is changed almost beyond recognition, with restaurants of all nationalities, stylish furniture shops, enticing artisan cafes and blocks of smart student housing. Abject poverty can still be found in backstreets or behind Georgian façades and the battered doors of Victorian tenements, but the general mood is cosmopolitan and upwardly mobile. This is the quarter where more discerning tourists flock to drink and eat.

From the docks, the coast of Fife, across the Firth of Forth, appears close enough to reach in a single leap. Running through the centre of the port is the Water of Leith, which starts in the Pentland Hills and passes through some of the city's best-known locations where, since the Middle Ages, mills have been powered by the fast-flowing water.

At the crossroads in the centre of Leith, by the main bridge, stands The King's Wark. A popular bistro pub, it was once a fifteenth-century royal complex, begun by James I, including shipbuilders' workshops, accommodation for merchants and warehouses. Like Fontainebleau and Falkland, it included a tennis court. Whether anything from the 1400s remains is uncertain, but the present inn retains its olde-worlde charm.

Little in Leith survives from the 1560s, other than fragmentary evidence of English ramparts, and St Ninian's Chapel. An appealing building, painted a pale terracotta, it is thought to have been left in ruins by English raids and rebuilt as a Protestant kirk after the Reformation. When Mary landed, it might already have been under reconstruction, although its distinctive Dutch spire, an attractive feature of the Leith skyline, was not added until late the following century.

Despite the plush high-rise apartments and serried parked cars, the layout and the character of the modern port are not so very different from its sixteenth-century forebear: outward-looking, independent, perpetually awash with incomers and visitors, and with a fringe of poverty that acts as a sharp reminder that while Leith is steadily gentrifying, not everyone is a beneficiary. Although the docks are now far distant from the river, there are permanently berthed barges tied up along the riverside. One is called the *Mary of Guise*, another *La Belle Esperance*. Both would have been in Mary's mind on that unpromising summer's day.

Not surprisingly, Mary had left France in tears, watching the coastline slip out of sight as she bid it *adieu*. She feared she would never see it again, and she was right. It was a rare episode of anxiety and regret in a life lived, to this point, with high hopes and confidence. Nevertheless, when she disembarked in Leith, it was with a bright face. This was the aspect she always showed in public, in whose presence she never failed to raise her game.

In part because of the speed of her journey there was no great crowd, and certainly no officials, to form a welcome party on the quayside. Taken aback at the suddenness of her arrival, there was consternation among those who greeted her over what to do. The solution was to usher her to the house of the rich burgess Andrew Lamb, close to The King's Wark, where she and her companions could dine, and recover from their trip. The original burgess's house is long gone, but in its place is a red-pantiled seventeenth-century whitewashed building of the same name. With its box-hedged parterre and crow-step gabling, it is like many houses in east-coast Scottish fishing communities, built to resist the salt winds that seek out instead the faces of the townsfolk.

Accounts suggest the party spent an hour here, by which time Mary's half-brothers Lord James Stewart and Lord Robert, along with the Duke of Châtelherault, and his mentally unstable son the Earl of Arran, had hastened to Leith. The horseback procession bearing the queen that subsequently made its way up Leith Walk towards the royal palace at Holyrood was greeted with enthusiasm. It was a reception that, for the first five years of her reign, Mary was to enjoy wherever she went. Even her fiercest critic, the scholar and Protestant reformer George Buchanan, conceded that 'she was graced with surpassing loveliness of form'. That day, and for several years to come, she was in mourning, as were her ladies-in-waiting. Their white-and-black dress code was strikingly French and chic and, for one of Mary's auburn hair and pale complexion, flattering too. Given her unusual height – she was approaching six feet tall – she was the embodiment of nobility. Many who saw her must have believed that the misery that had followed the battles of Flodden and Solway Moss, and the bitter conflict during her absence, were finally ended. Had they paused to reflect that a mere twelve months earlier the established church had been overthrown, to be replaced with a harsh brand of Protestantism, they might have had an inkling of what lay ahead. Then again, it is probable that a great many of the cheering crowd were still Catholic at heart, and hoped their queen would turn back the religious clock.

Treated with deference and adulation as she rode towards the palace, Mary was allowed a glimpse of royalist Scotland at its best. How much did she know of her own country? In some respects, she had carried her birthplace into France with her as a child. There, she learned to speak and write in fluent French, but with her Maries and guardians she spoke in Scots. The year-long visit of her mother in 1550 would have been a strong reminder of home, and what was lying in wait for her return. Yet it would be natural if, during the thirteen formative years she spent in France, it had usurped Scotland in her affections. She had been very comfortable with the luxurious way of life it provided. Those who trained her in the arts of queen-ship had done so, metaphorically, in a French accent. By the time of her homecoming, her cast of mind might therefore have been far more French than Scottish. And if this was not in itself a barrier to ruling well, her lack of day-to-day knowledge of how the Scottish court worked emphatically was.

Under Henri II, and briefly when her husband was king, Mary had adopted a Gallic regal attitude. In France, the monarch held absolute power, or was encouraged to believe that was the case. In Scotland, by comparison, the nobility liked to think that they were the king's equals, and that their ruler was on the throne dependent upon their consent. The reality was far more complicated, and power much more firmly held by the Crown than might at first appear. But it was to the Scottish monarch's advantage to cultivate this belief, allowing him or her to divide and rule, bringing lords in and out of the inner circle as best suited the Crown's purpose.

Mary might have hoped that keeping her Maries by her side would help dispel any notion that her court was to become the French bastion her mother had created. All the same, the question remains of what sort of woman she had grown into during her absence. It is hard to know with any certainty – this is part of what makes her so unendingly fascinating. No historian has ever been able fully to fathom her. Professor Ted Cowan wrote that 'Historians will never agree as to her character.' In person, she was beautiful by the standards of the day, with a lily-white complexion that had survived unscathed from three attacks of smallpox. This was no small advantage in an era when many faces were as pitted as orange peel. Evidence shows that she loved dancing and music as much when an adult as when a child, and was a keen needlewoman. Embroidery was an art she would spend much time on in middle age when she was imprisoned, but from her earliest days in Holyrood Palace she would take out her tambour frame and stitch during meetings of the Privy Council. She was a reader of poetry and the classics, not just in English, Scots and French but also in Latin, Italian and probably Greek, and owned a substantial library of 240 books. Its influence can be detected in her letters, which show an easy flowing style that allows her to open her heart and speak her mind. It is in her own words, especially in personal correspondence, that we detect a hint of her personality: her concern for the welfare of her servants and friends, her hauteur, her innate vivacity and optimism, which faded as her situation grew increasingly grave.

Like her mother, she was a card player, and would stay up half the night, sometimes playing dice or billiards, gambling for money. She was also an enthusiastic horse rider. In the opinion of one hyperbolic historian, she 'never looked handsomer than seen on horseback'. In France she had adopted the Italian fashion for wearing breeches beneath her riding skirts (made from Florentine serge) which allowed her to ride astride rather than side-saddle. Daring enough in France, such a sight was new to Scotland, causing some to mutter disapprovingly. Among her many outdoor pursuits were croquet, bowls, hawking and shooting the butts, which was excellent practice for hunting. If the number of places where she allegedly played golf is accurate then she cannot have had much time to rule. It's not clear either if she played tennis, but what is certainly true is that she was an athletic and energetic woman with a natural *joie de vivre*. For her, a day spent wholly indoors was a day wasted.

Mary's strength of character had already been severely tested by the age of eighteen, and it says much for her composure and confidence that when she reached Scotland, it was not as someone bowed down by bereavement but eager to embrace a challenge. And yet, she was entering a quagmire that was partly of her own making.

Jenny Wormald writes that for over a year, while she remained in France and contemplated remarrying, Mary had left Scotland adrift: 'she simply sat back and allowed the Protestant rebels of 1559–60, who had illegally deposed her regent, and set themselves up as "the Great Council of the Realm", to control the affairs of her country. It can hardly be overstated just how remarkable this was.' Had Mary returned to rule her country on the death of Francis, rather than hope to find a spouse on the Continent, the Reformation could conceivably have been stymied. In so doing she would also have shown commitment to her country and an understanding of her royal duty, as well as of the religious factionalism that was carving up Europe. In Wormald's view, and it is hard to disagree, 'Mary put marriage before monarchy'.

Unaware or heedless of this, Mary's sense of entitlement as she rode towards the Palace of Holyroodhouse would have been absolute. It was exactly a year since the Reformation had been declared, in August 1560, with the firebrand preacher John Knox in the vanguard. As with all great political upheavals, it did not happen overnight but was the result of years of gathering groundswell. The religious tide had been turning since the 1520s, and the more corrupt the Catholic Church was seen to be, the more the austere principles of a Calvinist strain of Protestantism, introduced by Knox, took hold. Thus the brand of Christianity that gripped the country was intensely judgemental and unforgiving.

Mary's arrival came at the very moment when the Church was doing away with the priests who acted as intermediary between people and their God. Translations of the Bible, still punishable by death in some countries, were spreading the sacred word, allowing parishioners to read the gospels for themselves without someone interpreting them. You could say that the Reformation was the ecclesiastical equivalent of republicanism, and a very unsettling precedent for all who sat on a throne. In 1558, the year before his own return to Scotland, John Knox wrote to Scotland's nobility and citizens, declaring that they would be justified, and indeed were honour-bound, to rise up against unjust monarchs. The man had many faults, but he was not duplicitous. Mary was not long in Scotland before he paraphrased his long-winded warning for her at their very first meeting: 'The sword of justice is God's, and if princes and rulers fail to use it, others may.' It was a sinister threat, and a courageous one, since it was also treason.

The trouble this precept was to cause lay far off. For the moment, Mary was allowed to practise her Catholic faith in private, so long as she tolerated Protestantism within her realm. In the following weeks, despite a handful of violent protests about her and her retinue's 'popery', she showed herself wisely tolerant. Or was she merely indifferent? This was an age when almost everyone professed to being a Christian. To do otherwise was to risk accusations of heresy, sorcery or witchcraft. Mary was conventionally pious, but there are no signs in her early years that she was exceptionally devout. It was not until she was imprisoned in England that the strength of her Catholicism emerged. By this stage, her insistence that she was being persecuted, and eventually martyred, for her Catholic beliefs looks more political than spiritual. And yet had she not been Catholic the danger she posed, as a figurehead around whom a Catholic uprising could be rallied, would have been far less worrying for her captors.

Before she sailed from Calais in August 1561, Mary had been visited by John Leslie, later to become one of her most trusted friends as Bishop of Ross. He urged her to land not in Leith but in Aberdeen, where she could summon the Catholic nobles in that region. Supporting her was George Gordon, Earl of Huntly, who could muster an army of 20,000, to march on Edinburgh and overturn the new-born Protestant Parliament. Huntly was a Catholic magnate of such standing he was effectively king of the north. He warned Mary not to trust her half-brother Lord James Stewart. She ignored this advice, although on discovering that James had been briefing William Cecil at the English court about their conversations she should have treated him with greater caution.

More pressing than religion was the question of the Scottish nobility's loyalty. It was on this group, and her relationship with them, that Mary's fortunes were to depend. To believe many histories, she had landed in a serpents' pit. The Austrian novelist and dramatist Stefan Zweig was virulent in his denunciation of these lords. In 1935, the year after he fled the Nazi regime for England, he published *Maria Stuart*, an impassioned psychological biography. His views on the lords were trenchant: 'in their amoral combativeness and cupidity they resembled the Italian condottieri, though lacking the latter's culture, and being even more unbridled in their instincts'.

Zweig's opinion was exaggerated, and possibly coloured by events of his own times, yet he is worth quoting because his was a commonly held view: 'these autocrats of the clans knew only one genuine pleasure, and that pleasure was war. "A bonnie fecht" was their delight; they were goaded on by jealousy; their one thought was to have power and ever more power. The French ambassador wrote: "Money and personal advantage are the only Sirens to whose voices the Scottish lords will lend an ear . . ."' Even Robert Burns, who might have been expected to be more sympathetic, considered them a 'pack of rascals'. Not until cooler historical minds addressed the subject was this perspective tempered by fact.

It was true, admittedly, that a steady income of pensions from the French king helped persuade many of the lords to support the queen. As a result, at the time of her arrival the consensus among her nobles was in her favour, especially since she had the confidence, and the ear, of her half-brother, who was in the Protestant ascendancy.

* * *

In 1561, the year Mary landed in Leith, another Scot returned home. If this were a thriller, you would see him stalking her from Calais to Leith, his ship gliding into port under cover of darkness. The reality was quite different and above board, but in every other respect, George Buchanan was to be as arch an enemy to the queen's reputation as Shakespeare was to Macbeth's.

An internationally acclaimed poet, he had been forced to leave Scotland in 1539 because of his satirical broadsides against Franciscan clergy. He mocked them long before it was safe to show contempt for the established religion. Setting up as a teacher, first in Bordeaux, then Portugal, he moved finally to Paris. Here he absorbed humanist ideas, which were the foundation of the Protestant Reformation. It was here too that he became tutor to Thomas Randolph, the future English diplomat and direct conduit to Elizabeth I. Even more significant was his friendship with Mary's half-brother, Lord James Stewart, later to become Earl of Moray. They may have met in Paris, where Buchanan moved in Huguenot circles, strengthening his Reformation views and connections. Moray appeared to him the ideal ruler for Scotland, and for the rest of his life this conviction is almost as much an explanation for his behaviour as his Protestant fervour.

Buchanan's return from his long exile might have been Moray's doing, since in the early days of her court at Holyrood, he became the queen's 'instructor', helping her to read and discuss such writers as Livy. He also wrote masques for her entertainments. Their rapport was initially good, and Mary granted him a pension (£250 Scots a year), a sum that was doubled three years later. But the accord was not to last. Buchanan was from the Knox school of ideology and misogyny. When Lord James broke with Mary, he did not hesitate over where his loyalty lay.

The court painter Arnold Bronckorst, who was a pupil of Hilliard, made a portrait of him in 1581, close to the time of his death. Buchanan is holding a book, signifying his erudition, and beneath his scholarly cap and clipped beard he looks intelligent, and tough. Anyone who has attended the General Assembly of the Church of Scotland will recognise the type: highly educated and self-confident, trenchant and unshakeable in their views.

Buchanan's influence was baleful enough while Mary was queen, and worse when, in captivity in England, she faced charges before an English tribunal. His *Ane detectioun of the doinges of Marie quene of Scottes* (1570) produced a string of accusations against her which the commissioners of the court read. This was the first official accusation against her. The editor and historian W. A. Gatherer writes, 'It was his work that introduced his party's case to the cultivated readers of Europe.' Allowing no room for doubt, it insisted on Mary's involvement in her husband Darnley's murder, and the adulterous passion for Bothwell that was the trigger for that crime. Here he is describing their tryst at Jedburgh, a few months before Darnley was killed: 'When he [Bothwell] had been brought there, their staying together and familiarity were hardly consistent with the honour of either. Then, either because of their daily and nightly exertions, which were dishonourable to themselves and infamous in the eyes of the people, or by some secret dispensation of providence, the Queen fell into so severe and dangerous a sickness that there remained little hope of her recovery.'

Buchanan was also in part responsible for Mary's son all but disowning her. Appointed James VI's tutor, he was a famously strict and punitive teacher. There is little doubt that he helped inculcate the idea that Mary was wanton, and that James was far better off without her.

But it was posthumously that Buchanan did Mary Stuart most lasting harm. Much of his History of Scotland – *Rerum Scoticarum Historia* (1582) – was written after Moray's assassination in 1570 and became a set text for the following two centuries. In it he levelled devastating and often wildly inaccurate accusations against Mary, dismantling the reputations of his enemies in passing. A further scurrilous work, *De Jure Regni apud Scotos* (1579), attempted to justify the way Mary had been treated by her disaffected courtiers, proving it was right for an unworthy monarch to be removed for the national good. Between them, these effusions painted a picture so blackly fanciful they should be regarded as historical fiction. But their influence was enormous and enduring. Not only did they defame and denigrate Mary, but they effectively denounced all women, especially those who dared rule.

In the middle of the 1500s, a controversial debate flourished in Europe. Known as the *querelle des femmes* – the woman question – it raised the issue of women's status and worth. At court, and in wider society, it was being asked whether women were capable of ruling, and should they be allowed to? When she was twelve, Mary wrote a series of formal letters on the subject of Worthy Women, showing her education kept abreast of modern ideas. Was she aware of how relevant it would be to her?

With several women in positions of influence and authority, such as Mary Tudor and Marie de Guise, soon to be joined by Mary, Queen of Scots, the *querelle des femmes* was more than an abstract question. Historian David Parkinson writes that 'its prominence around courts may be related to the rise of female patrons like Catherine de Médici, Mary Tudor, and Elizabeth, and to the opposition such women provoked.' According to Parkinson, by the 1550s and 1560s, 'in France as in England and Scotland sovereign queenship is a "burning issue"'.

Even before Mary was on the throne, attitudes towards female rulers were being tested and in many cases – notoriously so in Scotland – hardening in opposition. While in exile, John Knox issued his famous diatribe, *The First Blast of the Trumpet against the Monstrous Regiment of Women*. This salvo was directed at Mary Tudor, but being as crude in its aim as a nail bomb it wounded many beyond his target. One of its unintended consequences was to scupper his chances of ever gaining Elizabeth I's favour. But while he protested it was Mary Tudor he was reviling, his comments about Marie de Guise, in his *History of the Reformation of Religion in Scotland*, are additional evidence, should it be required, of his inability to see high-ranking women as equals, whoever they were. When she was appointed Regent, he wrote that putting a crown on her head was 'as seemly a sight (if men had eyes) as to put a saddle upon the back of an unruly cow'. Such misogyny must at times have made life for women of the period, whatever their rank, very hard to bear.

Then again, perhaps the better-educated, in positions of power, feared women more than ordinary folk did, because of the threat they posed to their authority. We will never know if that was the case, but whatever the reasons for widespread male mistrust and denigration of women, the environment in which Mary had to prove herself was a minefield. It would be pleasing to report that her husbands were exceptions to the rule but, apart from her first junior husband, the docile and adoring Francis II, her spouses were prime examples of unbridled male chauvinism.

Chapter 8

An Île de France

THE PALACE OF HOLYROODHOUSE

The Palace of Holyroodhouse, towards which Mary's homecoming procession advanced, was one of the Crown's finest symbols of authority and prestige. The James V tower, containing the royal apartments, was strikingly contemporary and luxurious. A four-square structure of three storeys, with turrets at each corner, it demonstrated her father's ambitions for a court as elegant and cultured as any in Europe. When first constructed it had a moat and an iron drawbridge, over which Mary passed into her new home.

There is no record of Mary's reaction on seeing Holyrood, but the response of the chronicler Brantôme, who arrived with her, suggests that she too might have been pleasantly surprised. He described it as a fine house, and 'much grander than was to be expected in so poor a country as Scotland'.

Sitting in a hollow below Arthur's Seat, an extinct volcano, and the cliffs of Salisbury Crags, Holyroodhouse was often swathed in smoke that billowed and belched from the many coal and wood fires in the palace and its environs. Situated at the foot of the High Street, or Royal Mile, which runs uphill from its gates to Edinburgh Castle, the palace was begun by James IV as a residence for his soon-to-be-bride, Margaret Tudor. His palace was substantially enlarged and embellished by his son, and very little of it remains today. Long after both kings were gone, it was fashionably remodelled in the seventeenth century by the stalwart Jacobite supporter Sir William Bruce. His airy cloistered courtyard and classical façades bring a glimpse of

Italy to the city. But for those interested in Mary Stuart, on approaching the palace the eyes are drawn immediately to the fortified medieval wing. It was behind these windows that some of the most dramatic and bloody events of Mary's reign took place.

The James V tower was designed on the same lines as the French chateau of Chambord, which had been built by Francis I in honour of his daughter, James V's first wife, Madeleine de Valois. Mary was very familiar with Chambord, and her father's palace might have reassured her by its familiarity. So too its gardens.

It was to become one of Mary's great pleasures to stroll in the gardens, and whenever possible she would hold meetings there, rather than stuffily indoors. The gardens at Holyrood were a refuge, offering a breathing space from the clamour of courtiers and the weighty demands of office. They also carried a reminder of her mother.

The palace gardens had their origins in the twelfth-century Augustinian monastery attached to Holyrood Abbey, and up until the time of James IV were tended by monks. He commissioned a queen's privy garden, in 1511, for Margaret Tudor, which was later redesigned for Mary's father, who employed the French gardener Bertrand Gallotre both here and at Stirling. For half a century the head gardener was John Morrison, who was in charge from 1546 until 1598. Morrison was under orders to employ two servants a day for 'rewling [rolling] and dressing' the gardens, and providing 'caill, herbis and sellatis to oure soverane ladyis'. He would also have taken instruction from Marie de Guise on shaping the layout to remind her of the great chateaux of her homeland. Mary would have been familiar with him, if only from her daily walks in the grounds.

Shortly before Mary's return, the abbey fishponds were drained and more church land purchased to extend the gardens. The focus was mainly on herbs and vegetables, with walled orchards for fruit. A sixteenth-century formal garden was a tranquil, fragrant space. Function and pleasure went hand in hand, and gravel pathways between raised beds and box hedge parterres allowed people to wander, even in poor weather. As at Stirling Castle there was also an enclosed deer park, Holyrood Park – which was among the grandest of its kind.

Although Mary had been raised in the presence of Catherine de' Medici, who was renowned for her interest in gardening, she showed no interest in imposing her own image on Holyrood's gardens. Instead, she used them as the stage for a variety of spectacular events, including jousts, tournaments and sporting parties. Edinburgh had never seen anything like it.

Despite the abundance of associations with her mother and father, Mary never warmed to Holyrood. The palace was to be her main residence for the rest of her reign, but even before it had become tainted with misery and terror, she was not entirely at ease here. Perhaps the knowledge that her most outspoken critic John Knox lived only ten minutes away up the Royal Mile was unsettling. Possibly the dankness of the palace's location made it hard to like. Or maybe in these surroundings she was too close to her citizens whose mood, as she well knew, was unpredictable.

After night-time curfew, when the town's watchmen guarded the city's eight gates and patrolled the walls built hastily after the Battle of Flodden, Edinburgh fell quiet. At all other times, its clamour and tumult would have reached the queen's ears. In the 1560s the population of Edinburgh was in the region of 12,000 to 15,000, crammed within its walls. The Royal Mile was a warren of back streets and passageways, filthy and riddled with disease. Almost every imaginable trade took place here, as some of the street names suggest: Blackfriars Wynd, Fleshmarket Close, Bakehouse Close, the Cowgate, Grassmarket and Lawnmarket. By day it was teeming with porters, tradesmen, hawkers, minstrels and townsfolk, by evening its taverns, alehouses, inns and brothels came to life. Work would start before daylight, as bakers stoked their ovens, butchers hefted dripping carcasses from the slaughter house, and the religious community in the Canongate, a minute's walk from Holyrood, rose before dawn, at the four o'clock bell for matins, their first observance of the day.

The High Street was a narrow funnel, leading straight to the portcullis of Edinburgh Castle. Wooden and stone houses rose on either side, up to six storeys high, with forestairs on which women would gather to watch the world go by. When more space was required, wooden additions were built onto the lower tiers, creating vertiginous buildings that were liable to collapse. As they grew higher, the streets below became darker. The houses of the poor might last only twenty years, but those that were better constructed could endure much longer. The greatest risk to their survival was fire, which, with the overhanging projections almost touching the buildings opposite, could rip through a street in minutes.

Historian Elizabeth Ewan writes that 'medieval towns were not pleasant smelling, even to contemporaries'. Whenever Mary ventured into the High Street, or its surroundings lanes, she would have been assaulted by the stench as well as the noise. Even the capital retained a rural air, as boys herded cattle or sheep into the fields beyond the city early in the morning and brought them home at night. The narrow-fronted town houses that lined the Royal Mile had long thin rigs at the back, which were used for vegetables, orchards or animals. They might contain doocots, brewhouses or kilns. For visitors, and the religious community and hospitals, horses were generally stabled on the outskirts of the city. This was also where trades such as skinning, tanning and fulling took place, closer to running water.

The city teemed with animals as well as pedlars, merchants and beggars. In addition to horses and mules, cats and domestic dogs, there were strays or 'midden dogs'. Pigs roamed freely, feeding on scraps, and chickens and poultry got under people's feet. Fish were gutted and their entrails cast aside. So much filth ran down the street that some wore wooden pattens to raise them above it. Over everything lay the fug of smoke from coal fires and dust from building work and unpaved streets. Ewan writes that sinusitis was a common and chronic complaint of town dwellers in this period. But for odour, nothing could compare to that of middens and foul-smelling privies, or the corpses of beasts and humans left too long unburied.

Yet not all was muddle, confusion or dirt. Above the cries and curses of traders and customers came church bells, or public bell-ringing ahead of proclamations. With Holyrood at its foot, the Royal Mile was filled with the well-dressed and wealthy, their brightly coloured cloaks setting them apart from the 'rude people'. They would have stood out amid the sea of labourers in white and grey, and the common folk, in coarse and drab woollen cloth.

By the 1560s, Edinburgh was a centre of scholarly professions associated with government and the courts of law. East-coast merchants were the most prosperous, and none more so than those with access to the Port of Leith and the international trade that flowed through it. As a consequence, there was much money in Edinburgh to be lavished on crafts, trades and the arts. The richest burgesses of the town took their cue from the luxuries they saw at court, at the end of the street.

Today, with the exception of Balmoral, said to be Elizabeth II's favourite residence, Holyrood is the property most strongly associated in Scotland with the royal family. Open to the public for much of the year, it is also used for stately civic occasions. Most popular of these is the Queen's summer garden party where she circulates among the throng, whose heads bob at her approach like ducks after breadcrumbs in a pond.

It was the week before Christmas when I visited, and the palace courtyard sparkled with frost. Shortly after the doors opened I followed behind a party of pre-schoolers in their fluorescent vests. Holding hands, they disappeared in pairs through the entranceway like a procession of jelly babies. They were later to be found cross-legged in Charles II's Throne Room, close to a gigantic twinkling Christmas tree. They did not seem to register the stern-faced portraits all around the walls studying them while their teacher talked.

Of all the locations associated with Mary Stuart, Holyrood feels most majestic. A living palace, where the Queen and her family regularly visit, it is undeniably magnificent. It is also unexpectedly lovely. The rooms are decorated with chandeliers, paintings, and richly upholstered furniture and tapestries. The Royal Dining Room table is laid out with silverware and crystal as if a banquet is about to begin. Under the benign gaze of portraits of the Queen Mother and the Queen herself, it offers a keyhole into the style, and formality, in which today's royals live and work.

The most fascinating of the high-ceilinged and spacious seventeenth-century quarters is the Great Gallery. The walls are devoted to dozens of portraits of Scottish kings, real and mythical, whose gaze is disconcerting for dinner guests. They are by the Dutch artist Jacob de Wet, who painted them for Charles II at a rate, it is said, of one a week. This gallery could as well be called the Pinocchio room. To affirm the Stewarts' age-old right to the crown, De Wet stretched the portraits' noses as if they were wax. Sir Walter Scott, on examining them, found himself wondering why all the royals were depicted 'with a nose like the knocker of a door'. It is one of the happy accidents of Mary Stuart's life that she did not inherit the Stewart nose.

The splendour of William Bruce's seventeenth-century palace is undeniable, but it is in the darker medieval apartments of the fortified James V tower that Mary's story is found. When she first arrived in the palace, her fashionably high heels would have echoed as she walked from room to room. Her mother's furniture had been removed after her death, and the place was almost empty. What little remained was under dust sheets. Fortunately, Mary brought sufficient furnishings to turn the barren palace into a home. Along with a large contingent of domestic staff from France, foremost of whom was a chef, Mary had also travelled with trunks filled with tapestries and wall hangings, bedding, linen, decorations and warm clothes for a cold climate. Over the years her interior decorating gathered momentum, as did the roll call of her staff.

A list from 1567, signed by the queen and by David Rizzio's brother Joseph, gives an idea of the size to which the queen's household eventually grew. By this point it numbered around 170 members, all paid from the queen's income from France as dowager queen. Other than the gardeners, the majority of her staff were French. They included a surgeon, two medical men, an apothecary, a tailor, an upholsterer, a painter and a lutenist. There were ladies of honour and esquires of the table and of the stables, ushers, a confessor and a chaplain. There was a barber, a stocking-maker and a shoe-maker. Her six masters of the household were French, as was Nichola, La Folle, a fool or entertainer who had travelled over with the queen's party. The Secretary's Department employed seven staff, all with foreign names.

When the trunks had been unpacked, and additional items ordered, the palace grew sumptuous. Inventories show forty-five stately beds, one of which was draped in cloth of gold and silver, with violet and grey silk drapes, fringed with gold and violet silk. There were thirty-six Turkish carpets and twenty-three sets of tapestries. The queen's dining room was hung with black velvet, and the library decorated in green. This wasn't Little France, this was an Île de France.

The editor's preface to the Lord High Treasurer's Accounts of Scotland covering the years 1559 to 1566 makes an interesting if tantalising point. While there is a great deal about beds in these accounts, he comments, 'it is surprising to find how little the stirring incidents of the time are reflected in the prosaic pages of the Treasurer. They go placidly on, recording the purchase of dresses, the payment of wages, the prices of provisioning garrisons, and sundry other little dry details, just as if Scotland had not been taking the most tremendous turning-point in her history.' That is one of the reasons, perhaps, why these accounts, which range from 1473 to 1635, make such absorbing reading. They are the worm's-eye view of ordinary business, their appeal lying in the detail of what was worn, eaten, fed to horses or given to servants, rather than significant matters of state.

The queen's rooms were on the second floor of the tower, directly above the king's. They were connected by a poky corkscrew stair-case, set within the walls, which was for private use. For other visitors, Mary's suite was entered formally from a wide stairway which opened onto her audience room. This is a gloomy chamber, panelled in wood, its ceiling embossed with royal monograms. It is now a museum, with cases containing jewellery and other objects connected with Mary. Among them is a gold pomander that opens in segments like a chocolate orange. This was filled with sweet scented herbs and spices, to ward off unwelcome smells which were not just unpleasant but considered a source of disease (hence the bird-like masks worn by plague doctors, who hoped the herbs stuffed into their beaks would protect them). There is also a cabinet displaying gifts that Mary apparently gave to her most devoted lady-in-waiting, Mary Seton. These include a stunning set of earrings, necklace and brooch.

In this room too there are reminders of the personalities of this court, and its European contemporaries. These include one of the best-known portraits of Mary by François Clouet, painted around 1558–60, before she arrived in Scotland. She wears a rose-pink high-collared dress and pearl headdress, a serene and thoughtful expression on her face as she slips on a wedding ring. There is also a copy of Nicholas Hilliard's glazed miniature of the queen, from the 1570s, by which time she was in captivity. Hilliard is thought to have painted Mary in watercolours before she left France, and it is likely he used an earlier sitting for this work. A cross on a chain is worn conspicuously over her dress.

At the far end of the audience room is a severe and dark full-length portrait of Mary, holding a crucifix, wearing a cross, and carrying what one assumes must be a tiny Bible. Closer inspection reveals a picture inset within this. It shows her kneeling, blindfolded, on the scaffold at Fotheringhay, the executioner poised to bring down his axe.

Every available space is hung with portraits, from Isabella, Queen of Denmark and Eleanor of Austria, to Philip the Fair, Archduke of Austria, and Erasmus. There is a wide fireplace with Dutch blue tiles, and four deeply set windows. Before one window is Mary's oratory, with the illuminated fifteenth-century Holyrood Oratory

Bible she used for her private devotions. Nearby is the place where Rizzio was stabbed to death. The bloodstains his corpse left on the floorboards before he was dragged down the stairs are still visible, some insist, although the floor has since been replaced. A copper plaque commemorates where the deed was done.

Chapter 9

'Ower sair'

A FIRST ENCOUNTER WITH JOHN KNOX

What John Knox made of the queen's oratory is not hard to guess. Nor did she make any attempt to hide it from him. Within a few days of her return, Mary summoned Knox, to accuse him of inciting disobedience and disrespect towards her among the people. She had ample evidence for the charge.

Initially, all had seemed well. The evening of her arrival, bonfires had been lit, and enthusiastic singers had serenaded her beneath her windows for several nights, keeping her awake. In one of the more choreographed celebrations, as she processed down the Royal Mile she was handed a Bible, in English, and the Book of Common Prayer. The message was pointed, and she believed she knew who was behind it.

That first meeting set the tone for what was to follow. Mary received Knox with her half-brother Lord James. Showing none of the deference she was accustomed to – indeed, speaking to her as she had probably never been spoken to before – Knox launched into an impromptu sermon. He told her of the duty of citizens to bring down an unfit ruler, speaking so intemperately Mary could not bring herself to reply for several minutes. When she did, she expressed dismay that he was effectively suggesting civil disobedience: 'I perceive that my subjects shall obey you and not me, and shall do what they like and not what I command, and so I must be subject to them and not they to me!'

Their argument continued. Since the record of it was written by

Knox in his *History of the Reformation*, its accuracy cannot be assumed. He replied:

> God forbid that ever I take upon me to command any to obey me, or yet to set subjects at liberty to do what pleases them! My travail is that both princes and subjects obey God. Think not, Madam, that wrong is done you, when you are willed to be subject to God. It is He that subjects peoples under princes, and causes obedience to be given unto them. Yea, God craves of Kings that they be foster-fathers to His Church, and commands Queens to be nurses to His people. This subjection, Madam, unto God, and unto His troubled Church, is the greatest dignity that flesh can get upon the face of the earth; for it shall carry them to everlasting glory.

Mary replied that she considered Rome to be the true Kirk of God, at which point Knox's harangue shifted up a gear. Mary listened, eventually dismissing him when she was called to dinner by saying he was 'ower sair' – too clever – for her. For his part, Knox left the palace to tell people, 'If there be not in her a proud mind, a crafty wit, and an indurate heart against God and his Truth, my judgement fails me.'

The twentieth-century poet William Soutar wrote in his diary, 'We cannot recall Mary Stuart without seeing the shadow of Knox at her back.' Knox was not by any means the author of her misfortune, but he played a significant part in cutting the ground from beneath her feet and stirring mistrust or even hatred of her. Moderation or compromise were not words he understood. In common with any religious fanatic, he was all or nothing, black or white, for or agin. That he believed it acceptable to commit violence, or worse, in the name of God gives an idea of the lengths to which he and the most passionate reformers were prepared to go to safeguard their infant revolution. In his mind, Mary was a mortal threat to the Reformation he had brought about. It still rankled that she had been promised the right to continue to practise her own faith in private when she reached Scotland. He thought she should have become Protestant like the rest of her subjects.

When he first met Mary, Knox was around forty-seven years old. Originally ordained as a priest, he acted as bodyguard to the Protestant reformer George Wishart, who was burned at the stake in St Andrews for his beliefs by the corrupt, cruel and clever Cardinal David Beaton. The execution took place conveniently close to the castle, where Beaton could sit at a window and watch. Knox was not involved in the subsequent assassination of Beaton, but heartily approved of it. After spending eighteen months as a galley slave for the French, who had captured him and other Protestants in St Andrews, he lived for several years in England. When Mary Tudor came to the throne, and the Catholic flame was briefly reignited, he fled for the Continent.

In Geneva he fell under the spell of Calvinism, which he described as 'the most perfect school of Christ that was ever on earth since the days of the apostles'. He was soon hell-bent on making others see the light. He returned to Scotland in 1559, and within a year, with the help of the Lords of the Congregation, foremost of whom was Lord James, had ushered in a radically different religious regime. When pontificating from the pulpit he could become heated. A scribe who witnessed his sermons said he would grow so excited, 'he made me to grue [shudder] and tremble, that I could not hold pen to write'. It was with a performance like this, in St John's Kirk in Perth in 1559, that the Reformation in Scotland truly began. Knox's inspirational and inflammatory words led to a riot and the destruction of altarpieces and other signs of Catholicism throughout the town and far beyond. Among his followers were fanatics who considered Catholic 'idolatry' a worse sin than adultery or murder.

In hindsight, it is hard to understand why Mary did not try to challenge a Reformation so recently introduced. So much of Europe was still Catholic that it might well have been possible, perhaps with the help of France, to reverse it. That she did not attempt to do so speaks to her broadmindedness, and her toleration. It might also suggest a lack of imagination. So long as nobody interfered with her own practices, she believed she could rule comfortably and effectively in a land where very different attitudes were gaining ground. Despite the bloody reprisals against Huguenots that she had already witnessed in France, she seems to have foreseen neither the ideological clash her own position might involve, nor, for that matter, the strength of her religious opponents' beliefs. Opinion on this strategy diverges. Some historians take the view that it was the wisest position to adopt, being long-sighted and pragmatic; others are incredulous that she would so meekly accept the situation without protest.

Lord James was at this point acting as Mary's closest advisor and confidant, even though he was known to be conveying information about her to Elizabeth I's minister, Sir William Cecil. More than ten years her senior, James Stewart was her half-brother by the king and his mistress Lady Margaret Erskine. James V had a string of illegitimate children, including Lord Robert Stewart, whose mother was Euphemia Elphinstone, and Lady Jean Stewart, whose mother was Elizabeth Bethune. As a young girl, Mary would have known those of the king's children who were raised in the royal household. Lady Jean was to become one of Mary's closest companions, and was with her when Rizzio was murdered.

Lord James was a serious-minded and shrewd political operator. A sombre portrait of him by the Flemish exile Hans Eworth, painted the year Mary returned to Scotland, shows him in distinguished courtly dress looking seigneurial. He bears a strong resemblance to his father. His narrow mouth and the fixity of his eyes suggest implacable determination as well as a powerful intelligence. He was said, by Antonia Fraser, to lack his father's charisma, but was trusted by the English – not always correctly – as a breed of less self-seeking Scottish noble. In their eyes his saving grace was his Tudor grandmother.

Lord James has been depicted by his critics as ruthlessly ambitious for the throne, but some believe his drive stemmed not from personal gain but from his Protestant convictions. The English ambassador Nicholas Throckmorton, who sported a ginger forked beard, was impressed by him. Lord James, he wrote, was a man who 'seeks to imitate rather some who have led the people of Israel than any captains of the age'. Either way, he was to prove an unreliable friend and dangerous enemy to Mary, who was too quick to assume that a relative with whom she had shared a roof in childhood would automatically be her ally.

Mary's audience room is the outer ring of her inner sanctum at the palace, beyond which lie her bedchamber and supper room. As at Stirling Castle, which her father had designed to give the royals privacy, Holyrood allowed the ruler to live almost separate from the other business of court. As Jenny Wormald writes, 'Mary's lifestyle is a devastating example of the dangers inherent in the opportunities offered by the architectural layout of sixteenth-century royal palaces which enabled monarchs to withdraw to the remoteness of their private apartments and render themselves inaccessible if they so wished.' In Mary's case, she was frequently absent from meetings of the Privy Council, which took place downstairs. These sessions could be held without her councillors catching sight of her, and vice versa. It allowed a *cordon sanitaire* between private and political life, which carried great risk.

* * *

Three weeks after settling into Holyrood, Mary appointed her Privy Council, the royal equivalent of a First Minister's Cabinet. It was a crucial occasion for a monarch, laying the foundations for their rule. Yet in this too she showed no desire to interfere with the Protestant ascendancy. A quarter of her councillors were Catholic: the earls of Huntly, Atholl, Montrose and Erroll. The rest were Protestants, among them Lord James, whom she made her chief advisor, the Earl of Glencairn, a devout follower of Knox, the Earl of Argyll, one of the largest landowners in the country, the fearsome Earl of Morton, and the gifted William Maitland of Lethington, who retained his influential post as secretary, but was one day to turn Judas. She also included Lord Ruthven, a man of whom she was wary from the outset. He was rumoured to be a warlock.

At no point in her reign did Mary try to augment the number of Catholics on her council. It was as if she could not imagine the possibility of trouble ahead, when their support might be necessary. Indeed, she actively alienated her fellow believers. One of her earliest decisive actions was a deliberate rebuff and rebuke to George Gordon, Earl of Huntly, the country's leading Catholic noble. Her treatment of him snuffed out any immediate hope of a Counter-Reformation. Had Mary been eager to restore her own faith, this might conceivably have been achieved, though not without bloodshed. That, perhaps, was the key to her seemingly supine toleration. In France, she had seen the beginnings of religious persecution. With the Dauphin she had been witness to torture and executions, and walked past the dangling corpses of Huguenots, left hanging for the public's delectation and instruction. Possibly she took to heart the warning they conveyed and wanted no further part in state-sanctioned persecution.

Not all her advisors had such scruples. Among the most important members of the Privy Council was James Douglas, Earl of Morton. He was utterly ruthless and cruel, although many of his worst crimes against humanity were committed after Mary had departed Scotland, during his Regency (1572–78). Perhaps because of his granite heart, he proved a successful politician. His family owned the magnificent red sandstone castle of Tantallon, overlooking the Bass Rock off the East Lothian coast, and it might be a fanciful version of this, or of Aberdour Castle, another Douglas property, that lies in the background of his portrait presumed to be by the artist Arnold Bronckorst. By the time of this painting, which is held in the National Galleries of Scotland, made around 1580, Morton was puffed up with power and prestige. His face suggests a pitiless nature. Although slow to join the Protestant cause until sure of its success, he proved a remorseless enemy of Mary. As John Guy writes, 'Although a Protestant, Morton was too venal and lascivious to be an ally of Knox and the Calvinists.' Unlike some of the lords who rebelled against the queen out of ideological conviction, his primary interest was always his own survival and gain.

The third member of the triumvirate which dominated the council and effectively controlled matters of state was William Maitland of Lethington. In his early thirties, he had been secretary to Mary's mother, and served her well. Canny, clever and quick on his feet, 'the Scottish Machiavelli' or, as he was known in his homeland, 'Meikle Willy', had eventually deserted Marie de Guise to join the Lords of the Congregation. George Buchanan was no admirer, writing of him: 'There is a certain kind of beast callit Chamaeleon.' A studious-looking young man, he was the son of a poet. He was not from a noble family, but he was a typical Scotsman of this and later periods, a highly intelligent, educated and ambitious man. His home was Lethington Tower, near Haddington. His loyalty to Mary, as to her mother, did sometimes waver, but his marriage to one of her four Maries, Mary Fleming, helped strengthen his attachment. In his favour, in an age that encouraged fanaticism, he kept a cool head over religion. He is said to have hotly refuted the claim that he once heretically called God 'a bogle of the nursery', but that the accusation was made is telling.

Maitland's first task on being reappointed to the Privy Council was to leave for London and try to negotiate a way out of a critical political impasse. The cause was the infamous Treaty of Edinburgh, contracted in 1560 before Mary left France. Intended to bring peace between England, France and Scotland and, by the withdrawal of French troops, leave Scotland to its own affairs, it also, crucially, stipulated that Mary would relinquish any claim to be Elizabeth's successor in the event that she, and any of her children, should die. Learning of this treaty, made without her agreement, Mary refused to ratify it. It was Maitland's task to broach this sensitive subject with Elizabeth and persuade her that if she acknowledged Mary's claim to the throne, she would agree to the treaty.

With hindsight, it is possible to see Mary's insistence on her right to the English throne as the stumbling block that led her eventually to the scaffold. Her single-minded pursuit of this right shows stubborn ambition and entitlement, but above all a lack of political acumen. With Scotland recently turned Protestant, making her personal position precarious, it is revealing that she focused on her own hypothetical elevation, even when Elizabeth was likely still to marry and produce a nursery of heirs.

Although Elizabeth admitted she preferred Mary to all other contenders, she would never formally concede Mary's right to the throne, or see her as anything other than a potentially dangerous rival. That she did not even raise Henry VIII's explicit exclusion of foreigners from inheriting the throne suggests that her objection was not legal but personal. As she told Maitland, to name Mary would risk fomenting a Catholic uprising: 'The desire is without example to require me in my own life, to set my winding sheet before my eyes . . . Think you that I could love my own winding sheet?'

Nevertheless, whether mendaciously or in good faith, she gave Maitland sufficient grounds for hope that an agreement could be reached that would satisfy both sides. Doubtless Elizabeth's advisor, William Cecil, who was present during the discussions, had his own thoughts on that.

Chapter 10

'An orgy of greed'

CRICHTON CASTLE HOSTS A WEDDING

Shortly after Christmas, in January 1562, Mary left Holyrood with her attendants, a baggage train and a substantial and heavily armed escort. The party, which included her half-brother James, rode unhurriedly south out of the city, and was soon in open country. Their destination was Crichton Castle, twelve miles beyond Edinburgh, which was the base of James Hepburn, the Earl of Bothwell.

The occasion of the outing was the forthcoming marriage of the queen's half-brother John Stewart to Bothwell's sister, Lady Janet Hepburn. Lord John was the Prior of Coldingham, a bleak religious outpost close to the border. Despite his clerical position he, like his sister, loved to dance, and was a most urbane and civilised courtier. Like so many of James V's illegitimate children, John had risen vertiginously; his status was further elevated when Mary bestowed Dunbar Castle on him.

Mary's love of partying was to become well known during the years to come, but at this point, so shortly after her return, she had enjoyed few opportunities for public gaiety. Her brother's wedding was a chance briefly to throw off the burdens of state and have fun.

Throughout her life the queen was generous to her friends and retinue. When they got married, she often paid for the bride's dress, along with other expensive items. She enjoyed making people happy, and few were as quick to reward those they liked or wanted to thank. Her letters are filled with mentions of bequests, emoluments and gifts.

Crichton Castle sits on the edge of a steep valley, guarded by gorse. As the queen rode closer, she would have seen a severe medieval fortress, at odds with the mood of the celebration and festivities it was soon to host.

Mary had met Bothwell once before. In 1560 he had brought letters to her in France from her mother. Although he had a well-earned reputation as violent, reckless and untrustworthy, his unwavering support of Marie de Guise endeared him to her daughter. It also made him a mortal enemy of the rebel Protestant lords when, in November 1559, he audaciously intercepted money sent by Elizabeth I to help them.

In 1562, the castle would have felt far distant from the city and its smog and filth. Today, even though it lies only a few miles from a busy road, it is as good as buried in the countryside. Massive and plain, it rises intimidatingly from its high vantage point. In the gorge beneath runs the River Tyne. In medieval times the castle would have been enclosed in a high protective wall, sheltering the buildings within, a landmark and refuge for neighbouring hamlets and villages.

Entering the central courtyard immediately dispels any thought of the Middle Ages. Richly ornamented façades date from the 1580s, when Mary's godson, Francis Hepburn, the fifth Earl of Bothwell, fell under the Renaissance spell. Around this time, Mary was imprisoned in England.

The interior, which lies open to the sky, is so haphazardly ruinous it's like an Escher drawing. Stairways run up walls and disappear into dark interiors, the whole a mishmash of seemingly disconnected doorways, windows and soaring walls. Roofless rooms suggest a spaciousness in the older as well as the newest wings, but some are miserably poky. The pit prison, in the ancient fourteenth-century tower, has a low entrance and a sickening drop. It was intended for common criminals, awaiting trial in the lord's court upstairs. Air and light came through a needle-like opening. This hellhole is close to the original lord's hall, but the walls are so thick there was no fear of prisoners' cries spoiling dinner.

Crichton Castle has a long and eventful history. After centuries of ownership, it passed from the high-ranking but treacherous Crichtons into Hepburn hands as reward for Patrick Hepburn, the Earl of Bothwell's loyalty to James IV. Patrick's father Adam, Lord High Admiral of Scotland, had died with James IV on the battlefield at Flodden. It was Patrick's rambunctious son James Hepburn who became the fourth Earl of Bothwell and, eventually, Mary Stuart's third husband. His part in her life was to prove disastrous, but at this stage, not only did Mary barely know him, her mind was circling around the possibility of her second marriage.

On the south-west side of the courtyard is a six-storey tower, dating from the mid fifteenth century. Four floors were devoted to bedrooms, and below them were service rooms for domestic staff. The grandest of these were the kitchens, designed to feed hundreds. This wing dates from the same period as the Great Hall block in the south wing, which once contained a magnificent hammer-beamed room where the wedding banquet would have been held. The splendour of all this suggests the castle was a hub of activity whose inmates were players on the national stage. The original owners of Crichton Castle were men of their age – that is to say, ruthless. The same can be said of the Hepburns, and of James Hepburn especially.

Lord John and Lady Janet were probably married in Crichton Collegiate Church, a quarter of a mile from the castle. This squat building, founded in the middle of the fifteenth century, oozes rural charm. Surrounded by weathered headstones, it sits embedded in well-tended grass in the pretty hamlet of Tynehead. When I visited on a dazzlingly bright summer's morning, the sky was cornflower blue and the song of yellowhammers filled the air. In the depths of January, when the royal party entered its doors, it is more likely they were greeted by the cawing of crows and rooks.

After the ceremony, the party would have made a procession across the fields from the church to the castle. This was a chance for locals to gawp at their newly arrived queen, and for the guests to display their finery. Many would doubtless have preferred a larger audience for their parade, but at least they would have the satisfaction of knowing that the 'carls' out here – a derogatory term used by townspeople of the peasantry, or anyone they wished to insult – would never have seen such a brilliant array of wealth and sophistication.

The queen was still dressed in mourning, but with such style as the country had rarely before seen. In winter her dress was of the warmest fabrics, possibly velvet or brocade. Her headwear might have been plumed or bejewelled, while the austerity of her black and white outfit was brightened by sparkling earrings, rings and necklaces. Pointed shoes were in vogue, and Mary had a love of heels that enhanced her height as well as her glamour.

For many years the prevailing fashion in Europe had been in the Italian style, with vividly embroidered corsets, gilded hair nets and wide, puffed and slashed sleeves. By the early 1560s, however, the political dominance of the court at Spain was influencing how the rich dressed. A portrait of Lord Darnley and his brother, the year after the Crichton wedding, shows him in the severe Spanish mode: an all-black ensemble of doublet, hose and tight-fitting jacket. A chin-high collar shows a glimpse of lace at the neck, as also at his cuffs. The austerity of this costume was a volte-face from the peacock brilliance of recent years, when the aristocracy wore expensively dyed robes. To prevent them aping their betters, commoners were forbidden to wear silks, velvets or embroidered materials, and could only indulge in bright colours on special occasions specified by strict sumptuary laws. Needless to say, not everyone complied. Second-hand clothes stalls allowed the less well-off to pretend they were from a higher station, although it took courage to flout the rules.

Those watching the wedding guests progress back to the castle would have looked much like peasantry anywhere in Europe in this age. Their homespun tunics, hose and dresses would have been drab, and their shoes or boots – their only pair – round-toed and hard-worn. By this century, rural peasantry were wearing short jackets rather than the longer tunics of the early Middle Ages. Combined with close-fitting hose, the effect shocked some onlookers, who felt little was left to the imagination. At the same tmie, women's bodices grew increasingly revealing.

The wedding party would have thrown coins for the crowd before disappearing into the castle for a spectacular and lavish wedding feast. Presided over by Bothwell, the entertainments that followed over the next few days impressed even the English ambassador, Thomas Randolph, who spoke of enjoying 'much good sport and many pastimes'.

To begin the celebrations, guests took their places at long trestle tables beneath the Great Hall's vaulting hammer-beam roof. The queen sat at the 'hie burde', or top table, alongside the bride and groom, with a canopy over her head to indicate her status.

In the days before the wedding, the countryside around the castle would have been plundered in honour of the newly-weds. In this era, despite the rise of elegant cuisine in some quarters, the principle behind banquets was, as historian Fernand Braudel writes, 'ostentatious quantity rather than quality'. Meat was the dominant feature, and as many as seven different plates would be offered at once, sometimes with various boiled, roasted, potted and pâtéd meats, grilled, baked and boiled fish, as well as vegetables, piled in pyramids on top of each other. Rich sauces were, thankfully, served separately.

Diners were offered venison, rabbit, partridge, woodcock, plover, turtle doves, pheasants, blackbirds, larks, duck and goose. There might have been heron, moorhens and coots as well as lampreys, eels, salmon, trout and shellfish. Wine flowed, along with the ale that everyone, including children, drank. Like many castles, Crichton had its own well, cellars, bakehouse and a well-equipped brewhouse. It would often be an ale-wife who was in charge. Bread-making was mostly a male occupation, while the humble oatcake was women's domain.

At the other end of the scale were oranges, a luxury only the very wealthy could afford. They arrived in Scotland in early winter and were hoarded to last until spring. When she was a girl, Mary loved to make marmalade, spending hours stirring vats of the bubbling fragrant liquid. It would be a remarkable oversight if the Crichton Castle chefs had not provided oranges for their guests.

The relay of servants bringing more food from the kitchens, and the copious supply of alcohol, turned the celebrations into a riotous occasion or, in Braudel's view, 'an orgy of greed'. Yet, some pretence of manners still had to be observed. Since everybody served themselves from the same dishes using their fingers, they must first clean their hands in water bowls on the table. Goblets might be passed from one diner to the next, or in the most extravagant households each guest might be given their own glass. Place settings might be laid with spoon and knife, but men especially might have used their own knives, worn in their belts for either eating or self-defence. Spoons were by now widely used, but to eat with knife and fork was a refinement for the next century. Even when forks were introduced, the French essayist Michel de Montaigne continued to use his fingers, being a fast eater, and remarked, 'I sometimes bite my fingers in my haste.' He seems also to have eschewed spoons.

If it was unacceptable to return a half-eaten chicken leg to the main platter, or to pick off it with dirty hands, it was even worse to wipe your mouth on the tablecloth or – unthinkably – to blow your nose on it. In his guide to manners, *Civility*, Erasmus indicated the correct way for people to behave in polite society: 'To wipe the nose on the cap or sleeve belongs to rustics; to wipe the nose on the arm or elbow to pastrycooks; and to wipe the nose with the hand, if by chance at the same instant you hold it to your gown, is not much more civil. But to receive the excreta of the nose with a handkerchief turning slightly away from noble people is an honest thing.'

Given the quantity of food those in aristocratic and privileged circles could consume, one pictures the upper classes as a stout breed tending towards obesity as they became less active; the lower orders by contrast would have been muscular and fit, if increasingly bent by a lifetime's hard work. Those in the country probably ate less meat than their urban counterparts, since it was in towns that animals were slaughtered, but they would have had ample opportunity to catch rabbits or gamebirds to add to their pots. It is likely that those who lived near the castle were able to dine on the wedding left-overs for days to come.

A reconstruction of the castle's kitchen suggests how it might have looked under pressure to feed dozens upstairs. Beyond the arches that led inside the enormous fireplace, cauldrons would have hung over the fire. These would be stacked with food, separated by dividing boards with holes punched in them, to allow steam to rise. At the bottom of the cauldron there might be a wrapped cut of bacon, submerged in water and allowed to stand there until it was cold. Above this were 'bag puddings' of cereals and beans, contained in what look like money pouches tied at the neck. On top of them sat a jar of poultry, eggs and onions, and one of beef laid on a bed of twigs, which was intended for use in soup. Hams and fish were smoked in the chimney itself, and for those keen to escape these pungent smells, a trapdoor in the kitchen floor gave access to the storerooms below.

The banquet for Mary's half-brother might well have lasted for several days. Part of the festivities included a masque and possibly a torch dance, where the guests were led across the floor by servants bearing enormous torches on poles. Added to all this was a fireworks display, the like of which had almost certainly never been seen in the area. What those in nearby villages made of the lit-up night sky is not reported. Among the books Mary Stuart left in Edinburgh Castle was one called *The Art of Fyir*. It was a family passion, evidently. The first fireworks display in Scotland was held in 1507 by James IV near Edinburgh Castle, in what is now King's Stables Road, below the castle walls. Years after, James V ordered fireworks for the coronation of his first wife Madeleine de Valois; later he personally designed those for the coronation of his second wife Marie de Guise. The Lord High Treasurer's Accounts read: 'fyre werk schot devisit be the Kingis grace' at the not inconsiderable cost of £57 6s 1d.

Mary's short visit to Crichton Castle is not in itself of any great historical significance, but there is a thread that binds this innocent occasion with other matrimonial schemes hatched by the Hepburn family. Bothwell's father Patrick was a first-class opportunist, a trait inherited by his son. Shortly after the death of James V, the third earl decided to marry the beautiful and very rich Marie de Guise. To make this possible he divorced his wife, Agnes Sinclair. Marie de Guise was not so amenable, however, and rejected him. Many years later the fourth earl was in a similar position. He was not long married to Lady Jean Gordon, Countess of Bothwell, when Mary Stuart was once more widowed. Seeing a swift route to power, he too divorced his wife, although their connection remained close – too close for Mary's liking. Lady Jean had brought a substantial dowry to the marriage, which allowed the frequently debt-ridden Bothwell to redeem the wadset, or mortgage, on Crichton Castle and its lands. Because of this, his first wife was allowed to stay in the castle after their divorce, leading Mary to believe that Bothwell was still attached to her.

In 1562, with all this far distant, the significance of the wedding for Mary's story lay in her first sociable encounter with Bothwell. Crichton Castle was the earl's main residence, convenient for the capital when business called, but uncomfortably close when things went wrong. After intercepting money sent to the Lords of the Congregation in 1559, Bothwell had narrowly escaped reprisals. Lord James and his heavily armed men had marched on Crichton. Half an hour before their arrival, alerted by his lookouts, Bothwell leapt bareback onto a horse and made off with the loot, estimated at around 4,000 crowns or £1,000. The Bothwells also owned Hailes Castle in East Lothian, but in terms of security, his preferred havens were Dunbar Castle, on the east coast, and Hermitage Castle, his own terrifying fortress in lawless Liddesdale.

In 1562, when he was in his mid to late twenties, Bothwell was in his prime. A single portrait of him exists from around the time of his marriage to Lady Jean four years later. Although he has a weaselly face with a dandified whiskery moustache, in other respects he was a typical Borderer: dark-haired, powerfully built, not particularly tall. Some see evidence of a broken nose which, given his belligerent temperament, would not be surprising. His eyes suggest a quick mind, and events add to the impression of impatience and impetuousness, the haste of a man who has no qualms about settling a score with violence.

He was in many ways a thug, famously profane and crude despite being educated by his uncle, the Bishop of Moray, and at the University of Paris. On his father's death in 1556 he inherited the title of Sheriff of Edinburgh, and also the role of Lord Admiral. It was he who chartered the ships bringing Mary Stuart's goods back to Scotland. (Her uncles arranged the galleys in which she and her retinue sailed.) The position of Lord Admiral was lucrative, since it allowed him to pocket a hefty percentage of any forfeited goods taken at sea and the bounty from shipwrecks. He was unusual in loathing the English, despite being a Protestant. This hatred was possibly the result of his family's role in keeping order on the Border Marches; he had been often involved with the most villainous of his neighbours.

The role of march warden was unenviable, involving keeping the violent and treacherous family clans, or 'surnames' of the Borderlands in check. Evidence of how dangerous and unruly they were is seen in the time of James IV when he and Henry VII colluded in catching and executing the worst offenders, despite their countries being often at loggerheads. When it came to the Borders, national loyalties counted almost for nothing. The Borderers used guerrilla tactics, but Bothwell, who was a shrewd military operator, had their measure and fought steel with steel.

A curious building beside Crichton Castle is evidence of how he kept control of the region. Within arrow's shot of the castle gates is a buttressed and crow-stepped roofless stone building. It looks like a chapel, even though the Hepburns were famous for their impiety. An iron padlocked gate stands where there was once a doorway, beyond which is a simple arched stone vault. There are windows on either side, and at each end is a barred entrance, above which is a horseshoe-shaped gap, the clue to its purpose. This was not a place of worship but a stable. The main floor was for the animals, who would have been tightly packed, and the upper storey was used for storing hay and for the ostlers' accommodation. Possibly they slept on pallets, but more probably they just bedded down on hay.

The horses would have been small by today's standards, more like Eriskay ponies than racehorses. In the Borders they were known as 'hobbies'. Sturdy, strong and prized for their stamina, they were expected to cover forty, fifty or even sixty miles a day, carrying heavily armed soldiers in full armour. After a night's rest, they continued, as fresh as when they first set out.

The Crichton Castle stable, which was built about fifteen years after Mary left Scotland, is probably the finest physical testimony in the country to the importance of horses in the sixteenth century. In this region, close to the Borderlands, they were not only a sign of wealth but also enabled the area's most influential figures to maintain power. Without them, lords, rulers and indeed the criminal clans would have exerted far less authority and terror.

* * *

At the time of the Crichton Castle extravaganza, Mary was contemplating her own marriage prospects. Her preferred candidate was the highly unsuitable Don Carlos, the insane son of Philip II. Sickly from childhood, he had grown increasingly volatile and violent, and was eventually barred from the succession by his father (and later arrested for plotting against him, dying a few months later in prison, at the age of twenty-three). As she watched Lord John and Lady Janet make their vows, Mary might have been envisaging her own nuptials. That reports of Don Carlos's condition did not deter her pursuing this possibility shows that dynastic ambition was, at this point in her career, paramount. No matter how unprepossessing a spouse he might prove, she aspired to a powerful political alliance that would allow her to continue to rule Scotland, even if her husband remained in Spain. It was a successful recipe for royal marriage already pioneered by Mary Tudor and Philip II.

The wedding was a short break from the queen's working schedule. Mary had been home for less than six months, but that period had been used to assert her authority and set the tone she intended to take as ruler. Within days of her arrival, she had made a proclamation, upholding the new religious settlement for the moment, and showing that, while she was still worshipping privately as a Catholic, she had no intention of threatening the status quo. Doubtless she hoped that this would put an end to the fierce protests that her celebration of Mass had roused. On her first weekend in Holyrood, Master Patrick Lindsay, the hot-headed son of one of Knox's staunchest supporters, had tried to attack the priest at Holyroodhouse as Mary was at Mass. He was prevented by his friend, Lord James, who stood guard. Lindsay was to feature often in aggressive confrontations during Mary's reign. The queen's situation was not helped by John Knox, who announced that the celebration of a single Mass was worse to him than the advance of an army of 10,000 intent on restoring the old religion.

There is a curious and unsettling postscript to Mary's visit to Crichton Castle. A few weeks later, Bothwell clashed with the Duke of Châtelherault's son, the Earl of Arran, who was clearly not of sound mind. Bothwell, who enjoyed a long-running feud with the Hamiltons, provoked a fight. In the fallout, the young Earl of Arran, who was besotted with Mary, claimed that Bothwell had plotted with him and his relative, Gavin Hamilton, Commendator of Kilwinning, to kidnap the queen. They were to kill her chief ministers and incarcerate her in Dumbarton Castle. At this, both were immediately imprisoned for treason. Bothwell was thrown into jail in St Andrews, and then Edinburgh Castle, before escaping some months later and fleeing abroad. Arran spent four years in Edinburgh Castle and after his release, in a very sorry condition, was confined at home for the rest of his sad and long life.

It was believed initially that Arran had been raving, but as Antonia Fraser writes, given what was later to ensue, 'One must bear in mind the possibility that Bothwell was at least toying with the idea of an abduction'. If that were true, it casts Mary's visit to Crichton in a different and more sinister light. In his guise as genial and generous host, Bothwell might already have been envisaging his guest one day becoming his hostage.

Chapter 11

The Cock o' the North

HUNTLY CASTLE

The small market town of Huntly sits amid lush, rolling farmland, fifty miles south-east of Nairn. Its central square is dominated by a castellated clock tower, and the place is formal-looking and quiet, even on a Saturday afternoon. Huntly Castle is not visible from the centre, where I parked, but it is only a short walk away, along a narrow road that leads through a stone arch and down a long avenue of lime trees. At the end of the avenue lies the castle, partially hidden by trees. Even a glimpse confirms that it is one of the finest ruins in the country. Despite lying open to rain and wind, which have tried to batter it into submission down the years, it retains an air of authority and assurance. The afternoon of my visit it was bathed in autumnal sunlight. The shouts of a lively school rugby match nearby were a mere echo of the drama it once witnessed.

This was the lair of George Gordon, Earl of Huntly, cousin of Mary, Queen of Scots. A leading figure in her Privy Council, he was one of the richest and most powerful noblemen in the land. His territory sprawled across the north-east, and his influence reached even farther. Huntly was his stronghold, known in those days as Strathbogie, but he had castles all over the region. Only the Earl of Argyll could match his position. And as Huntly's influence waxed, so did his waistline.

As the country's leading Catholic magnate, the earl had been close to Marie de Guise. He had travelled with her through France, whose Renaissance chateaux inspired the transformation of Huntly Castle. Under his instructions, in the mid 1550s it was turned from a medieval tower house into a palace. On one of the Regent's visits to the north, in 1556, the castle was newly renovated. Marie de Guise brought with her the usual entourage of soldiers and courtiers, maids and servants, trailing a baggage train longer than Huntly's high street. Uneasy at the strain her household was putting on the earl's hospitality, she suggested she might leave earlier than planned.

You can picture the earl's expression, as he led Marie down the stairs to his cellars. Set in the basement, below the vast kitchens, these stone-vaulted storerooms were so well stocked she almost gasped. With barrels of wine, tubs of butter and lard, jars and vats and pots of preserved meats, vegetables and fruits, there was enough to feed the castle and its guests for months. But Huntly's love of bragging was not wise. Although Marie de Guise was reassured that he could afford to host her retinue for as long as required, she was also unsettled at this ostentatious display of wealth which was intended to show the resources at his command, and not only in terms of comestibles. So great was the earl's overweening confidence that later, in conversation with the Regent, the French ambassador told her she should 'clip the Cock o' the North's wings'. Marie de Guise did not disagree, but she was so fully occupied with controlling the Protestant forces gathering against her – who were joined briefly at one point by the notoriously perfidious Huntly – she never did. It would fall to her daughter to thwart the earl's ambitions.

In the castle's heyday, this part of the country was the original northern powerhouse. Robert the Bruce granted the land to Adam Gordon de Huntly after the Battle of Bannockburn, and over the centuries the Gordons built their base and their influence until they rivalled that of the monarchy.

There has been a fortress here since around 1190, and the remains of the motte and bailey are still visible: a wooden tower on a high motte, or mound, which was protected by a wooden palisade, as was the bailey, or courtyard, below, which held houses and livestock.

Later, around 1400, a large tower house was constructed, built on an L-shaped plan with a round tower adjacent to the main rooms.

Although dilapidated, the castle's former glory is palpable. Imposing but elegant, it is approached from the west, with visitors walking beneath its massive drum-like tower. An eye-catching frieze decorates the southern wall, bearing the name of the marquis and marchioness of Huntly, scrolled in pink sandstone like icing on a cake. The castle was partially destroyed by James VI, who did not hesitate to crush the family, but until then there was an Italianate loggia along the base of this façade. It was proof that, contrary to stereotypes of the frozen north, this corner of Scotland can be balmy.

The frieze and loggia were part of Strathbogie's renovation at the end of the sixteenth century, after George Gordon's time, but what he achieved in his lifetime was spectacular. The English ambassador, Thomas Randolph, wrote of his visit in 1562 that 'Huntly's house is the best furnished of any house I have seen in this country; his cheer is marvellously great; and his mind then such, as it appeared to us, as ought to be in any subject to his Sovereign'. Randolph was not so naive as to think the earl's loyalty unimpeachable. He also observed that 'no man will trust him either in word or deed'. Even so, it is not entirely clear at what point the earl decided upon outright rebellion against the Crown.

The entrance to the castle lies at the rear, through an ornately embellished doorway designed to parade the owner's status. Although much of what remains dates to the period after Mary's era, more than enough survives to evoke its lustre. The rear courtyard contains a brewhouse and bakehouse, and while the cobblestoned floor of the stables probably is from the early 1600s, the narrowness of the stalls, big enough only for a motorbike, is another reminder of the diminutive stature of horses at the time.

It is in the main part of the former tower house that the Earl of Huntly's ambitions are palpable. His apartments, and those of the countess, were high and spacious, with deeply recessed windows and massive fireplaces. As sightseers wander from room to room, they are accompanied by chirping swallows darting in and out of the empty windows and emerging at full speed from their roosts in the chimneys. On my visit, one flew several laps around a vaulted chamber before perching on the top of a studded wooden door, close enough to touch. At the top of the castle, on the tumbledown parapet, a brood of swallow chicks waited, like communicants at the altar rail, to have food popped in their mouth.

At the other extreme, in the castle's depths, lies the basement prison, into which captives were dropped fifteen feet or more. Lifelike models of prisoners sit on the earthen floor, a reminder of how grim incarceration would have been. The eyes of one stare straight up from the gloom, unnerving in the way of all dolls.

Yet it is not the individual rooms that make Huntly Castle memorable so much as the overall impression. The luxurious tapestries, furniture and silk-draped beds that caused sixteenth-century visitors to gape might be beyond memory, but its personality persists, the echo of previous lifetimes reverberating, long after the last chord was struck. To look beyond the windows or from the parapet is to see a kingdom that in the 1560s might as well have been on the other side of the moon, so distant does it seem from Edinburgh and the seat of royal power. The architectural splendour and artistic vision are a rebuke to the Lowlands' innate sense of superiority. The Highland stronghold of the Gordons was on a par with any French chateau or Italian palazzo. Coarse, unsophisticated, unworldly it was not.

While Huntly Castle does not rival Stirling or Linlithgow in scale, it shows the hubris of the Gordon clan. It feels like the residence of a king, and sets you speculating how the country would have fared had the capital been in the rich and fertile north, in Huntly territory, where it could draw on Baltic and Scandinavian connections for trade and political contacts. What sort of nation would Scotland have become, with decisions made so much further from the border with England, when its closest neighbours were across a rough sea? Had Huntly and the Gordon family's ambition prevailed, might this have become the heart of Scotland? Was Huntly's eventual humiliation a lost opportunity for the country to shift its axis?

* * *

Long before 1562, and for many years after, the Highlands and Islands were a headache for rulers. People here lived to a different beat. They were bound by more personal, immediate loyalties, based on kinship rather than king. During her royal progress, in the early autumn of that year, Mary came to know the Highlanders well. Despite their thrawnness and ferocity, and the threat they potentially posed, she warmed to them immediately. Thomas Randolph was amazed at how happy she felt in their company. In Antonia Fraser's words, 'She evidently looked on the Highlanders as noble savages, a category she found more sympathetic than their opposite numbers, the savage nobles, in the south.' In an effort to show her appreciation, Mary hastily ordered Highland dress for herself, and plaid for her courtiers. Thereafter she retained a soft spot for the people from this part of her kingdom.

But there was no sentimentality behind the journey that brought her here. Setting out from Holyrood in August, the queen had a long itinerary and agenda ahead of her, and many appointments to keep. She was an accomplished and enthusiastic horsewoman, but the prospect of making her way with her enormous following of staff and soldiers over a distance of more than 250 miles, even in late summer, must have been daunting. Randolph reported that reaching Aberdeen, on 27 August, had been a hard slog in bad weather.

The young and athletic Mary would have accepted the privations of the trip as an unavoidable part of her role. This was, after all, no jaunt. Royal progresses were an exercise in flaunting royal authority and reminding her citizens who was in charge, while at the same time allowing the monarch to become acquainted with their realm. This particular foray had a specific purpose: to curtail the Cock o' the North as Mary's mother had not. The fact that Huntly was her cousin – he was James IV's grandson, by his illegitimate daughter

Margaret Stewart – made no difference. As she approached the earl's
bailiwick, it gradually became clear that her original intention of
bringing him to heel peaceably was not going to be enough.

Until Mary ascended the throne, the Gordons' Catholic faith had
never been a source of conflict. Now, the mood was different. Huntly
had, perhaps rashly, proposed to help Mary raise a Catholic rebellion in the north on her homecoming. Fearful of showing any pref-
erence for Catholic nobles lest it turn Protestants against her, the
queen had rejected his offer, making it plain that she had no immediate intention of upsetting the new religious settlement. At the
same time, her attitude to the earl was coloured by Lord James –
another of Huntly's cousins – who encouraged her to put him in his
place. It was a far from altruistic suggestion.

Mary had not originally intended to deal with Huntly so early in
her reign. Since taking up her throne, her priority had been to
arrange a meeting with Elizabeth I, at which she hoped to coax her
cousin into formalising her place as next in line to the English crown
after Elizabeth and any offspring she might bear. Surprisingly,
Elizabeth had agreed to meet in York, in August or September of
1562; less surprisingly, as the time drew near, she postponed. It was
not hard to see why. In France the Wars of Religion had broken out,
pitting Catholics against Huguenots. Elizabeth was anxious not to
antagonise English Protestants by engaging with such a high-profile
Catholic, especially one who had already voiced a rightful claim to
the English throne. This was the closest the queens ever came to
meeting face to face, and Mary recognised its cancellation as a significant setback.

Unwisely, the Earl of Huntly had made no attempt to hide his
dismay that Mary wished for a meeting with Elizabeth. He considered it tantamount to consorting with the enemy, and playing into
the hands of the scheming Protestant lords. His was a powerful
voice, not just as the leading magnate in the north. As James IV's
grandson, he had been raised at court with Margaret Tudor as
his guardian, and James V his cousin, playmate and friend. He was
also Chancellor of Scotland.

Thwarted in her expectation of seeing Elizabeth, Mary started to make other plans. Arrangements were put in place for what was to be the grandest royal progress of her reign, through the north-east of the country. Her first progress had been made shortly after her arrival. That tour embraced her childhood haunts of Linlithgow and Stirling, as well as Perth, Dundee and St Andrews, and over the following years she would visit all quarters of the country, except the islands. But it was the three-month journey between August and October 1562 that stands out, in part for her own certainty of purpose, but mostly for its almost theatrical drama.

Mary rode out of Holyrood on 11 August and reached Old Aberdeen via the castles of Glamis, Edzell, Dunnottar and probably Balvenie on August 27. She left the city in summer and arrived in the north-east in conditions more like winter. At Aberdeen the Earl of Huntly had gathered his men to meet her: not the 100 Mary had stipulated, but a body of 1,500. The martial overtones could not be mistaken. Also present in Aberdeen was Huntly's courageous wife, the Countess Elizabeth. Requesting an audience with the queen, she pleaded with her, not on her husband's behalf, but for her wayward son, Sir John Gordon. Sir John had recently escaped prison, after being convicted of assaulting and wounding another noble, and was now an outlaw. Impressed by the countess's concern for her son, Mary promised leniency. It seems the women felt an affinity, despite for the moment being on opposite sides of a potentially deadly disagreement. In later years, the countess would become the queen's friend and attendant. For the moment, Mary stipulated that if John would present himself at Aberdeen Tolbooth and agree to put himself into ward at Stirling Castle, the matter would be settled. Persuaded by his mother, Sir John agreed, and surrendered himself.

The original tolbooth prison or wardhouse where he handed himself in was rebuilt in the early seventeenth century, but a glimpse of the grisliness of these days can be found in Aberdeen's Tolbooth museum, at the east end of Union Street. Conditions for inmates awaiting sentence or execution can still be imagined from the claustrophobically narrow turnpike stairs, and the dark stone cells, where criminals would have been fighting for space and fresh air. The heavy leg cuffs or fetters, which bound their ankles to an iron post or wall, are on display, while the blade of the guillotine, called 'the maiden', speaks for itself. So too the thick metal grilles at windows, and doors so heavily studded and padlocked that dynamite would be required to open them if the key was lost. Nevertheless, it was not the miserable conditions that changed Sir John's mind. When he learned that his keeper was to be his family's arch enemy, Lord Erskine – uncle of Lord James – he reneged on his promise and fled. From this point, events swiftly escalated.

Instead of going into hiding, as would have been wise, Sir John summoned his men and began to harry the queen's party as it made its way towards Inverness. It appears his intention was to abduct and marry Mary, with whom he was infatuated, despite being already married. Whether Mary was aware of the full extent of the Gordon plot, a warrant for Sir John's seizure was issued.

Weeks earlier, when the royal progress was being organised, it was agreed that Mary would visit the Earl of Huntly in his castle at Strathbogie. She allowed two of her entourage, including Thomas Randolph, to do so, but, after hearing of John Gordon's perfidious plans, she would not risk walking into a trap. Instead, she bypassed Strathbogie and made for Darnaway Castle, near Forres on the Moray Firth. While here, she officially pronounced Lord James as Earl of Moray. This was a formality, since he had already been granted the title. Until now, his elevation had been kept secret for fear of enraging Huntly, who for many years had administered the estate of the unassigned earldom and taken the revenues, along with those of the earldom of Mar.

This insult was well-judged. It also affirmed that any appearance of amity was futile. Meanwhile Lord James, from this time forward referred to as the Earl of Moray, must have felt gratified that Mary was acting in his favour at every turn. He had humiliated his cousin George by usurping his lucrative role and had persuaded the queen to quash him for his insolence and presumption. The dubious influence of Mary's half-brother on her decisions and allegiances was evident already. In future years she might have had time to regret how much trust she had placed in his judgement, but for the present she remained blinkered.

From Darnaway, Mary reached the royal castle of Inverness on 11 September. The medieval, towering, turreted castle, little of which remains today, was in the charge of Alexander Gordon, another of Huntly's sons. Being told of his father's treatment by the queen, he refused her entry. This was treason, and, the following day, when she and her men forced their way in, he was promptly captured and hanged from the battlements for public view.

There was no mistaking the queen's mood, but her intention utterly to crush Huntly was not confirmed until she heard the lurid rumour that he planned to kidnap her himself and marry her to whomever he chose.

Despite the seriousness of such threats, and the danger she faced, Mary was exhilarated by her first experience of the campaign trail. Famously, she told the Highland chieftains who visited her in Inverness that she wished she were a man, 'to know what life it was to lie all night in the fields, or to walk on the causeway with a jack and a knapscall, a Glasgow buckler, and a broadsword'. It was Thomas Randolph who noted her words for posterity. There were times when the English ambassador could not hide his admiration for Mary's spirit, but in the four years he spent at her court he drip-fed information to William Cecil that was often highly disadvantageous to her image and reputation.

Keeping low at Strathbogie, Huntly deputised Sir John to capture Mary as she and her men advanced over the River Spey. The plan came to nothing since, at the sight of the army Mary had mustered at Aberdeen, which was three times as large as his own, Sir John turned heel. The fortunes of Huntly Castle were, for the moment, on the ebb. With the Gordon clan outlawed, and Huntly in hiding, the property was ransacked. The sumptuous furnishings and plen-ishings were shared between the queen and her half-brother Moray in what, to modern eyes, looks like avarice. Among the treasures they lifted were the contents of St Machar's Cathedral in Aberdeen, which had been given to the earl for safekeeping after the Reformation. Most important of these was the silk tent in which Edward II slept the night before the Battle of Bannockburn. Its whereabouts remain unknown to this day.

Chapter 12

The Lap of Luxury

SPYNIE PALACE

Of all the locations where Mary made history, few are as beguiling as Spynie Palace. Elevated over a plain that sweeps down towards Elgin and the Moray Firth, it is surrounded by rich agricultural land. In the distance is the glint of the sea.

Mary arrived from Inverness on 17 September 1562, 'convoyed by great numbers of horse and foot'. She stayed only for two nights, on her way back to Aberdeen, possibly to evade the predatory Sir John Gordon. Spynie was to offer a brief haven during a military campaign that by now was focused on removing Huntly from power and emphasising to the northeast who was in charge. While her visit was short, it underlined Spynie's symbolic importance. Conveniently placed for a stopover between Inverness and Aberdeen, it was also a reminder of the queen's Catholic convictions. After weeks spent in a presbyterian climate, a few hours in the company of the last Catholic Bishop of Moray offered a chance to be among like-minded believers. Whether Mary found a soulmate in the notoriously worldly and ruthless bishop is unrecorded. The fleetingness of the visit suggests not.

Few church properties better evoke the opulence of the Catholic church in the high Middle Ages, and the tangible evidence of pomp rather than piety. Spynie was no hermit's retreat. The palace was buzzing with vigorous life, unlike the contemplative calm and strictly observed hours of silence of the more austere religious houses.

No sign was visible of poverty, humility nor, in the bishop's case, of chastity.

Whether or not she was aware of the bishop's reputation, on her arrival Mary was shown to lavishly appointed apartments, and her retinue of soldiers and servants found beds in the palace's warren of rooms. The kitchens roared into life at news of their exalted guest and a surfeit of food was prepared. Servants were sent hurrying through the passage below the Great Hall to draw water from the loch, and the courtyard and corridors saw a ceaseless procession bringing food and drink from bakehouse, brewhouse, cellars and pantry.

The bishop – who was famous for enjoying the finer things in life, and had fathered nine children – enjoyed himself as immoderately as the royal soldiers, courtiers and perhaps also the queen. After all, she loved a convivial occasion. The enormous dining hall, which had been enlarged from a more modest original, allowed some privacy for the bishop and high-status guests before dinner, with a partition creating a private chamber for their use. Conveniently, it had its own fireplace and latrine. They took dinner on a dais, near the Great Hall window, elevated above the rest of the company.

Even in its present ruinous state, Spynie Palace soars into the sky, severe but beautiful. In early autumn, when I arrived, a forceful wind kicked up copper leaves, making the avenue of gnarled beech trees leading to the palace thrash overhead as the main tower came into sight. In a ploughed field alongside the palace a metal detectorist was working his way slowly across the ground, like a latter-day Piers Plowman.

The complex is huge, and the most complete structure, called David's Tower, is the largest tower house in Scotland. Built in 1465, it is six storeys high. Originally entered at first-floor level, its wooden door was guarded by an iron yett. The need for security is written on every wall, with gunholes on the upper storeys, while wide-mouthed gun-loops at basement level allowed weapons to be fired at attackers' legs. Before reaching this point, enemies had to pass through the east gate, which was equipped with a portcullis and 'murder holes', through which defenders could disable their foes. It seems that men of the cloth were no less violent in the Middle Ages than their secular counterparts. The bishop was instrumental in the execution of at least two religious reformers, including Patrick Hamilton, who was burned at the stake.

Spynie's origins lie in 1208, when the Pope authorised the Bishop of Moray to create a cathedral at Spynie. A few years later the bishop decided to move the cathedral to nearby Elgin, for greater safety. This he did, while keeping Spynie as his private residence. No evidence remains of the very earliest buildings, but the basement of David's Tower shows stonework from the 1300s, as does the south range of buildings, part of which contains a chapel. A piscina for washing altar vessels can be seen, high in a wall.

By the fifteenth century Spynie comprised a sophisticated range of buildings, including two towers, a great hall and formal gardens just beyond the fortified walls. In those days, it overlooked a large sea loch, which acted as a fishing and trading port and almost lapped its walls. Royal guests were frequent. James II spent Christmas of 1456 there, eating salted Spey salmon. James IV visited in 1493 and again in 1505. On that occasion he was on one of his many pilgrimages, this time to St Duthac's shrine at Tain. Records note that maidens were employed to sing for the king and paid 14 shillings for their efforts.

David's Tower no longer has its roof and leaves no trace of the gloriously painted walls with which the palace was decorated. Even so, its scale and the depth of the recessed windows speak of grandeur. Patches of the original white plasterwork remain, but the rest is for the imagination to fill, with blazing fires, canopied beds, Turkish carpets and Flemish tapestries. Unless the bishops of Moray were a different breed from other high-ranking clergy of their era, they would have spared no expense in pursuit of comfort and prestige. The high-walled complex included a tennis court and a bowling alley, along with vaulted wine cellars. Nor was luxury confined to the later Middle Ages. A well-preserved ceramic jug from the 1300s, decorated with shells, was found in the west and oldest ranges, while the remnants of a glazed ceramic medieval urinal also hints at style and elegance, when even basic functions were an opportunity for artistry.

On the spacious first floor the bishop held ecclesiastical and barony courts. The floors above contained the bedchambers, allowing the bishop a bird's eye view of his diocese. As the Church's wealth grew, so did Spynie. The Great Hall, in the northern range, built around 1500, could seat hundreds. The well in the north range remains, as do two corbels, carved into faces, on which the Great Hall's steeply pitched roof stood. Close by is the water gate, which led to the loch, where water was also drawn by servants and brought into the Great Hall by a lower passageway.

The lavishness of the castle and its surrounding land indicates how far the medieval church had come from its humble egalitarian beginnings. For many centuries now, bishops had become political and powerful figures. They were as much to be feared as revered. The splendour of Spynie also reveals the affluence and influence in this part of the country. It was another reason why a queen might want to stamp her authority firmly upon the region.

Spynie's ruins lie in the shelter of a horseshoe of trees. From the top of David's Tower the tranquil scene below would be familiar to medieval peasants: green and gold fields were fringed with trees, like fur around a cuff. Along the edge of newly harvested fields ochre bales of hay were stacked, ready for the barn. What remains of the sea loch was steely grey under the clouds.

In 1562, the bishop, Patrick Hepburn, had less than ten years to live. A hard-hearted character, he had joined Huntly in urging Mary, before her return to Scotland, to overthrow the Reformation. While this came to nothing, he managed to secure his position and a substantial part of his income from the benefice for the rest of his lifetime. Perhaps Mary's visit was intended to keep him in line, rather than seek spiritual advice. He was responsible for educating her future husband, James Hepburn, Earl of Bothwell, who was brought up at Spynie. It could, however, be argued that Bothwell learned as much from the bishop's dubious behaviour as from his lessons. Certainly, he never forgot his childhood home. After the

Battle of Carberry when all hope for Mary's cause seemed lost, it was to here that Bothwell fled.

While Presbyterian church governance was ratified towards the end of the century, and on Patrick Hepburn's death the bishopric fell out of Catholic hands, episcopacy was never formally banned. As a result, Morayshire and parts of the north-east continued, for many centuries, to be an outpost of Episcopalianism.

While Mary was in residence in Spynie, the Earl of Huntly was stewing. Aware he might be apprehended at any moment, he flitted from one residence to the next, making sure not to stay in any place for more than a night. By day, he would return to Strathbogie, and his well-stocked cellars.

In early October, when Mary was back in Aberdeen, it became clear that not only was he refusing to surrender but he was also attempting to persuade the south of the country, under the Duke of Châtelherault, to join the north-east against the queen. Having suggested a rebellion to her the year before, he was now engaged on his own (suicidal) revolt. On learning this, Mary pronounced him and his son John outlaws. At Moray's urging, she sent for reinforcements to join them at Aberdeen; these included the fearsome Lord Lindsay and Kirkcaldy of Grange, a seasoned soldier.

An attempt was made by Kirkcaldy to capture the earl at his castle while he was dining, but, alerted just in time, Huntly managed to escape over the back wall – no easy feat for one so overweight – without weapons or boots. Kirkcaldy's men gave chase, but the earl's horse outrode them.

Even at this point Huntly might have survived had he remained in hiding rather than heeding his wife's advice. Unfortunately, like many ditherers, he was easily swayed by those who were decisive. The fearless Countess Elizabeth, inspired by witches' prophecy which suggested her husband would come to no harm, urged him to challenge the queen in battle. Consequently, Huntly gathered his 700-strong army, and marched towards Aberdeen in late October.

On 28 October 1562, on the Hill of Fare at Corrichie, fifteen miles west of Aberdeen, Huntly's troops confronted Mary's. The previous evening, dismayed at the size of the royal army and the numbers melting away from his own side, he had decided to retreat when morning came. But, too unwell to rise at daybreak, he woke late, by which time the battle had begun. He had no option but to follow through with his wife's plan.

With Moray in charge, and Maitland at his side, the queen's 2,000-strong force was briefly outmanouevred by Huntly's skilful men. Had they prevailed, Mary would have been humiliated, her standing shaken. Fortunately, her army was well equipped with guns, and her artillery saved the day. Under fire, the earl's men were forced off their hill and into the swampland at its foot – reminiscent of the Battle of Flodden – where, for all their courage, they became sitting ducks. Carnage followed, with more than 220 men killed and 120 taken prisoner, including Huntly and his sons John and Adam. The trio were being led to Moray in handcuffs, on horseback, when Huntly suddenly toppled to the ground in his heavy armour. The cause was probably apoplexy, either a stroke or a heart attack. In the words of Randolph, 'the Earl suddenly fell from his horse startk ded'.

It was an inglorious and pathetic end for one of the most powerful men in the kingdom. Such was his girth, a pair of creels was placed beneath his corpse, to roll it from the battlefield. The ignominy of this sight was in contrast to the authority he once wielded, and the threat he had posed to the Crown. Further indignity was to come. Huntly's embalmed corpse, in its coffin, appeared before Parliament the following summer, to have a decree of forfeiture and attainder passed upon it. In order to make it appear as if Huntly was actually present at his indictment, the coffin was placed on its end. It was four years before his remains were returned to the north, where they were buried in the precincts of Elgin Cathedral.

Sir John Gordon fared even worse. He was executed in November, in Edinburgh, with Mary present. When his neck was on the block, the axe-man repeatedly missed his target. The scene became so gory that Mary fainted.

It had been a difficult month. Shortly after her return to Edinburgh from the north, Mary fell ill. As Randolph reported to Cecil:

Immediately upon the queen's arrival here, she fell acquainted with a new disease, that is common in this town, called here the 'new acquaintance', which passed also through her whole court, neither sparing lord, lady, nor damoysell, not so much as either French or English. It is a pain in their heads that have it, and a soreness in their stomachs, with a great cough, that remaineth with some longer with other shorter time, as it findeth apt bodies for the nature of the disease. The queen kept her bed six days. There was no appearance of danger, nor many that die of the disease except some old folks.

It has been speculated that this was the first appearance in Scotland of influenza.

Mary's swift reprisals against the captain of Inverness Castle and Huntly do not suggest a timorous nature, but nor was she bloodthirsty or vengeful. Huntly's youngest son Adam Gordon, who was captured on the field, was pardoned and given a post at court. In 1565 the lands and title were restored to Huntly's eldest son George. He became the fifth earl and in due course Chancellor of Scotland and one of Mary's most trusted allies. His mother Elizabeth Keith and his sister Jean Gordon were to become valued companions of the queen as ladies-in-waiting. Lady Jean (who later married and happily divorced the Earl of Bothwell) became a particularly close friend.

Chapter 13

Home for 'a country girl'

FALKLAND PALACE

The Royal Palace of Falkland, in Fife, was one of Mary's favourite haunts. Here, she said, she could play at being a 'country girl in the park and woods', and she visited it as often as her duties allowed. In the sixteenth century, the palace was set in the Forest of Falkland, embedded, like Fontainebleau and Versailles, in a sea of trees. It was the royal family's main hunting lodge, where they could relax, and where the thrill of the hunt replaced the back-stabbing at court.

The county of Fife, in which the village of Falkland lies, was described by Mary's son James VI as 'a beggar's mantle fringed with gold'. Even in the 1560s its star attraction was St Andrews, with its prestigious university and ancient cathedral, to which pilgrims flocked. The coastline was studded with harbour villages, such as Anstruther, Crail, Pittenweem and Elie, where today drying nets and stacked creels on the quaysides await the boats' next sortie. Away from the sea, the mood changes. Few tourists are found in former mining towns such as Cowdenbeath, Methil and Lochgelly. In the 1980s they became a byword for post-industrial deprivation and hardship, and many of the old pit towns have still not recovered. It would seem, from James VI's portrait, that these industrial towns were far from affluent even then, compared with the fishing and merchant trade of their coastal cousins.

In Mary's reign, coal mining was becoming so important that in 1563 a law was passed banning the export of coal. Mines were simple open shafts sunk as far as water and wooden props allowed, around eighty feet deep. Descending by ladders into what were called bell-pits or stair-pits, women and children carried creels of coal to the surface on their backs. The earliest Scottish miners, in the thirteenth century, are thought to have been labourers who were feued – under a feudal contract – to local landowners. Employed in agriculture for part of the year, they would go down the mines in wintertime for fuel for their masters and themselves. Theirs was an unenviable position, but in the following centuries things got much worse. By 1650 there were fifty mines in Fife, and demand for coal was soaring. Legislation in 1606 turned miners into virtual slaves, with no rights and no prospects. When underground excavation began, conditions could be horrendous. As before, women and children bore the brunt of the carrying. Mary probably knew little about the back-breaking toil of the coal trade and, even though it was tucked in the heart of Fife, near rich coal seams, the palace's grates were more likely to have held wood than coal.

Compared to the sober town around it, Falkland Palace represents a realm of luxury and leisure completely at odds with Reformation joylessness. With the Lomond Hills as a backdrop, and rose-filled cottage gardens, even now the village feels as if it is rooted in another age. When I first visited, as a student, it was the almost soporific peace of its backstreets that struck me. On a shimmeringly hot summer's day nothing moved. Bees among the honeysuckle made more noise than traffic. It would have been easy to assume that this was a sleepy backwater where nothing happens. Decades later, and living in a far smaller and sleepier village myself, I realise how wrong first impressions can be. But what was not in question, centuries ago or in the present, is the exceptional glamour and panache of this architectural gem.

The palace gatehouse entrance, with its heraldic shields, stout walls and enchanting French turrets, make an indelible impression. It is the benchmark of Stewart self-confidence, a Narnian door into a world where to be royal involved pageantry, display and something almost mystical. Regal is too weak a word for the palace's enveloping aura of opulent elegance. Restored from a ruin in the late Victorian era by the Marquis of Bute, its surprisingly intimate rooms spill one onto the next. Their painted beamed ceilings are the cause, one suspects, of a thousand cricked necks.

Mary had known Falkland Palace since she was a child, when its richness and seclusion must have seemed sensational. On her first return as an adult in September 1561, by then a connoisseur of France's chateaux, would she have felt a pang of disappointment? It seems unlikely. Falkland might have been on a smaller scale than the grandest Scottish castles, let alone those in the duchies of Burgundy or Lorraine, but its charm lay not in its size but its perfection, a mark of which was its setting.

The Forest of Falkland brought an extra dimension to its appeal, one that Mary, like her father before her, found irresistible. Across the north of Europe, forests are synonymous with fairy tales, depicting the sometimes malign nature of wilderness, where danger lurks behind every tree in the shape of wolf, bear or witch. In this context, Mary would have made quite an impact on the people of Falkland: a young, beautiful queen in a citadel protected by a shield of trees. Viewed like this, the palace takes on an almost allegorical aspect. Within its walls and estates she was safe; beyond lay danger.

Situated midway between the Firth of Tay to the north and the Firth of Forth to the south, the palace's position was originally of strategic importance. With time, its function became less political and more personal, as it became the royals' country bolthole. In 1501, James IV ordered work to start on an updated palace. Over the next decade this took shape: a Renaissance quadrangle alongside the courtyard, and a Gothic chapel and hall. After the king's death there was a lull, although an aviary and stable block were added, and work was begun on the gatehouse.

James V inherited his father's passion for building. He began extensive renovations and additions in 1537. Inspired by what he had seen in France, he employed French stonemasons and artisans, among them the notable Nicolas Roy. Also hired were local builders, as well as plasterers and sculptors from the Netherlands. The palace's design was intended, initially, to make his ill-fated wife Madeleine de Valois feel at home. It was his second wife, Marie de Guise, who was to benefit.

The similarity between the gatehouse at Falkland and that which James V built at Holyrood is striking. Echoes are also found of his improvements to Linlithgow and Stirling. All these royal palaces evidently came under the same shaping hands. The young queen would have met her father's artistic and ambitious personality in palace after palace, expressed in brick and mortar. She had never known him, yet in this sense at least, he played a tangible part in her life.

Nowhere is the effect of the late Gothic and Renaissance style more pleasing. While Stirling, Linlithgow and Holyrood are magnificent, Falkland is a jewel box, containing everything precious in a bijou space which, for all its pomp, is homely. By the reign of James IV, its function had become that of a royal retreat. No doubt a wealth of happy associations helped seal its place for both Jameses and Mary as one of their favourite residences. It also represented sanctuary, for it was here that James V took to his bed after the Battle of Solway Moss, to recuperate or die.

Marie de Guise also sought solace within its walls, immediately after sending Mary off to France for safety as a child. At the palace she would have space to compose herself and master her sorrow before facing the court once more. Even today, the palace orchard and its formal gardens, dominated by giant, clipped cypress trees, have a calm, untroubled atmosphere that creates a sense of timelessness and ease. The gardens, begun in the middle of the fifteenth century, were a graceful, and productive, feature of Falkland. By 1485, the kitchen plot was producing barrel-loads of onions. The gardens created for James IV at the same time as the glorious south and east ranges, were enclosed in 1513 by a high stone wall.

Their seclusion and privacy emphasised Falkland's role. An invisible cordon was wrapped around the palace, encouraging strangers to keep their distance. In this it resembles Balmoral, the royal retreat in the Highlands built for Queen Victoria by her doting husband

Albert, which remains the summer holiday destination of the House of Windsor. Indeed, Mary Stuart's personality and interests have much in common with modern royals, especially her love of horses, sport and outdoor pursuits.

At the hunting lodge of Falkland, she could indulge in these as she wished. Hunting – as in riding through the forest to shoot wild animals in great numbers – was its *raison d'être*. Other than jousting, the chase was probably the pastime that set aristocracy apart from the rest of society, not just in the sixteenth century but until recent generations. Indeed, the word 'forest' indicates royal privilege. In Middle English its meaning did not merely indicate an abundance of woodland, but very specifically described a wooded area reserved and protected for hunting. Forest law, introduced into England originally by William the Conqueror, ferociously protected game for royal use. A remnant of this proscription is found today in the law banning the harming or killing of swans anywhere in the country, because they are Crown property.

The penalties for hunting on royal estates in the sixteenth century were clearly not deterrent enough. One of the few personal complaints Mary ever publicly made was to bemoan the lack of deer for her and her husband Darnley to hunt. She was vexed that they had 'na pastyme' when they went on holiday. But it was not just poaching that was outlawed in royal forests. Grazing animals, gathering kindling, and many other prohibitions made the forests a no-go area. Cutting down trees was utterly forbidden, wood being such a valuable resource for construction and shipbuilding. Permission might be allowed to hunt creatures deemed harmful to deer – badgers, foxes, otters and squirrels – but the rights of the royal forest were fiercely guarded, and those who broke the rules might be imprisoned, or worse.

The huntsman was an important figure at court. It was his role to search for prey – he might bring back an animal's spoor embedded in moss in his hunting horn for inspection – and then to lead their hounds towards it. Almost as important was the man in charge of the dogs. Three breeds were used in hunting: bloodhounds, which were kept on a leash, from which their name lymers came; smaller hounds, which chased by scent and were called brachets; and a large type of greyhound, called levriers, which were powerful and ferocious enough to kill a deer.

Dogs played a large part in Mary's life, on the hunt, and at home. The treasurer's records note the allocation of bread allowed to them each day; at one point she had as many as thirteen. They would have worn collars, as did the working hounds, in leather or cloth. Favourite dogs' collars were decorated with studs or gems, as befitted a member of the royal household. An inventory records blue velvet bought for her lapdogs.

Out on the hunt, horns sent signals across the forest, their distinctive calls alerting the party to what was happening, and where. The royal leader of a hunting party might use a horn known as an olifant which, as its name suggests, was carved from ivory. Once the hounds had the quarry at bay, it fell to one of the party to drive his lance or shoot an arrow into its heart. When the beast had been gralloched – disembowelled – the dogs were given their share before anyone else.

That Mary loved blood sports is interesting in one who in other spheres tried to avoid unnecessary violence. Nor was the chase as she enjoyed it truly sporting. To ensure a good day's fun, deer and other game were captured and transported to wherever the hunt was to take place. When the party was over, the survivors would be recaptured and taken to their next event. Although Scotland was not short of wild boar, they would also be imported from France to add to the smorgasbord of beasts on offer. Once they had been released in the forest, beaters – often Highlanders, skilled in this Gaelic style of hunting – would be employed to flush the animals and herd them towards the royal party. They would lie in wait in the undergrowth, armed with arrows, spears, crossbows and cudgels, as the creatures were driven into their sights. It was a highly dangerous tactic since, if things got out of control, the terrified beasts might head straight for those in the heather and trample them to death.

This happened at least once. The occasion was a special Royal Hunting arranged in August 1564 by the Earl of Atholl, who would soon be appointed Lieutenant of the North. It was held at Blair Castle, on Mary's way back from Inverness. Many years later one of her entourage, a young man called William Barclay, recalled the day. The earl, wrote Barclay, had 'with much trouble and vast expense', organised a stupendous day's sport. In the space of two months, 2,000 Highlanders had driven 2,000 red deer, and also roe deer and fallow, from the hills and woods of Atholl, Badenoch, Mar, Moray and elsewhere, to the Forest of Atholl, where the hunt was to take place. His account suggests that so much preparation went into a royal hunt it was like a military expedition. The following is a translation from the original Latin.

The Queen, the great men and others were in a Glen when all the deer were brought before them. Believe me, the whole body of them moved forward in something like battle order. The sight still strikes me and ever will, for they had a leader whom they followed close wherever he moved. This leader was a very fine stag, with a very fine head. The sight delighted the Queen very much, but she soon had occasion for fear upon the Earl (who had been accustomed to such sights) addressing her thus: 'Do you observe that stag who is foremost of the herd? There is danger from that stag; for if either fear or rage should force him from the ridge of that hill, let every one look to himself, for none of us will be out of the way of harm; for the rest will follow this one, and having thrown us under foot, they will open a passage to the hill behind us.'

What happened a moment later confirmed this opinion; for the Queen ordered one of the best dogs to be let loose upon a wolf; this the dog pursues, the leading stag was frightened, he flies by the same way he had come there, the rest rush after him, and break out where the thickest body of the Highlanders was. They had nothing for it but to throw themselves flat on the heath and allow the deer to pass over them. It was told the Queen that several of the Highlanders had been wounded and that two or three of them had been killed outright; and the whole body [of deer] had got off, had not the Highlanders, by their skill in hunting, fallen upon a stratagem to cut off the rear from the main body. It was of those that had been separated that the Queen's dogs, and those of the nobility, made slaughter. There were killed that day 360 deer, with 5 wolves, and some roes.

Stags could be deadly, as could wolves, but even more dangerous were wild boar. Cannier than deer, and fearless when cornered, they could slit open a huntsman with their tusks, and frequently did. Hunting was seen as a pleasurable occupation, but it was also a rehearsal for the battlefield, where similar quick wits and dauntless courage would be required.

Shooting the butts was far less savage or risky, and wherever she went Mary had targets set up in the gardens or grounds. Wearing a velvet glove, she would practise her archery skills. The orchard at Falkland was an ideal location for such sport. It is a far cry from this noble pursuit to the dartboards of working men's pubs, yet the principle was much the same. The diplomat Thomas Randolph described the scene at Holyrood, in April of 1562, in a letter to his master William Cecil: 'after the council was risen, the queen's grace, as she doth oft, did in her privy garden shoot at the butts; where the duke and other noblemen were present, and I also admitted for one to behold the pastime . . . [It] would have well contented your honour to have seen the queen and the master of Lindsay to shoot against the Earl of Marr and one of the ladies.'

But perhaps above all, Mary enjoyed hawking. In this, as in many things, she was like her father and grandfather. James V had a master falconer, James Lindsay, who had seven assistants to help him raise, train and keep the birds. By Mary's time this number had been reduced to four, although when she married Darnley, two more were employed, because of his fondness for the sport. The Treasurer's Accounts in 1562 show her sending hawks as a gift to Elizabeth, when she still hoped to secure a meeting. A man called James Gray was paid £80 to take them to London.

The royal aviary or mews would have included hawks or owls, trained to fly off their keeper's gauntlet and return to the wrist with small prey in beak – rabbits, squirrels, mice – sometimes still wriggling. That she could watch them rip open and devour their catch says much for Mary's stomach. So too does the training these birds went through before they were allowed to fly unleashed, trusted to bring back their kill. Falcons – the name given by falconers to all female hawks – were prized for hunting, outstripping their male counterparts – tercels – in skill and size. A young falcon would take many months to train, during which period its eyelids would be sewn closed, to force it to use its other senses. Once the stitches and its leather hood were removed, and it had become reaccustomed to daylight, the bird would be taught to catch easy prey. Birds such as cranes would be tethered, with raw meat on their backs (their eyes were also 'seeled' and their claws clipped). It was not a sport for the squeamish, but once fully trained, a falcon was a priceless asset for its owner. They became such favourites, they might sleep in their lordship's bedroom and be carried everywhere on his wrist.

As well as hunting, there was another sport for which Falkland Palace was famed, namely tennis. While there were tennis courts in Stirling, Perth and Holyrood, none was as fine, at this date, as the one built for James V. The earliest surviving open-air court in Britain, it allows visitors to catch a glimpse of royal leisure. Today real tennis is a niche pastime, like playing Bach on a clavichord. In the sixteenth century it was all the rage among the aristocracy. As the cloistered design of the court suggests, the game's origins are monastic or clerical, but very quickly it was adopted by royalty. Using a small ball stuffed with wool, the game was first known as *jeu de paume* – played with a hand (later gloved) – but by the sixteenth century rackets were coming into use. In Scotland it was called caitch or caitchpule, in England tennis, from the cry '*tenez, j'y mets*' that players made before serving.

James IV's losses at caitch are recorded in the Treasurer's Accounts for 1496–98, along with wagers on the game, and the cost of tennis equipment. James V was also a keen player, and the court was one of his priorities for the palace redesign, although its construction was frequently delayed because work on the building took priority. Falkland's design is, like the palace, on the French model, a *jeu quarré* rather than the English *jeu à dedans*. The intricacies of the court's architecture are for aficionados. Falkland, for instance, has no *dedans* penthouse and *tambour*, but is equipped with *lunes* (holes), and an *ais*, or stave. It is the oldest such court still in use.

That royals as obese as Henry VIII enjoyed the game suggests that the standard of fitness required was low. Nevertheless, it could be hazardous. James I was murdered in his palace at Perth because of his love of tennis. He had blocked up the hole in his privy, which adjoined the tennis court, because the tennis ball kept getting lost in it. Had he not done so, he might have managed to escape when his attackers broke into the palace, and tracked him to the 'foule hole' below the latrine. Years later, James VI specially repaired the court at Whitehall for his son Henry to enjoy, urging him to play for his health. It was said that the boy died as a result of catching a chill during a game.

From what one knows of Mary, who enjoyed dressing in men's clothing and occasionally passing herself off incognito with friends in the streets of Edinburgh, it is not impossible that she would have played, whether in her cumbersome riding skirts, or in male garb. Yet there is not a single reference to this in the screeds written by and about her. Other hobbies – cards, embroidery, bowls, drawing, croquet, reading, dancing, music, etc. – are frequently listed, but tennis is conspicuously absent. It could be an oversight, or simply that she played so infrequently that it did not merit comment.

Yet although the palace custodians like to think otherwise, tennis experts Thomas Puttfarken and Marietta Crichton Stuart say that it 'was not a fitting sport' for a queen. As a result, they write, the

Falkland court fell into disuse during the time of Marie de Guise and her daughter. Whatever the truth, even if she did play, Mary did nothing to keep the court in good order. After years of neglect, it was restored by James VI. The main allure of Falkland Palace lay not in the small, cloistered court but in the forest and its freedoms.

Chapter 14

'Exercing hir one day richt oppinlie at the feildis with palmall and goif'

SETON PALACE

In the course of her reign, Mary would often feel the need to escape the confines and intrigue of the court in Edinburgh. Falkland involved a long ride and sea crossing, but among the most accessible and appealing retreats within reach of the capital was Seton Palace. This was the home of one of the country's most powerful families. Her closest lady-in-waiting, Mary Seton, was the half-sister of its present owner, George, fifth Lord Seton. Like his father before him, George was one of the queen's staunchest supporters and encouraged her to consider his palace her own whenever she liked.

A twelve-mile ride from Holyrood, within view of the East Lothian coast, it was a refuge she often sought. On a sunny day in early summer, I drove into the dusty car park for those following the Prestonpans Battlefield Trail or visiting Seton Collegiate Church, which stands just outside the gates of the former palace. Nearby, a train rattled towards North Berwick, a few miles down coast.

This fishing port was a precursor of Salem in Massachusetts, and would be indelibly associated with Mary's son James. Fear of witches and warlocks was not unknown in the 1560s, but it was far from the hysterical pitch it was to reach towards the end of the century and thereafter. This vengeful mood was fomented, in part, by James's obsession with the supernatural. His treatise *Daemonologie*, published ten years after his mother's death in 1597, bears testimony to his assurance in the power of the Devil and his malevolent handmaidens. James considered women especially susceptible to witchcraft; he wrote, 'for as that sexe is frailer then man is, so is it easier to be in trapped in these grosse snares of the Devill'. In 1590, convinced that East Lothian witches had plotted his murder at sea, he set about rounding them up, thereby triggering a spiral of vengeance that put the county on the map for the worst of reasons.

A plaque in the car park commemorates the Battle of Prestonpans, where Prince Charles Edward Stuart's Jacobite army enjoyed a resounding victory. The third train in a matter of minutes passed. Whatever peace this place once offered has long since departed. The noticeboard made no mention of the area's close association with Mary, Queen of Scots.

On passing through a latched iron gate into woodland, the sound of road and rail was swiftly muffled. Strings of lightbulbs in the trees led away from a field of horses towards the immaculate high walls surrounding the church. Outside, near grazing horses, the guide and ticket collector was grappling with messy undergrowth. Against the odds, this corner was blooming with clematis, jasmine and buddleia, which he had planted to brighten it up.

Leading me through an archway into the gardens that encircle the church, he gave an impromptu tour. A robin hopped close, keeping up with him at every step. A row of lush lavender bushes decorated one of the tumbledown walls between us and the remains of the building where the monks lived. The well is still visible, and the site of a water wheel, but by 1561 it would have been all but empty, its purpose ended.

On her visits to the palace, Mary would have been able to enjoy the restful atmosphere in Seton Collegiate Church. Built in the shape of a cross, the church was damaged by Henry VIII's army during the Rough Wooing and, after the Reformation, lost its function as a place where its resident community of monks would pray for the souls of the Setons. Despite this, it would have been redolent of the old faith, in which Mary could take comfort. There are few finer collegiate churches in the country, and this one feels more inviting than most. In part this is because it is so airy and unadorned. It is not famous like Rosslyn Chapel, but where that is a design disaster, Seton is tasteful and calm.

In a sheltered corner of the garden lie fragments of stone armorial bearings taken from the former palace. They are almost all that remains of the L-plan palace, which is thought to have had a high square tower and pedimented roof. Or at least all that can be seen by the naked eye. Leaning on the iron gate separating the church grounds from those of the grand Seton Castle (also known as Seton House), built in 1789 by Robert Adam, the guide pointed to the huge sward of grass, the size of a football pitch, in front of its walls. Fragments of the old palace have been incorporated into it, but they are negligible. Hence the thrill in 2017–18 when the owners allowed excavation of the grassed area, which they were planning to returf. Archaeologists discovered that part of the old building lay beneath the green and continued under the present house.

A few months after my visit, Seton Castle was put up for sale. The estate agents' photos offered a chance to see inside, and it is palatial. The outlook alone is priceless: on one side the sweeping East Lothian fields, and on the other the Firth of Forth. From the tower of its medieval forebear, the views were equally good. Mary would stroll the gardens and orchards, or enjoy a contest of shooting the butts. There is a record of her winning an archery competition nearby in February 1567 – shortly after the murder of her husband Darnley – in which she and Bothwell competed against the earls of Argyll and Huntly (the restored son of the 'Cock o' the North'). But Seton Palace is significant in Mary's story principally for two reasons: one that was to be important for her future, the other for her posthumous reputation.

It is widely assumed that among Mary's favourite sporting pastimes was the game of golf. She is said to have played all across Scotland, from Bruntsfield Links, Musselburgh, Tantallon and Wemyss castles and Leith, to the most famous of them all, the Old Course at St Andrews, in the construction of which she was allegedly involved. Credited with introducing the word 'caddie' to

Scotland from the French military cadets who carried the royal clubs, she often supposedly played with her ladies-in-waiting. Once, the story goes, she gave Mary Seton a splendid necklace as her due for beating her in a game on Musselburgh Links. Down the years historians have considered Mary's enthusiasm for golf too trivial to authenticate or disprove. And yet, according to Professor Neil S. Millar, a pharmacologist at University College London with an interest in the early history of golf, there is only one piece of evidence that associates Mary with golf, and that reference does not offer definitive proof.

The single mention is made in a polemic, written to discredit her. This is known as the Hopetoun manuscript, an early draft for the *Book of Articles*, which gathered information and evidence intended to implicate her in the murder of her husband Darnley. After this shocking event, Mary spent several days at Seton Palace, perhaps contemplating her next move, and possibly for her own security. According to the Hopetoun fragment, she did not behave as if she was devastated at her spouse's killing. She seemed so unconcerned that she played sports and consorted with her presumed lover, the Earl of Bothwell, the prime suspect in Darnley's death: 'Few dayes eftir the murther remaining at halyrudehouse she past to seytoun, exercing hir one day richt oppinlie at the feildis with palmall and goif, And on the nicht planelie abusing hir body with boithuell.'

Pall-mall was similar to croquet, played with a wooden ball and mallet. It's well known that Mary played this, which was another common royal pursuit. It is also the first, and only, reference in contemporary records to her playing golf. The intention behind this description of Mary's carefree behaviour is malign, hinting that she was an accessory to murder. By pointing the finger at her callousness, and her behaviour with the man widely believed culpable for the deed, the intention was to tarnish her reputation beyond repair.

Seen in this context, whether Mary ever picked up a golf club seems irrelevant. Perhaps she did. If so, however, it is odd that her harshest critic, George Buchanan, who compiled the *Book of Articles* presented at her trial at Westminster, and relished any opportunity

James V, who died following the Battle of Solway Moss, when his daughter Mary Stuart was six days old. (Ian Dagnall / Alamy Stock Photo)

Marie de Guise, Mary, Queen of Scots' mother and a member of one of the most powerful families in France. (GL Archive / Alamy Stock Photo)

Linlithgow Palace, where Mary Stuart was born. On special occasions its fountain, originally brightly painted, flowed with wine. (Author's collection)

Mary, Queen of Scots drawn by François Clouet around 1549, the year after her arrival at the French court. (Artokoloro / Alamy Stock Photo)

The future Edward VI in 1546. Henry VIII's plan for him to marry Mary led to the brutal Rough Wooing. (Pictorial Press Ltd / Alamy Stock Photo)

Stirling Castle. Marie de Guise retreated to this redoubtable Renaissance fortress to keep her young daughter safe. (Author's collection)

Above left. James Hamilton, Duke of Chatelherault and Earl of Arran. Regent from 1543 to 1554, he was famously indecisive and self-serving. (Juri Swimmer / Alamy Stock Photo)

Above right. Portcullis Arch, Dumbarton Castle. Despite being almost impregnable, the castle was heavily guarded while Mary was in residence in 1548. (Author's collection)

Left. Catherine de' Medici, Queen of France, by François Clouet. The Florentine wife of Henri II, Catherine became Mary's mother-in-law. (GL Archive / Alamy Stock Photo)

Francis II and Mary as King and Queen of France, from Catherine de' Medici's *Book of Hours*. (World History Archive / Alamy Stock Photo)

Left. James Stewart, Earl of Moray. Mary's illegitimate half-brother and son of James V, he was politically astute and regal in bearing.
(Art Collection 2 / Alamy Stock Photo)

Below. Holyrood Palace. Mary's luxurious apartments in the James V Tower were on the second floor, above the king's rooms.
(Author's collection)

John Knox preaching in St Andrews. Knox's sermons were so impassioned he made his listeners tremble. Note the hourglass. (FALKENSTEINPHOTO / Alamy Stock Photo)

Huntly Castle. George Gordon, Earl of Huntly, was called 'the Cock o' the North'. Mary was keen to clip his wings. (Author's collection)

Above left. Spynie Palace, the Bishop of Moray's sumptuous residence, where the Earl of Bothwell was for a time educated. (Author's collection)

Above right. James Douglas, Earl of Morton. Arnold Bronckorst's portrait of a ruthless opportunist, who allied with the rebel lords. (GL Archive / Alamy Stock Photo)

Left. Miniature of Mary, by François Clouet, painted between 1558 and 1560, while Mary was still in France. (Ian Dagnall / Alamy Stock Photo)

Above. Crichton Castle. One of Bothwell's strongholds, it was large enough to garrison a small army and its horses.

Right. Henry Stuart, Lord Darnley, with his younger brother Charles, by Hans Eworth. Darnley is dressed in the severe and fashionable Spanish style. (The Picture Art Collection / Alamy Stock Photo)

James Hepburn, Earl of Bothwell. The only surviving portrait of Mary's third husband, it shows him with signs of a broken nose. (Archivart / Alamy Stock Photo)

The murder of David Rizzio. This 18th-century engraving by Isaac Taylor, after John Opie's painting, captures the romanticised chaos and terror of the scene. (Classic Image / Alamy Stock Photo)

Right. The tiny chamber in Edinburgh Castle where, after a long and difficult labour, Mary gave birth to James.
(Cindy Hopkins / Alamy Stock Photo)

Below. Traquair House, a medieval royal hunting lodge that was once set in the heart of the teeming Ettrick Forest.
(Author's collection)

Craigmillar Castle. It was here that Mary and her inner circle deliberated what to do about the troublesome Lord Darnley. (From R.W. Billings: *The Baronial and Ecclesiastical Antiquities of Scotland*, 1845–52)

Elizabeth I, the Ermine Portrait, attributed to Nicholas Hilliard. The monarch wears the magnificent black, grape-sized pearls once owned by Mary. (incamerastock / Alamy Stock Photo)

Right. James VI, aged about eight, by Arnold Bronckorst, c. 1574. From early childhood, James was raised by his mother's enemies. (Heritage Image Partnership Image Ltd / Alamy Stock Photo)

Below. A tattered yet glamorous shoe believed to have been discarded by Mary in Jedburgh because of a broken heel. (Author's collection)

Mary, Queen of Scots' House, Jedburgh. This is either the original building, or one on the same location, where Mary stayed – and nearly died – in 1566. (Author's collection)

Hermitage Castle, an outpost of royal authority, where the Earl of Bothwell tried to maintain order among ferocious Borders clans. (Author's collection)

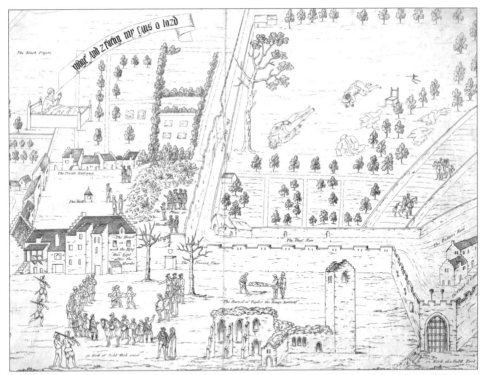

A drawing, sent to Sir William Cecil, showing the explosion at Kirk o' Field, and Darnley and his servant's murder. (Chronicle / Alamy Stock Photo)

Dunbar Castle, a formidable east-coast fortress, where Mary was taken after her abduction by Bothwell, and possibly raped. (Author's collection)

Borthwick Castle. Mary hurled abuse from the ramparts at the Confederate Lords gathered below. (Author's collection)

Carberry Hill. A contemporary drawing showing Mary being led from the battlefield by Kirkcaldy of Grange after her surrender. (Chronicle / Alamy Stock Photo)

Right. Lochleven Castle. A romanticised scene showing Mary's escape from captivity, with the help of the devoted Willie Douglas. (Lebrecht Music & Arts / Alamy Stock Photo)

Below. Dundrennan Abbey, where Mary spent her last night in Scotland before crossing the Solway Firth to England and life-long captivity. (Author's collection)

to accuse Mary of sporting activities 'clearly unsuited to women' did not include golf in his litany. Had there been proof, he would certainly have used it against her.

The Hopetoun manuscript, Professor Millar writes, appears to have drawn on second-hand accounts, whereas an eyewitness to these events, the English statesman Sir William Drury, recorded that she played a 'match at shooting', i.e. archery, but makes no mention of golf. As Millar concludes, while there was evidence of her practising archery 'often' when in St Andrews, there are 'no reports dating from this period of her playing golf during her visits to the town'.

Two months after Darnley's murder, in early April 1567, Mary was once more at Seton Palace. She was accompanied by Bothwell who, days earlier, had begun to woo her, hoping to become her husband. He would soon be put in the dock for his alleged part in the murder, but this was a shamefully biased trial from which he would emerge unscathed. What was about to happen, however, could have altered the course of her reign and, possibly, averted her own tragedy.

While Mary was walking in the grounds of Seton Palace, arm in arm with Bothwell, she was approached by an old man. He had been one of Darnley's servants but had fallen into destitution. He asked for money, and it is likely that Mary would have been generous, as she typically was. Bothwell had other ideas. Railing at the beggar's impudence, he began to punch and kick him. His assault was so savage that the old man hobbled away, blood pouring from his mouth. Two days later he died.

The horror of this incident showed Mary the dark side of Bothwell she had not previously witnessed. As John Guy writes, 'He strove for personal pre-eminence over his rivals among the Lords, which he sought to win in any way he could. His loyalty to Mary and her mother had all along been directed to this end.' Yet, as Guy points out, even at this stage in his relationship with Mary, she could have halted his ambition to marry her by disassociating herself with a man about to stand trial for her husband's murder, and thereafter continuing to keep a distance. That she did not act, even after experiencing first-hand his almost psychopathically violent outburst, casts her in a decidedly unflattering light. At best, she was besotted and saw this as an aberration; at worst, she was untroubled by his aggression or even, conceivably, saw it as confirmation that he was a man on whose strength she could depend. Whichever way one views it, that stroll in the precincts of Seton Palace was a sinister revelation.

Chapter 15

'I died for love of your beauty'

ST ANDREWS

Where Falkland was tucked out of sight, keeping its head low, St Andrews was a bustling centre. It was a hive of religion and politics, which went hand in hand. Although today it looks quaint and appealing, in 1563, when Mary visited on one of her progresses through the country, it had already seen more than its fair share of murder, martyrdom and vengeance. This was not her first visit after taking up her throne, but it was particularly unsettling, not just for what happened but for what, in hindsight, it foretold of her own career.

Mary had obviously taken a liking to St Andrews, because by 1563 she owned a house in South Street near St Andrews Cathedral. Here she would regularly stay with her four Maries, enjoying an almost illicit taste of ordinary domestic life, cooking and keeping house in a manner not possible elsewhere. Like thousands of young women students in later years, the town allowed her a degree of liberty and self-expression she had never before experienced.

The story begins in Burntisland, a few miles down coast, in the commanding Rossend Castle, a stone's throw from the harbour. On her way to St Andrews, Mary broke her journey here. In the evening, when the grooms of the chamber were checking her room before she retired, they came upon the poet Pierre de Châtelard, hiding behind the bed's canopies. He was armed with sword and dagger and was dragged out to explain himself. With remarkable sangfroid,

he claimed that he had grown sleepy while Mary's meeting with
Maitland and Moray dragged on late into the night, and had gone
into her room to rest.

The young man was one of the queen's favourites. He had sailed
with her from France and was part of her inner coterie of companions, with whom she would exchange light-hearted verse. His courtly
poetry was so mannered and arch it could have come from a template
of formal Renaissance flirtation:

> Immortal goddess
> Give ear to my song
> (You who have me in thrall,
> To whom my will is subject)
> So that if my life
> Be cut short in the prime
> Your cruelty
> Shall at least avow
> That I died for love of your beauty.

It is impossible at this distance to know if the sentiments in this
eerily prescient effusion were genuine, or part of courtly ritual and
convention, but Mary would have appeared gauche and even ridiculous if she had appeared to take seriously such doggerel. Instead,
as was the custom, she replied in kind. It was a game, or so she
thought.

The degree of licence allowed a young unmarried queen was slim.
It is likely that when on one occasion Mary was seen to dance with
Châtelard, resting her head on his chest, she had overstepped a line.
She made the error of confusing strait-laced Scottish court convention with that to which she was accustomed in France. The seeming
impropriety of this gesture played into Knox's hands, and he
denounced Mary's behaviour as being 'more like to the bordell than
to the comeliness of honest women'. Perhaps Châtelard also read too
much into it. Or perhaps he had encouraged her lapse of judgement,
knowing the damage it would do.

Whether or not his excuse was believed, Châtelard was marched out of the queen's chambers and banished forthwith from court. This was deemed punishment enough, but it would have been better for him had he been flogged and sent home. That he continued to pursue the queen suggests either idiocy – and he was clearly no fool in other respects – or something more calculated. When the queen's party left for St Andrews, he followed. She and her ladies-in-waiting settled themselves in their house, unaware of his presence. Waiting for darkness to fall, he found a way into the house and burst into her chamber, just as her maids were about to prepare her for bed. Mary screamed so loudly the whole place was roused. In seconds her half-brother Moray was in the room. The queen was badly shaken, so much so that she called on Moray to run Châtelard through on the spot.

She was lucky to have a man like Moray at her side. Cool-headed and quick-witted, he realised that the situation needed delicate handling. There was no way to contain a story like this which, if it became public before they had it under control, would besmirch Mary's reputation. Rather than kill the poet himself, he had Châtelard arrested and imprisoned. After a swift trial, he was sentenced to death. For months thereafter, Mary would not sleep alone, insisting Mary Fleming share her room, to protect her against further intruders.

Until his execution, Châtelard was kept prisoner in St Andrews Castle. It is not hard to imagine how unpleasant this was. When the tide is running high, rolling waves crash at the foot of the cliffs where the castle's crumbling remains stand. The North Sea is so strong here that the pier has often been destroyed or badly damaged by storms, from the Middle Ages to our own times.

On one of my most recent visits, children were paddling on the narrow beach beneath the castle walls, and a man was playing Icarus with his drone, trying to impress the seagulls. The castle is built into the rocks, and you get an idea of its impregnability from two mines that burrow beneath it. One was dug by besiegers in 1546–47, trying to get into the castle from below; the other is a counter mine, made by the castle defenders as they attempted to find and block their enemies' mine. Among the many reminders of this ferocious period, in which John Knox was one of the besieged, is a bottle dungeon. Now blocked with a grille, it was a formidable prison, cut deep into rock. As its name suggests, a narrow neck led to a larger windowless chamber from which escape was impossible. It is said that, after Cardinal Beaton's murder in 1546, his mutilated body was preserved here, in a chest of salt.

As a student at St Andrews, I'd often stand by the castle railings, where the wind tried to whirl people off their feet. Hundreds of years after Mary's time, it was still possible to see traces of the town she knew so well. Patrick Geddes's map from around 1580 shows a tidy grid of streets and squares leading to the castle and cathedral, very similar in shape to today. The cathedral has long been ruinous, following the Reformation, but St Rule's Tower stands proud.

St Andrews is the oldest university in Scotland. The town had made its name initially as a pilgrim destination, after the relics of St Andrew arrived in the fourth century: an arm, three fingers, a kneecap and a tooth. The university was founded in 1413, and a century and a half later students would have passed Mary and her companions as they strolled the streets, trying to look inconspicuous. It is doubtful whether anyone could miss these striking and well-groomed women, shadowed at every step by guards. Perhaps, as when Prince William was an undergraduate, they simply pretended not to recognise them, allowing an illusion of privacy.

St Mary's College, where divinity and theology are taught, is one of the loveliest corners of the town. The original college was built around 1538, at the same time as the renovation to Falkland Palace, and the same French mason who worked on Falkland, Nicolas Roy, was probably involved in its construction. An archway leads into a bright, hushed quadrangle, dominated by a magnificent spreading holm oak. Within the quad is the King James Library, founded by Mary's son in 1612. There is also a gnarled hawthorn tree which continues to produce red berries every year despite, as legend has it, being planted by Mary in 1563.

The queen was well disposed towards the university. Since childhood she had kept company at court with men and women of genius. And, although she did not, by all accounts, possess a brilliant mind, she was intelligent. Reports of her talent for composing poetry have been exaggerated, but her interest in literature and fondness for the arts appears irrefutable. She would not have been tongue-tied in the presence of intellectuals and recognised the importance of universities to the country's international prestige.

Shortly before she gave birth to James, in 1566, Mary revised her will, in case she died in childbirth: *'Je laysse mes liuures qui y sont ceulx en grec ou latin a luniuersite de sintandre pour y commancer une bible.'* ('I leave my books which are those in Greek or Latin to the University of St Andrews to start a library there.') Since she survived, it was to be decades before those of her Greek and Latin books that were not looted when she was taken captive were eventually given to the university by her son.

Despite the olde-worlde air of St Mary's Quad, it is in the town's narrow cobbled wynds and pends that the medieval character of St Andrews is most tangible. Many of these narrow passages lead to the market square where, standing at the crossroads, it is easy to imagine the clamour of stallholders and fishwives as they touted for business, and the noise of farm animals and poultry being driven past their carts and creels. In the sixteenth century the town would have resembled today's Italian hill-towns and villages, where church bells still punctuate the day. Church and cathedral bells in St Andrews rang from before daylight and at regular points during the day, until they finally announced the hour of curfew. They alerted citizens to meetings, festivities, public declarations, and summoned the devout to the devotional observations that marked the days and weeks. The sing-song music of bells elevated all towns of that age, raising the tone above the grubbier dealings at street level.

Picturesque though it is, St Andrews has witnessed terrible deeds. There was nothing quaint about the market square on 22 February 1563, the day of Châtelard's execution. The townsfolk thronged to watch a very grisly kind of entertainment. Stepping onto the scaffold, and looking out across the crowd of strangers, the poet showed great composure and courage. He began by declaiming from Pierre de Ronsard's 'Hymn to Death': 'It's done. I've unraveled the thread of my fate'. Then, before putting his head on the block, he turned in the direction of Mary's house and spoke his last words: 'Adieu, the most beautiful and the most cruel princess in the world!'

Antonia Fraser is not alone in speculating whether there was more to this story than first appears. To contemporary eyes, Châtelard's actions are those of a stalker, so deranged by his own compulsions he was deluded into thinking they were reciprocated. Indeed, his behaviour was so suicidal it seems calculated to draw attention to his infatuation. That he was a Huguenot has fuelled suspicion that he intended not to seduce Mary, but to cause a scandal. The poet himself, according to Maitland of Lethington, had told the queen, while he was in captivity, that he was following the orders of a senior figure in France. Had this plan succeeded, he would have strengthened the Protestant camp's case for putting one of their own on the throne. If this was true then, unless he was prepared to be martyred for the cause, Châtelard fatally miscalculated Mary's response. Anticipating lenience, he found her pitiless.

An earlier compromising incident underlines the queen's vulnerability to sexual scandal. The previous summer, when entertaining an English guest, she was handed a note from a Captain Hepburn, seemingly one of her staff. The English ambassador Thomas Randolph described the scene to Sir William Cecil. The note, he said, contained 'as ribbald verses as any devilish wit could invent, and under them drawn with a pen the secret members both of men and women in as monstrous a sort as nothing could be more shamefully devised'.

Who was this captain, and why was he not dismissed at once? Did Mary share his obscene communication with Randolph and others, or did he later learn from gossip what it had contained? What struck

Randolph most was the queen's lack of response when she saw it. In his eyes, that was damning. Yet surely the real surprise is that it happened in the first place. Historian Alison Weir believes that Mary could be unwise in her dealings with men: 'She may have inherited her father's promiscuous nature, whether or not she indulged it, and she was no shrinking violet.'

The Captain Hepburn incident is certainly perplexing. Was it evidence of debauchery at court, encouraged by Mary; or was it proof of a predatory and salacious attitude in the men around her, who saw her as fair game? After all, there had already been talk of abducting and marrying her against her will by a string of noblemen, from the deranged Earl of Arran, taking his cue perhaps from a similar suggestion by James Hepburn, Earl of Bothwell, and most notably Sir John Gordon. John Knox was never in doubt: 'We call her not a whore but she was brought up in the company of the vilest whoremongers.' Yet not only is there no evidence of Mary encouraging flirtation, she positively recoiled from the attentions of all the above.

Stefan Zweig's musing on why Mary encountered lechery and lack of respect chimes with the views of those who in the years after her death came not to praise but to bury her:

> Maybe a few of the men who were brought into contact with her and who came to their conclusions on the strength of certain almost imperceptible signs, had a premonition that under the sensibility, the exquisite grace of manner, and apparently perfect self-possession of the maidenly woman, there lurked an infinite capacity for amorous passion, hidden as might be a quiescent volcano beneath a pleasant landscape . . . it is indisputable that Mary allowed the men in her circle of intimates to forget that a queen must be kept unsullied by any daring thought where the fleshly woman was concerned.

At this stage in her reign, nothing suggests Mary was anything other than high-spirited and occasionally incautious. Her outrage at

Châtelard's intrusion suggests horror at her honour being compromised. This unhappy event, whether provoked by passion or political malice, is a reminder of how exposed she was as a young queen, in possession of a considerable fortune, but in want of a husband.

That need was felt as urgently by Mary as by her court, and much diplomatic energy was expended on finding her a suitable consort. The complicated negotiations that dogged this search for several years finally came to a conclusion in St Andrews where, early in 1565, Mary gave an audience to the English ambassador and openly discussed choosing Darnley as her spouse.

There is a grisly postscript to the role St Andrews played in Mary's fortunes. Her nemesis, George Buchanan, was appointed Principal of St Leonard's College in 1566 by Moray. In the process of compiling his *Book of Articles* against her after Darnley's murder, he set out to prove that one of her servants had brought her news of the deed, thereby implicating her in its planning. The servant's name was Nicholas Hubert, a Frenchman formerly in Bothwell's employment before joining the queen's household as valet de chambre. Dragged back to Scotland from France, where he had fled, he was imprisoned in St Andrews in 1569. His chief interrogator was Buchanan. When at first he refused to cast suspicion on the queen, he was tortured. At this point he confessed to taking letters from Mary to Bothwell after the murder. The ambiguous missive to which he was referring was one of the infamous Casket Letters, produced as evidence before an English court, and indelibly damaging the queen's reputation. Hubert, who was known as 'French Paris', was then sentenced to hang. On the appointed day, he cried out to the crowd from the gallows that his confession had been forced from him and was entirely untrue.

Hubert's death, and the controversy over the Casket Letters – which continues to this day – lay far in the future. Soon after Châtelard met his end, Mary received bad news. Two days after the poet's execution, on 24 February 1563, her uncle Francis, Duke of Guise, had been assassinated by a Huguenot, who shot him in the back. If Châtelard really had been intent on her destruction by the

Huguenots, then on hearing this she would have felt beleaguered and unsafe. These were melancholy months for a queen who found herself in an isolated and precarious position.

Chapter 16

'More like a woman than a man'

THE FATEFUL MEETING AT WEMYSS CASTLE

The two years that lay between the Châtelard debacle and Mary meeting her future husband Darnley look, in retrospect, like limbo. The period between February 1563, when the poet was executed, and February 1565, when she and Darnley were guests at Wemyss Castle, can be seen as a bridge between the honeymoon start to Mary's reign and the increasingly fractious and ill-fated marriage and reign that was to follow.

By now, Mary was beginning to perceive the self-interest with which her half-brother James, Earl of Moray always behaved. Her trust in him diminished, and she appointed Maitland of Lethington to the position of right-hand man in Moray's place. From this point onwards, her relationship with Moray would see-saw, eventually plunging them into outright enmity. Seemingly aware that without his full support she needed better advisors around her, Mary brought fresh blood into her inner circle, notably the formidable Lord Ruthven, who was rumoured to be a necromancer.

The issue that was to underpin – indeed undermine – the rest of Mary's reign was her right to be in line of succession to the English throne. Thwarted in her hope of meeting Elizabeth the previous year, Mary was determined to gain Elizabeth's acknowledgement of the legitimacy of her claim. It was a stumbling block to Scottish–English relations that lasted to the end of Mary's life, and was not fully resolved until her son James inherited the English title in 1603. Elizabeth was initially willing to agree that of all the claimants, Mary was her favourite. Quashing that notion was her advisor William Cecil, who urged caution in expressing such sentiments. He poisoned Elizabeth against her cousin at every opportunity, working behind her back to sabotage the Scottish queen.

The week before the fateful visit to St Andrews, where Châtelard disgraced himself, Mary had sent Maitland of Lethington to London and Paris, to further negotiations for her marriage. Securing the best possible match was an overriding concern. Her priority was to make a dynastically suitable union that would bolster her entitlement as Elizabeth's heir. At the same time, she would be filling the yawning gap in her personal life: someone she could trust, who would put her interests above everyone else's, including his own. Widowed young, and motherless at this daunting stage of her life, Mary was surrounded by opportunists seeking her favour and hoping to influence her decisions. Yet even among those who truly could be relied upon to give her good counsel, such as her far-sighted courtier Sir James Melville, there was a tutelary air to their relationship, not one of informal and deep closeness.

So much has been written about Mary's beauty as a young queen, not to mention her wealth from both France and Scotland, that it is hard today to understand how difficult it was to find her a spouse. Part of the reason was that Scotland alone was not an enticing prize. It would be another matter entirely if its ruler was also in line to inherit the English crown.

The candidate Mary had initially seemed most likely to marry was her late husband Francis II's brother, Charles IX. Catherine de' Medici, unfortunately, had made it plain that this would never happen. Some years earlier, as a recent widow, Mary had been open to the possibility of Don Carlos, son of Philip II. In Scotland, she revisited this idea. A portrait by Alonso Sánchez Coello in the Vienna Kunsthistorisches Museum shows the nineteen-year-old Don Carlos, who suffered from epileptic fits and was rumoured to be violently insane. His face is shaped like a flat-iron, and he is dressed in canary-yellow doublet, hose and shoes, which was the height of fashion. Notes to another portrait of him by Coello, in the Prado in Madrid, mention that the artist minimised his deficiencies. Coello and other portraitists were said to flatter him, softening the horsey Hapsburg jaw, and hiding his distorted back.

As Mary had shown with the sickly and puny Dauphin, a man's lack of looks and health were not necessarily an obstacle to marriage or even affection. Nor did any aristocratic woman in this era, least of all a queen, contract a union on the basis solely of attraction or personal gratification. If she was in some ways ill-tutored for her role in Scotland, Mary had been schooled in many of the duties and responsibilities of a monarch. Marriage must be as much to the public benefit as to hers.

Apart from Don Carlos's obvious shortcomings, he would have brought political and religious advantages to the liaison. A Catholic groom would put Mary in a position to gain support across Europe, from France to Spain and the Low Countries, thereby putting pressure on Queen Elizabeth, who dreaded her Catholic subjects rising against her.

There was precedent for such a long-distance match, where the husband would not be perpetually, if ever, at his wife's side. Philip II had married Mary Tudor of England and had not interfered with England's religious struggles. Now, he was married to Catherine de' Medici's daughter Elisabeth de Valois. If Mary could attach herself to the Hapsburg dynasty it would bind her to two of the most powerful regimes in Europe. From Philip II's perspective, it would allow him control, through his son, of Scotland, England and Ireland.

It was Maitland's task to convince the Spanish ambassador in London of the advantages of this proposal. Despite being one of the arch-Protestants at court, he had no qualms in pressing the queen's case and trying to force Spain's hand by hinting, untruthfully, that if they did not agree, Mary would marry Spain's great rival, the Valois king. After this opening gambit, he went to Paris to gain the support of Mary's Guise relatives for the Spanish match. For several months Philip II appeared to consider this possibility, but he was bluffing, hoping to avert the risk of her marrying Charles IX. The Guises, for their part, made no attempt to hide their U-turn on the subject. Once they had thought Don Carlos a brilliant prospect. Now, with their influence at court severely diminished, and with Catherine de' Medici temporarily tolerating the Huguenots, they had other ideas.

Indeed, so confident was the Cardinal of Lorraine in his authority over his niece that he had already conducted nuptial negotiations on Mary's behalf. His choice was Charles, Archduke of Austria, the third son of the Holy Roman Emperor Ferdinand I, but she would not countenance such a match. For a start, the archduke was also being mooted as a possible husband for Elizabeth. More crucially, he was not wealthy enough. Mary had also reached a stage in her career where she profoundly resented such interference by her uncle, who was behaving as if she were still his protégée. Her outright refusal marked a turning point in her dealings with the Guises. Meanwhile, Catherine de' Medici added to her sense of isolation by suggesting she ought to marry the Earl of Arran, son of the Duke of Châtelherault. By this point Arran had grown so unstable he was kept out of the public eye.

In the peculiar and unhealthy atmosphere at both Scottish and English courts, a sort of madness took hold. William Cecil's influence was so profound that, in his bid to exclude Mary from the English succession, he created a situation where Elizabeth insisted that she had the right to veto whomever Mary intended to marry. Under these outrageous terms, Mary's choice would be decided in an English court. As John Guy writes, 'Simply by seeking to marry – and so fulfil the universally accepted obligations of a woman ruler as Cecil could only wish his own Queen would do – a course had been set by which Mary would be turned into an English suppliant.' It was an intolerable restriction and humiliation, but above all it was an ill-advised overstepping of English authority, indicating the depth of English anxiety.

If Mary felt intimidated by Huguenot conspiracies, Elizabeth was terrified of rebellion among England's diehard Catholics. It was a precarious time, with the start of the Wars of Religion in France making everyone uneasy. Stung by England's banishment from Le

Havre, after attempting to aid the Huguenot cause, Elizabeth was understandably fearful that her Catholic subjects might rise and rally around Mary if she married a Catholic. In this nightmare scenario, Mary would be aided and abetted by her Guise relatives, and the Pope himself. In Scotland, meanwhile, the Lords of the Congregation were almost as anxious on this subject, fearing the fragile new Reformation could be overturned.

While Elizabeth's determination to remain single was not yet set in stone, she recognised that Mary would soon remarry. Nevertheless she proved quixotic and inconsistent in trying to suggest a candidate of whom she would approve. A foreigner might be acceptable, so long as he was not French, Spanish or Austrian, but an English noble was by far the best option. Whomever Mary chose, he had to be fully behind the principle of harmonious Scottish–English relations, and ideally in Elizabeth's pocket.

It is symptomatic of Elizabeth's febrile state that she suggested Mary should marry her own favoured courtier, Robert Dudley. Elizabeth was widely rumoured to be having an affair with Dudley, and even, some speculated, to have secretly borne his child. Worse, Elizabeth suggested Mary should, in marrying him, move to London, presumably so she need not relinquish him entirely. To make Dudley a more attractive proposition, she raised him to Earl of Leicester in September 1564, caressing his neck during the ceremony, for all to see. Among the onlookers was the striking figure of young Henry Stuart, who bore the ceremonial sword. This is the point at which he starts to play a part in Mary's story. The initial impression he made was one of elegance and good breeding, thereby embodying the maxim that appearances can be deceptive.

If Mary ever did seriously contemplate Leicester as the way out of the impasse she found herself in, it would have been a marriage of convenience of the coldest and most demeaning kind, to secure her right to the succession. That she did not reject the suggestion out of hand indicates either fear of provoking Elizabeth into renouncing her claim or her overwhelming desire to inherit the English throne. But for all Leicester's influence at the English court, the master of horse and hand-me-down lover was far beneath the status she expected in her future consort.

In the event, Mary's feelings were irrelevant, since Leicester refused to agree to the marriage. Instead he began to pave the way for another candidate of whom Elizabeth and Mary might both approve. This was Henry Stuart, Lord Darnley, who would soon become an albatross around Mary's neck.

When Darnley's father, the Earl of Lennox, fled to England from Dumbarton Castle, he became an ineffectual accomplice to Henry VIII's ambition to subdue Scotland, promising far more than he could deliver. Optimistically anticipating that one day Lennox might become Regent, Henry had allowed him to marry his niece, Margaret Douglas. She was the daughter of James IV's widow, Margaret Tudor, and her second husband, Archibald Douglas, the Earl of Angus.

Margaret, the Countess of Lennox, was a formidable figure, staunchly Catholic and, in modern parlance, a tiger mum. She had long aspired for her son to marry Mary and, after Francis's death, had sent him to the French court to offer his condolences, hoping something more might follow. That occasion was Darnley's second audience with the queen, the first being at Francis's coronation, when he was dispatched to beg that his family's Scottish estates be restored to them. This was to no avail. The Lennoxes were eventually granted permission to return to Scotland and actively urged to go north by Elizabeth in the autumn of 1564. A few months later, Mary was introduced to Darnley for a third time. For the Countess of Lennox, this was a heaven-sent opportunity. It was to cost her a long period in the Tower of London, since Elizabeth was enraged at her encouragement of this marriage, but by then it was too late. One pictures the countess nursing her delight to keep her warm on cold prison nights.

Henry Stuart certainly looked like a Renaissance princeling. Records and portraits depict a tall, lithe and self-consciously attractive young man, with the arrogant confidence of one born to expect a life of distinction and privilege. Sir James Melville first encountered him at Leicester's elevation to his earldom, where Darnley was pointed out to him by Elizabeth. She teasingly suggested he was a more tempting prospect for Mary than Leicester, but the Scottish envoy seemed not to take the bait. Darnley, he said, was 'more like a woman than a man'. Time alone would show that the femininity in his face and bearing were offset by displays of machismo and a taste for violence. Nor did his appearance put the queen off. Quite the contrary. Melville later noted that when the nineteen-year-old Darnley and Mary met, she seemed taken with him. Perhaps his greater maturity, or maybe her longing for love, made him catch her attention at last.

Melville's observations throughout his years in service to Mary are often but not unfailingly reliable. He was an extraordinary character, sent by Marie de Guise as a page to Mary, at the French court, when he was fourteen. He returned to her service in Scotland after allowing himself to fulfil his dream of seeing Europe. Back at Holyrood Palace, he became a gentleman of the bedchamber and a member of the Privy Council. His memoir was written after James VI came to the English throne in 1603, but the events it records end in the year 1593. It was found in Edinburgh Castle by a kirk minister, Robert Traill, who was imprisoned there in 1660. Traill gave it to Melville's grandson George. When George died on board a ship bound for America after eating 'putrid' provisions – along with 100 Covenanter prisoners from Dunottar Castle – the manuscript was feared lost. It was later discovered in the keeping of the Earl of Marchmont.

Among the most interesting passages, apart from its recollections of Mary's reign, is its preface. This takes the form of a letter to Melville's son, explaining that he wrote his memoir to serve as an example 'concerning the service of Princes'. It offers a glimpse behind the scenes at court and illuminates how volatile the fortunes of courtiers could be:

> I won greatest favour with those who were wise, grave, aged and experimented . . . But when it chanced me after to serve Princes of younger years and of less experience, at the first by the like

diligence, care, and fidelity, I obtained their favour above the rest of their servants; yet at length they were carried away by the craft and envy of such as could subtilly creep into their favour by flattery . . .

The atmosphere of sycophancy and back-stabbing this depicts suggests that the royal court could be a quagmire of competing and often venal interests.

On being allowed back to Scotland, Darnley had crossed the border and ridden after the court, which was on a progress through Fife. It was wintertime, and the journey would have been taxing. Yet perhaps he was so fixated on his pursuit of the queen he barely noticed any discomfort. He arrived in Fife on 16 February 1565, and the next day he and Mary met. The scene of their fateful encounter was Wemyss Castle, a medieval tower house that lay between St Andrews and the ferry crossing at North Queensferry. Darnley had been back in the country less than a week, and Mary would not have known that she was the reason for his hurried journey northwards. At this point, Mary was still hopeful of marrying Don Carlos, although she remained amenable, in theory, to the Earl of Leicester's suit. Even so, it is possible that, knowing Darnley's pedigree, the prospect of him as a potential husband did cross her mind as he bowed before her, bending, as Georgette Heyer might have written, a shapely leg. Unlike his mother he was Protestant, but his interest in religion was superficial, and, as became apparent in many aspects of his behaviour, he swayed in whichever direction benefitted him best.

Although the old tower where the court was entertained is largely gone, the castle's position is still commanding, high above the water on the cliff front. In the depths of winter, with snow on the ground, its thick walls and deep fireplaces would have been welcome.

Since the queen's retinue carried her home comforts from one destination to the next, for the duration of her stay Wemyss Castle was draped in her tapestries to keep out the draughts and floored with an abundance of thick rugs. The royal canopy was pinned above her head as she ate and held court, and chests packed with cutlery, plate and linen provided everything her enormous party required. Beds were also transported, dismantled and reassembled like fore-runners of flatpack furniture.

After their initial encounter at Wemyss, Darnley left to visit his father in Perthshire. He later returned to join the royal party cross-ing the Forth and heading for Holyrood, where he quickly became part of court life. Mary's secretary David Rizzio and he became particularly close, to the extent that they were said to 'lie in one bed together'. Years later, James Melville referred, with obvious distaste, to Darnley's promiscuous proclivities, remarking that he was 'much addicted to base and unmanly pleasures'.

Chapter 17

'God save his grace'

THE MARRIAGE OF MARY AND HENRY LENNOX

Shortly after Darnley's arrival at the Scottish court, Elizabeth finally dropped any pretence of naming Mary as her successor. In the middle of March 1565, the queen received a message saying that even if she and Leicester married, Elizabeth would not confirm her title as heir, 'until she be married herself, or determined not to marry'. It was one of the occasions on which she proved most vexatiously awkward.

With the Countess of Lennox pressing her son's credentials as Mary's next husband – the great-grandson of Henry VII had both Tudor and Stewart antecedents – what followed appears in retrospect as almost inevitable. All other avenues of marriage had closed; Elizabeth was not to be trusted, but having paraded Darnley before Sir James Melville as a potential groom for Mary, appeared to approve of their union; and Darnley, skilled in courtly etiquette, turned on the charm. Possibly he was overconfident, because when he first proposed to Mary she firmly refused him. Yet the seed of the idea had been planted.

What happened next is more like the plot of a romantic novel than the behaviour to be expected of the ruler of a divided, fractious country. Darnley fell ill, purportedly with measles, which was a serious ailment, and frequently fatal for children. In a spontaneous and reckless act of kindness, Mary invited him to Stirling Castle, where he could recover and convalesce. Once he had been conveyed there, she spent much of April in the royal apartments, personally nursing him back to health.

It was an extraordinary privilege for one of such brief acquaintance. As he lay in his richly appointed guest room, Darnley must have realised he was greatly favoured. Perhaps he tried to downplay his symptoms in order to appear more manly. More probably he lapped up the attention and made no effort to minimise his afflictions, prolonging the pleasure of the queen's attention.

His acceptance of Mary's offer is understandable. Who would have refused? More astonishing was the queen's conduct. Rather than entrust his care to her staff, she undertook to restore him to health herself. Although she no doubt summoned her own doctors to attend him and offer advice, she would often sit by his bedside, staying alone with him late into the evening. Seemingly she was unconcerned at feeding salacious rumours. Unlike when Châtelard scandalised her in St Andrews, she was no longer worried about protecting her reputation.

Was this because she already knew that they were to marry? Or was she simply blinded by infatuation? Maybe the explanation is more prosaic, and poignant. Since her mother's death, Mary had been bereft of comfort and affection; suddenly here was a man with whom she might find both. Starved for too long of loving company, she grew heedless. In her role as nurse – bathing his fevered brow, changing his pillows, bringing him broths and herbal potions – she would have had ample opportunity to form an intimate bond. Since childhood, when she became a close companion to the sickly Dauphin, she had understood the connection between invalidism and love. Darnley's illness and her nursemaiding was an adult version of the same dangerous equation. Her error was interpreting desire for something more enduring.

This short but intense period was the hinge on which the rest of her life would turn. Antonia Fraser describes act one of the forthcoming drama: 'Under the influence of the proximity of the sickroom – and the tenderness brought forth by the care of the weak, the suffering – and the handsome – Mary had fallen violently, recklessly and totally in love.' Yet not everyone thinks she was genuinely smitten. Accounts of the queen looking and speaking increasingly unlike her usual self have led to speculation that she was using Darnley for her own ends, while perhaps not admitting as much even to herself. Meanwhile at court it was rumoured that she was bewitched.

Very likely the ailment that kindled their love affair was not measles but the early stages of syphilis, which was to afflict Darnley for the rest of his short life. The connection between syphilis and illicit sex had been quickly understood after its appearance in epidemic form at the end of the previous century. 'Licht women' were blamed for transmitting it, and in Aberdeen, where it was first identified in 1497, prostitutes were ordered to cease their trade, or face expulsion from the city.

Known as 'grandgore' or 'glengore', it did not carry the same stigma as leprosy – which was thought also to be transmitted through promiscuity – but its symptoms were disfiguring and mortifying. Most noticeable were great scabs. And, as with leprosy, and indeed the plague, the authorities sent the afflicted into enforced isolation until they appeared to be cured. Lepers, unfortunately, never had any hope of recovery. They were condemned to life outwith the town walls, carrying wooden clappers to alert people to their presence, and fed on unsellable scraps from the nearest market.

Had Mary known Darnley was suffering from syphilis rather than measles, would her feelings have cooled? It is certainly possible she would not have appointed herself so zealously as his nurse, but as this would not have been the first instance of the disease she had encountered at court, it is conceivable that she would have taken a matter-of-fact view. Syphilis was an occupational hazard for soldiers away from home on campaign, as it was for men of a certain class. Although there is no evidence that Mary's father suffered from it, he was famously libidinous, as were many noblemen. Incredible as it may seem, it is improbable that evidence of promiscuity would have been a barrier to romance.

As with so many elements in Mary's story, it is tantalising but ultimately fruitless to speculate. The fact remains that when Elizabeth heard of their increasingly close relationship, she sent her ambassador to inform Mary that she would never approve of their match. For her to take a husband who had a claim to the English throne could not be countenanced.

In reply, Mary bestowed the earldom of Ross upon Darnley. It could be read as today's equivalent of posting a 'save the date' announcement. It seems that, after two years of indecision, negotiation, rejection and disappointment, she had made up her mind. Or, as Randolph put it, 'seeing she is a woman, and in all things desires to have her own will'. The sexism can be dismissed, but not the sentiment. It is a measure of Mary's frustration during the increasingly demeaning and desperate months of finding a husband that when her options had narrowed to this most inadequate and venal individual, she lost common sense and patience, and behaved in a manner calculated to cause dismay and even ridicule. How easy she made it for those like John Knox who believed her to be, like all Catholic women, governed by lust. And what a gift for Moray to persuade others that by selecting a man like Darnley as the King of Scotland – the title she insisted he be given – she was endangering the realm.

Despite representations from her closest advisors, ambassadors and even her four Maries, Mary was intent on marrying Darnley. Why she did not heed the advice of her dearest friends is puzzling. Her ladies-in-waiting, drawn from the ranks of the aristocracy and raised at the far from puritanical French court, were experienced and worldly. They understood the difference between a passing lustful whim, which could be discreetly indulged, and someone worthy of a lifelong commitment. Yet Mary ignored their protestations. Perhaps this is the closest we will ever get to a sign that privately she knew she was making a terrible mistake.

Having gained the support of Philip II and Charles IX to the union, she was not dismayed, as she ought to have been, that Moray was appalled. He was to lose his position as one of her most trusted advisors to a young and foppish man described by her uncle Claude as a 'girlish nincompoop'. Even before this, there had been bad blood between them. Shortly after his return to Scotland, Darnley had let it be known that he thought Moray had too much power. It was a slur Moray would never forgive, and his loathing and mistrust of Darnley soon encompassed the queen.

It is little wonder that those who thought Ruthven was an agent of the devil considered Mary to have fallen under a spell. That might have been true at least in the humdrum sense that she refused to think clearly. She seemed entirely unconcerned that her nobles were beginning to align themselves into parties, for and against the queen's future husband. The political rift created by her rash choice became the fault line in Mary's reign. It would be the source of many of her future troubles, one for which she alone can be blamed.

Infuriated to learn that Elizabeth condemned the prospect of her marrying Darnley and had summoned him and his father Lennox back to England, Mary refused to let them go. She appointed her fiancé Duke of Albany, and a week later, around six on the morning of 29 July, left her rooms in a procession for her private chapel at Holyroodhouse to marry him. Dressed as ever in mourning black, with a large black hood, an outfit reminiscent of that she wore to her first husband's funeral, Mary was led to the chapel and up the aisle on the arm of Lennox, and attended by Atholl. Darnley placed three rings on her finger, the middle one with a magnificent diamond, and the couple knelt, to be blessed by the priest. Darnley then left the ceremony, before the nuptial Mass, and went to his wife's bedchamber to await her return.

Ahead of the wedding feast, Mary was ritually disrobed, guests symbolically removing her widow's weeds pin by pin. She was then dressed in a colourful gown by her ladies-in-waiting, as befitted the occasion, although in light of what was soon to follow, black would have been more appropriate. By now, the coolness between the Maries and the queen, caused by their reservations about Lord Henry, had hopefully been forgotten. Coins were thrown for the crowd, and an afternoon and evening of dining and dancing ensued, followed by several more days of celebration and entertainment.

On the morning after the wedding, Mary called a meeting of her nobles. The heralds announced Darnley as King of Scotland, and went on to inform them that henceforth all royal documents would be jointly signed by both the King and the Queen. There was stunned silence, until Darnley's father cried out, 'God save his grace'. Already the tension this marriage would cause was all too obvious. The only mistake Mary had not made was to ask Parliament to grant her husband the Crown Matrimonial. This title, were it ever given, meant that in the event of Mary's death, her husband, and any of his future heirs, would inherit the throne.

Only the queen and King Henry were truly happy at this point, although the lack of enthusiasm of Mary's friends must surely have dimmed her joy. Perhaps she did not care what they thought. In the previous weeks Mary had behaved differently with her closest companions, as if she were in the grip of ungovernable passion. Darnley, for his part, had shown himself so vicious, spiteful and arrogant that even his former friends found him intolerable. The only person who had supported the couple when they announced their intention to marry, and who seemed oblivious to its significance, was Mary's Italian secretary David Rizzio.

* * *

It has often been assumed that the nobles at the Scottish court were exceptionally unruly and venal. It has perhaps been too easy, and simplistic, to dismiss the north as a primitive region, run by near savages who lacked the cultivated manners of their southern and European counterparts.

Certainly Scotland was poor and rough, but the behaviour of its lieges was no more appalling than anywhere else. It could even be argued, as the saga of Mary, Queen of Scots unfolded, that its ruling elite showed greater respect for the realm's interests than in some other countries. The ideology that propelled John Knox and his followers was not self-interest, in the acquisitive sense, but a zealot's insistence on self-determination. If a ruler proved themselves unfit, they could be ousted, forcibly if necessary. It greatly aided the Protestant cause, and Moray's in particular, that their argument could be bolstered by religious righteousness and the claim to be upholding the country's new faith. With Darnley nominally converted to Catholicism, the conflict could be framed as the defence of the Reformation: noble, principled, without personal guile or grievance. Yet the source of the problem Mary was about to face was much more simple. She had proclaimed Darnley King of Scotland the day after their marriage, without consulting her Privy Council. To Moray and his closest allies, it was intolerable to put a man like Darnley in such a position of authority. With Châtelherault and Argyll, he signed a bond, opposing the Queen's Catholic marriage. Their main fear was Darnley becoming ruler and their positions of power nullified.

The barely contained resentments that began to fester during this phase of Mary's rule were potentially disastrous. There were rumours that Darnley planned to murder Moray, 'in the back-gallery of her highness's lodging in Perth'. For his part, Moray was said to be plotting to abduct Darnley and his father, the Earl of Lennox, and set them free in England, like wolves in the wilds. Mary publicly rebuked Darnley for talking so rashly, but Moray's attitude represented such a challenge to her authority that she summoned him to explain. When he did not appear, it was clear that she was facing the most serious crisis of her reign, a rebellion far more worrying than that of Huntly. This was civil war.

On 6 August 1565, Mary declared Moray outlawed, and confiscated his and the other rebels' lands. The traitors' army began to congregate near Ayr. Mustering her forces, and with Darnley exquisitely attired at her side in gilt armour, Mary rode out of Edinburgh at the head of her troops. She made an impressive sight, helmeted like Boudicca, and with pistols on her saddle-bow. Her stamina during the weeks that followed was widely remarked upon. Even Knox was impressed. Despite atrocious weather, he noted, 'the queen's courage increased man-like, so much that she was ever with the foremost'. Only one other woman, whose name is not recorded, could keep up with her.

While Mary headed west, Moray and his men entered Edinburgh, expecting to gather support. Instead, the cannons at Edinburgh Castle were fired at them, and the queen's outraged citizens rose up and forced them to flee. During these weeks, Moray pleaded with England for support in his Protestant campaign. Randolph recorded, 'They expect relief of more money from England. If her Majesty Queen Elizabeth will now help them, they doubt not but one country shall receive both Queens.' The rebels' intention was seemingly to dispose of Darnley, and depose Mary. Elizabeth, unsurprisingly, refused to countenance rebellion against a monarch. Who knew otherwise where that might lead?

Mary, on the other hand, was in the novel position of being able to ask the Pope for financial support, for what she could call her safeguarding of the Catholic cause, her intention being to 'restore religion in splendour'. She also received financial aid from Philip II of Spain. Yet before riding out against Moray, Mary had reassured her subjects that she intended no change in the religious status quo. In so doing, she was emphasising that Moray was a common rebel and traitor, not a champion of the people's religious rights. In hinting to her allies that she intended soon to restore Catholicism in direct contradiction to this assurance, she was either lying, or conniving.

That summer the queen and her husband rode through the country, by way of Linlithgow, Stirling and the vicinity of Glasgow, avoiding the city, where there was an outbreak of pestilence. During their pursuit of Moray, he zigzagged like a snipe. Little wonder his campaign was belittlingly referred to as the Chaseabout Raid. The armies came closest to battle in the south-west, near Dumfries, in early October. It has been speculated that Mary conceived her son during this raid, possibly while in the south-west. Her forces, by this stage reputed to be around 18,000-strong, were about to attack Moray's smaller band, when he crossed the border, seeking safety in England. He was to remain there, in Newcastle, for several months, not returning until shortly after the murder of Darnley the following year.

Soon after Mary realised the extent of Moray's disaffection and disloyalty, she sent a messenger to Paris to summon the exiled Bothwell to return. Despite English warships sent to intercept him, he landed at Eyemouth, a small, cliff-bound fishing port a few miles north of the border, and was soon reappointed to his old position as Lieutenant of the Scottish Marches. That he was also appointed Lieutenant General of the Queen's Army caused a rift between the newly married royal couple. As Randolph gleefully reported to Cecil, 'Jars have already risen, between the queen and Darnley; she to have her will one way; and he another: He to have his father, for Lieutenant General, and she to have Bothwell.' Since both men were Lieutenants General, one in the west, the other in the south, it seems a flimsy pretext for an argument loud enough to reach the court. Mary also pardoned Lord Gordon, son of the Earl of Huntly, and on 2 October, both he and Bothwell returned to the Privy Council.

There was also a cooling of Mary towards her secretary Maitland of Lethington, whose allegiance appeared to waver. He retreated to his family seat near Haddington in East Lothian. Known then as Lethington Tower, but today as Lennoxlove, in its grounds there is a 600-year-old chestnut tree, a rare survivor from Mary's day.

Chapter 18

'Smaller than their own scullery at home'

MARY'S SUPPER ROOM

Mary Stuart's little supper room in Holyrood is the kernel of the palace. Like the smallest in a nest of Russian dolls, reached through a series of bigger, grander chambers, this is where many sightseers feel they come closest to the queen.

The supper room is reached by a tight turnpike stair leading from Darnley's room on the floor below. The original stair, which was boared up in the seventeenth century, was used by him alone, as it opened directly into Mary's bedchamber, off which stands the supper room. Depending on your temperament, the first sight of these quarters is either thrilling or disappointing. In Muriel Spark's novel, *The Prime of Miss Jean Brodie*, the schoolgirl Sandy recalls the moment when she 'had been taken to Holyrood in an uncle's car and had seen the bed, too short and too broad, where Mary, Queen of Scots had slept, and the tiny room, smaller than their own scullery at home, where the Queen had played cards with Rizzio'.

The bedroom, with its sumptuously embroidered four-poster bed – not the original – is hung with rich tapestries. A frieze around the walls is painted in grisaille, a monotone grey that makes it appear to be carved from stone, but its coolth is offset by the warm, oak-panelled ceiling, embossed with the monograms of Mary's parents. How often did she raise her eyes and think of them? With deep and high windows, by tower-house standards this is a light-filled room, and it is easy to envisage how comfortable it would have been with a blaze in the blue-tiled fireplace and heavy curtains drawn against the night.

Off the bedchamber are two small rooms. One, possibly a dressing room where a lady-in-waiting might have slept, stands empty, save for tapestries and portraits on the walls. A Queen Elizabeth lookalike stares out expressionless, perhaps a member of European aristocracy. The other, in a turret overlooking the palace courtyard, is the fabled supper room. It is a step away from the low door to the private staircase, and it was here, on the evening of 9 March 1566, that the first of the desperate, dastardly events in Mary's reign took place. What happened bears out the historian Rosalind Marshall's verdict on Lord Darnley, that 'by having such a man at her side Mary was placing a dangerous weapon in the hands of her enemies'. Or, as Antonia Fraser puts it, 'Darnley as the tool of Mary's opponents could have a cutting edge.'

By the time Mary's pregnancy was well advanced, her marriage was already on the rocks. In retrospect, her romance with Darnley had lasted little longer than their honeymoon, which had been spent largely in pursuit of Moray. Once this joint endeavour to protect Darnley's honour was ended, cracks in the relationship quickly showed. The most obvious cause of the growing *froideur* between them was the queen's refusal to grant her husband the Crown Matrimonial. It was one thing to designate him King of Scotland, another formally to seal his position with a title that meant he could become ruler one day.

Mary was twenty-two when she married the nineteen-year-old Darnley. She has been accused of losing her wits over him, but in withholding the Crown Matrimonial she demonstrated a steely awareness of where the country's – and her own – best interests lay. Already she recognised that her spouse was not capable of holding the reins of power, or not yet at any rate. She would remind those who criticised her decision of Darnley's youth and immaturity, although these could not have been her only reasons. By now Darnley was twenty, yet Mary had ascended to the throne at nineteen, while her first husband became King of France at fifteen.

Encouraged by his scheming father, the Earl of Lennox, Darnley's ambitions were boundless. With a character as weak and vicious as his was soon to prove, it is disturbing to speculate that had he been granted his wish he might have found ways of disposing of a disgruntled wife. The lack of care he took of Mary in subsequent weeks and months is evidence that he took scant interest in her welfare.

King Henry was no longer the charming, entertaining fellow Mary had met at Wemyss Castle. Instead, he was behaving like a drunk, and had grown petulant and bullying. Like many men, he believed his wife should be governed by his whims and commands. Mary thought otherwise and grew to regret her insistence, when they wed, that state documents must be signed by the king as well as by her. Darnley was so frequently absent from meetings and consultations and occasions when documents must be countersigned that she had a seal made of his signature, to save the bother of tracking him down.

Had she been so inclined, Mary might have found him in the low dives around the Canongate and the Royal Mile, either its taverns, gaming parlours or brothels. Knox's account of this period describes the king as frequently hawking and hunting, but adds to this list 'other such pleasures as were agreeable to his appetites, having in his company gentlemen willing to satisfy his will and affections'. If one is tempted to dismiss the lemony tone as puritanism, other contemporaries refer to behaviour 'too shameful' to commit to the page. The English, it seems, were well aware that Master Lennox was 'bad', long before he left England.

One of Darnley's putative lovers was the Italian singer, lutenist, and stalwart of the court, David Rizzio, whose name has become a byword for tragedy. What concerned some onlookers most was not that the men slept together but the fear that Rizzio was a spy for the Pope. Whatever the truth, the evident closeness of king and courtier makes what happened next even more repugnant.

Dread of Catholic influence was infecting the Scottish court. Without consulting his wife – indeed, imagining himself acting alone – Darnley began to fancy himself as a great European Catholic king, restoring the old religion. He talked of bringing High Mass back to St Giles' Cathedral. After his investiture with the Order of St Michael, by the French king, on 10 February 1566, he and his friends waltzed up the Royal Mile, proclaiming that they had just overturned the Reformation. He seems to have interpreted this formality as the seal of approval from Catholic Europe.

Darnley was not alone in starting to rock the religious boat. Letters between Randolph and the English diplomat Nicholas Throckmorton from early February suggest that even the ultra-cautious and diplomatic Mary was considering proclaiming herself as the rightful Catholic ruler of England, thereby jettisoning her previously careful policy of presenting no threat to the status quo. In this volatile atmosphere, the disaffected lords, both Protestant and Catholic, and all far cleverer than Darnley, knew how to play him for their own ends.

When Mary first arrived in Scotland, she invited musicians to enliven the court, which was constantly filled with music. Rizzio was a singer, from Piedmont in north-west Italy, in the employ of Count Moretta, the ambassador of Savoyard. The court's musicians and singers performed during meals, in the evenings and whenever the queen felt the need of diversion. It seems her new husband was also fond of music. When he married, he brought a family of musicians, the Hudsons, from Yorkshire to Edinburgh, for their entertainment. The court's promotion of music continued that of Mary's grandfather and father. James IV had been the patron of the country's greatest Renaissance composer, Robert Carver. But within the palace, sonorous liturgical compositions would have taken second place to the conviviality of folk songs and traditional music, much of it influenced by French and English fashions.

Yet even as Holyrood rang to the sound of pipes, lutes, drums and singers, musicians were under threat. With the Reformation, great choral compositions, such as masses and requiems, all but died. The vicar of St Andrews, Thomas Wode, who was a keen collector of songs, predicted in the 1570s that 'Music sall pereishe in this land alutterlie'.

At Holyrood, however, music continued to play an integral role in everyday affairs. And so, gradually, did David Rizzio. When

Count Moretta and his retinue left Scotland, Rizzio was persuaded to stay on as one of the queen's valets de chambre. After three years of impeccable service, he had become such a favourite that, when Mary's French secretary Pierre Raullet was sacked for taking bribes, she appointed Rizzio to the post. This was a very different role from that of valet, and he proved far from satisfactory. In fact, he was so inept he caused more work for the queen as she undid his errors.

Yet Rizzio seemed not to notice his inadequacies. On his promotion, he would have been wise to keep a low profile, but evidence suggests he was an obnoxious peacock, who swiftly positioned himself as the conduit between Mary and her nobles and enjoyed flaunting his influence. He did a brisk trade in bribes, which in part explained the lavishness of his outfits. But while some described him as 'attractive', and he was reputed to enjoy playing sports, no silks or furs could hide the fact that he had a distorted back or shoulder. This led his enemies to describe him as 'a dwarfish and deformed person' and 'very ill-favoured'.

Mary, however, enjoyed his wit, conversation and music. Growing increasingly homebound as her pregnancy advanced, and with her husband out gallivanting most evenings, Mary allowed Rizzio to become one of her closest companions and would play cards with him into the small hours. Rumours that they were having an affair made her laugh. That was always her way, but it is odd that Rizzio, who hailed from Machiavelli's homeland, was either unaware of, or more probably unconcerned by, the hatred he was fomenting. And no matter how ridiculous the gossip, Mary should have known better than to give any appearance of misconduct. It is telling that, when prompted by her trusted counsellor Melville to keep Rizzio at a distance, she brushed off his concerns and refused to modify her blatant favouritism.

Maitland of Lethington, who was counting the days until he could regain his position at court, took advantage of the situation. It was he who told Darnley that Mary was being unfaithful with Rizzio. To one of Darnley's temperament, throwing out a suggestion of this nature was like leaving a lighted candle in a hay barn. The

Earl of Morton reinforced Darnley's suspicions and rallied his Douglas relatives, including Darnley's uncle, George Douglas, to nurse the first flames into a blaze. By the time they were done, Darnley was unsure if the child Mary was carrying was even his.

Darnley's loathing of Rizzio helped the lords gain their end. Forgetting that some of them had recently rebelled against him becoming king, they made an unholy and shameful pact with a man they neither respected nor trusted. Protestants saw their way back to power, and Catholics saw the reinstatement of Parliament as a place where they would not be unfairly excluded from the queen's presence by a trumped-up singer.

Parliament was due to meet in the middle of March 1566, at which time Moray and the rebel lords (with the exception of Châtelherault who had been pardoned) were to be charged with treason and have their lands forfeited to the Crown. To avoid this calamity, Moray and others agreed to ally with Darnley and support his claim, promising to secure him the coveted Crown Matrimonial, since Parliament alone, not the queen, could grant this honour.

Thereafter, upon gaining the Crown Matrimonial, Darnley promised to revoke his Catholic sympathies, pardon the rebels, restore their lands and titles and bolster Protestantism within the realm. Naturally, to explain his religious volte-face he needed someone to blame for indoctrinating him. Who better than one thought to be a papal spy and, even more damningly, bedding the queen?

A bond was drawn up in Darnley's name, which he was made to sign, to safeguard the rebels in case he later denied any involvement. It makes shocking reading to modern eyes. Few documents more starkly present the mindset of the political classes in Mary's time. It is worth quoting in full, not just for its affirmation of murder as a legitimate aid to good governance, but for the attitude it shows towards the queen:

> Be it kend [known] to all men by these present letters: We, Henry, by the grace of God, King of Scotland, and husband to the Queen's Majesty, for so much we having consideration of the

gentle and good nature, with many other good qualities in her Majesty, we have thought pity, and also think it great conscience to us that are her husband, to suffer her to be abused or seduced by certain privy persons, wicked and ungodly . . . especially a stranger Italian called Davie . . . we have devised to take these privy persons, enemies to her Majesty, us, the nobility and commonwealth, to punish them according to their demerits, and in case of any difficulty, to cut them off immediately, and to take and slay them wherever it happeneth.

And because we cannot accomplish the same without the assistance of others, therefore have we drawn certain of our nobility, earls, lords, barons, freeholders, gentlemen, merchants, and craftsmen, to assist us in our enterprise, which cannot be finished without great hazard . . . We bind and oblige us, our heirs and successors, to the said earls, lords, barons, gentlemen, freeholders, merchants, and craftsmen, their heirs and successors, that we shall accept the same feud upon us, and fortify and maintain them at the uttermost of our power, and shall be friend to their friend, and enemy to their enemies, and shall neither suffer them nor theirs to be molested nor troubled in their bodies, lands, goods, nor possessions so far as lieth in us.

And if any person would take any of the said earls, lords, barons, gentlemen, freeholders, merchants, or craftsmen, for enterprising and assisting with us for the achieving of our purpose, because it may chance to be done in presence of the Queen's majesty, or within her palace of Holyrood-house, we, by the word of a prince, shall accept and take the same on us now as then and then as now . . . In witness whereof we have subscribed this with our own hand at Edinburgh, the 1st of March 1565.

With hindsight, it is extraordinary to realise that the plot to kill Rizzio was widely known, at least two weeks before it was enacted. In late February, Randolph informed Queen Elizabeth of what was planned, and Melville, deeply disturbed at the rumours, urged Mary to pardon the rebels at once, to avert trouble. She wavered but, given the growing surge of anti-Protestantism on the Continent, and her hopes of winning Catholic support, decided against. Thus, by the end of February 1566, Rizzio's fate was sealed. It waited only the hour.

Chapter 19

'He must learn his duty better'

THE MURDER OF RIZZIO

As with most places where dreadful acts have been committed, it is our imagination that invests them with horror. The queen's supper room, furnished with table, chairs and Jacobean-style wing-backed armchair, could not look more innocent. It is more the setting for a book group than for murder. A high window looks out towards the palace gates and the road leading to Abbeyhill and Leith. Most commentators record how confined and cramped a room it was when crowded with Mary's retinue. The heavy furniture it holds certainly shrinks it, yet while small it is not poky.

It was here that, around seven o'clock on Saturday evening, 9 March 1566, Mary was enjoying dinner with several friends and members of her retinue. Among them was the 33-year-old Rizzio, her half-sister Jean, Countess of Argyll, the master of her horse, the master of the queen's household, her French apothecary, a page and a groom. Despite it being Lent, Mary was allowed to eat meat since she was six months pregnant. The table was lit with candles, and it would have presented a cosy tableau when Darnley pushed aside the tapestry hanging and entered. Taking a seat beside his wife, he amiably put an arm around her waist. Unknown to the diners, the palace gates and all doors were already guarded by Morton, Lindsay and around a hundred other heavily armed men. There was as yet no hint of what was about to unfold. That became clear minutes later with the terrifying appearance at the supper room door of Lord Ruthven, in a full suit of armour. He was pale as wax, in part because of ill health and the effort of moving beneath a second skin of steel, but doubtless also because of the gravity of the act he was about to commit.

Informing Mary that her secretary was guilty of a serious offence, he ordered Rizzio out of the room: 'He hath hinderered him [Darnley] of the crown matrimonial, which Your Grace promised him, and has caused Your Majesty to banish a great part of the nobility that he might be made a lord; he has been a destroyer of the commonwealth, by taking bribes, and must learn his duty better.' By now, the Italian was cowering behind the queen, clutching her skirts. Two of Mary's party tried to rush Ruthven, but he pulled out a pistol and waved them back. Then, with dagger in hand, he advanced on his victim.

More of Darnley's supporters were crowding into the room, led by Patrick Lindsay, Lord Lindsay of the Byers, a formidably pugnacious man in his early forties. The first blow the secretary received was very probably dealt at that point, being thrust into Rizzio across Mary's shoulder. Some believe that it was not Ruthven but Darnley's uncle who, snatching his nephew's dagger from his belt, lunged at the secretary. Whoever it was, the blade passed so close to Mary's throat that she felt the coldness of the steel. In the mêlée, the table with its dishes and glasses was overturned, but the candlestick was rescued by the countess and lit the scene. Darnley held Mary firm, preventing her from struggling. As Rizzio was dragged out, a pistol was pressed into her stomach. It was an act she never forgot or forgave. To the end of her life, Mary believed that she and her unborn child were also in mortal danger.

Mary's account of events in a letter, three weeks later, to James Beaton, Archbishop of Glasgow, rings with alarm and anger. When she tried to prevent Ruthven entering by assuring him that if Rizzio had committed any crime he would be publicly held to account, she added that if Ruthven took any further steps he would be charged with treason. This had no effect:

Notwithstanding, the said Lord Ruthven perforce invaded him [Rizzio] in our presence (he then for refuge took safe-guard, having retired him behind our back), and with his complices cast down our table upon ourself, put violent hands in him, struck him over our shoulders with whingers [a short stabbing sword], one part of them standing before our face with bended daggs [pistols], most cruelly took him forth of our cabinet, and at the entry of our chamber give him fifty-six strokes with whingers and swords, in doing whereof we were not only struck with great dread, but also by sundry considerations, were most justly induced to take extreme fear of our life.

The place where the killers finished the deed, with a further fifty-five stabbings, was in the audience chamber, beyond Mary's bedroom. The palace guidebook says that 'his alleged bloodstain can be seen in the place where his body was left', and given the number of blows he suffered, it would not be wholly fanciful to expect to see telltale signs, if the floor was the original. In his *Chronicles of the Canongate* (1827), Sir Walter Scott relays an anecdote that turns tragedy into humour. Mrs Policy, the housekeeper of Queen Mary's apartments, was appalled when, during a tour of the palace, a detergent salesman got onto his knees by the begrimed floorboards, scrubbing brush in hand: 'Two hundred and fifty years, ma'am, and nothing take it away? Why, if it had been five hundred, I have something in my pocket will fetch it out in five minutes.' The miraculous product was called Scouring Drops.

Above this spot hangs a portrait of the poor fellow, holding a lute and with the hint of a Mona Lisa smile. The ferocity of the attack upon him reveals the depth of personal grievance behind it. In a short career, he had outraged and alienated lords on both sides of the religious and royal divide. The same was beginning to be true of Mary.

In the calm, ordered surroundings of the palace today, it is impossible to envisage such frenzy. Rizzio is surely one of the most miserable figures in Scottish history. He was a talented man blinded by ambition and brought down by hubris and by a queen who refused to see how their rapport could be misconstrued or manipulated to her enemies' ends. Yet even had he, and Mary, acted with impeccable professionalism, the outcome might have been no different. Such was the political ferment, a sacrifice was required.

Rizzio's body was pitched out of the audience chamber, down the main staircase and onto a chest in the porter's room. It was a disgraceful episode, an indelible stain on the reputation of all involved. Even so, it was a very shrewd piece of realpolitik.

The town's common bell had begun ringing at the commotion from the palace. Hundreds of the town watch appeared at the palace walls, armed with spears and led by the provost, who called up to Mary's apartments to ask if all was well. She was prevented from screaming for help. If she made a sound, Lord Lindsay told her, she would be 'cut into collops' – sliced into slivers – and 'cast over the wall'. From the man who had had to be restrained from slaughtering the priest at Holyroodhouse, the threat was convincing. Darnley reassured them that an enemy had been justly dealt with and all was well. Satisfied, they departed.

Ruthven, Morton and their allies had planned to kill several of Mary's adherents this night, among them lords Livingston and Fleming, but in the end the only other victim was a Dominican priest, Father Adam Black. Formerly chaplain to Marie de Guise, he was stabbed to death in his bed not long after Rizzio's execution, by the fanatical Henry Yair. Before the party who had been at supper were allowed to leave, unmolested, Mary learned from her half-sister Jean, who had seen his body, that Rizzio was dead, and appallingly butchered. On hearing this, Mary said, 'No more tears. I will think upon revenge.' A childhood under the tutelage of her Guise uncles and Catherine de' Medici had schooled her in self-preservation and retaliation.

That night, Mary was kept prisoner in her bedroom, with a heavy guard at the door. She was allowed none of her ladies-in-waiting, but did have the company of Elizabeth, the Dowager Countess of Huntly, herself no stranger to ferocious reprisals and violent death. During the commotion the countess's son, the recently reinstated Earl of Huntly, and the Earl of Bothwell, had managed to slip from the palace and make for Dunbar, otherwise they too might have perished.

Early the following morning, a contrite and terrified Darnley was admitted to Mary's rooms. He begged forgiveness, clearly in fear of his own life among his brutal fellow conspirators. Now, he preferred his wife's protection to theirs. He showed her the bond he had signed with Morton and others, and told her that they planned to incarcerate her in Stirling Castle until the birth of her child. He was to become ruler, with this caucus at his side, and she would remain in captivity for the rest of her days. If, that is, they did not execute her. Learning this, and realising she must prevent them setting their plan in motion, Mary feigned labour pains. While she was ill, they could not abduct her to Stirling. Not entirely convinced, yet stymied, the lords allowed a midwife and her surgeon to attend her.

On the day after Rizzio's murder, Darnley had proclaimed Parliament cancelled, allowing Moray and the others under threat of forfeiture to return openly to the city. Not knowing of Moray's involvement in the murder, Mary summoned him to Holyrood. It was but a few months since her army had been on his tail, yet their conversation was unexpectedly friendly, and she took solace from his seemingly sympathetic company. When he later returned in the company of Morton and others who had burst into her rooms, they knelt before her and asked for her forgiveness. Morton knelt on the boards where Rizzio had been stabbed, and while doubtless most of the blood had been wiped up, his hose were nevertheless stained. He seemed unperturbed.

Mary said she could not forgive them at this point, but promised that, if they served her well in the coming months, she would consider it. As they began to cavil, she again feigned illness, and withdrew. It was left to Darnley to assure them that his wife would sign their pardons the following day when she felt better. Suspicious but temporarily stalled, the conspirators left for the evening.

Plans for Mary's escape had been discussed since the night of Rizzio's death. She had vetoed the idea of climbing down a rope ladder brought into her chamber in a warming dish, not least because she was heavily pregnant. There were also guards in the room above. Instead, she smuggled out a message to Huntly and Bothwell with the dowager countess, informing them that she would join them at Seton Palace. Her master of horse, Arthur Erskine, the captain of her bodyguard, John Stewart, Laird of Traquair, and a handful of soldiers were ordered to stand ready with horses at the rear gates of the palace at midnight on Monday evening. This small band would convey her first to Seton and then to Dunbar Castle, a place of greater safety.

The need to flee was urgent, but it was hazardous. In historical novels, people evade capture with aplomb, leaping roofs, shimmying down drainpipes and running like hares. But the reality would have been profoundly daunting, especially given the heightened nerves of those commanded to prevent the queen escaping at all costs. As you stand in the queen's bedchamber, the prospect of creeping through this huge building unseen seems almost impossible. Tiptoeing out of a bedroom without waking a partner or child is challenging enough. Boards and doors creak. The need to take great care makes hands shake, and things are often knocked over or slip through fingers that ordinarily would stay glued in place. The drop from Mary's bedchamber to the palace grounds at the rear of the tower could break a hip, and even if it were managed successfully by rope or sheets, with so many soldiers on the premises the distance to be covered before reaching the gates would be petrifying. That the queen did not waver at the prospect shows how deadly her situation was.

Once the dissatisfied Moray and Morton and their party had left, Mary and Darnley waited until the palace was asleep. The hours must have crawled until, at around one in the morning, they left her bedroom by the private turnpike stair, and once downstairs, hurried through the servants' domain of store rooms, pantries and wine cellars. Even had a servant spotted them, they would not be betrayed. Once in the garden, they made for the gate in the walls, near the cemetery, where the sight of Rizzio's freshly dug grave nearly unmanned Darnley. Perhaps his conscience was pricking for the friend with whom he had played tennis a few hours before he died.

Outside the gate they were awaited by Arthur Erskine, and a small party of loyal followers. Mary rode pillion behind her master of horse. It cannot have been a comfortable journey. By this point she had the measure of her husband, who had proved utterly faithless and treacherous. When he feared they were being pursued and struck his whip at Erskine's horse to make it go faster, Mary told him to gallop ahead if he liked. True to form, Darnley did just that.

Chapter 20

'Of truth we are so tired'

DUNBAR CASTLE

Riding through the night might sound the stuff of *The Three Musketeers*, but March is one of the coldest Scottish months, and in darkness it would have been punishing. Even if one of Mary's party had led the way with a torch once fear of pursuit was gone, they would still have relied heavily upon the horses to keep to the path, their night-time vision far sharper than that of the riders.

The road from Holyrood to Dunbar is twenty-six miles, but the detour to Seton lengthened the journey. Despite their haste, it took five hours to reach the small fishing town, thirty miles north of the border, huddled around the harbour. These days Dunbar is better known as the birthplace of the environmentalist John Muir than for its connection with Mary Stuart. By Muir's boyhood, in the 1840s, the castle had long been a ruin, but in 1566 it was a fortress. Perched on the lip of the sea, this towering red sandstone edifice was pounded and pummelled by the North Sea, and withstood it all.

As reward for helping her through this crisis, Mary handed its wardship to Bothwell. With crow's-nest views across the Bass Rock and the Firth of Forth, and down coast towards Berwickshire, it was fittingly situated for the Lord Admiral. From here he could glimpse some of the fortified islands in the Forth and keep an eye on ships entering Scottish waters. Darnley might have been interested to learn that two of these islands – Inchkeith and Inchgarvie – were used as isolation wards for those afflicted with syphilis.

On arrival at Dunbar, or so storybooks have it, Mary cooked eggs for breakfast. It might conceivably be true, since she had barely eaten since the night of Rizzio's murder, and she always enjoyed playing housewife. But she was also feeling sick. After two sleepless nights and the strain of events this was unsurprising, but prosaically she blamed it on her pregnancy. In a letter from Dunbar to Elizabeth I, she wrote: 'Some of our subjects and council . . . have slain our most special servant in our own presence and thereafter held our proper person captive treasonably . . . but of truth we are so tired . . . what through riding of twenty miles in five hours of the night, as with the frequent sickness and evil disposition by the occasion of our child.'

After the horror of the past three days, Dunbar offered sanctuary and security. She spent hours writing letters, and doubtless stood at the castle windows, staring out to sea. From here you can see the smooth wide sweep of Belhaven beach, and beyond it the woods and sands at Tyninghame. Southwards, these days, the chimneys of Dunbar's cement works belch out white plumes that create pillars in the sky.

I was brought up in Belhaven, a village on the edge of Dunbar, and there were few days when at some point I did not gaze out across the water to the gannet-whitened cliffs of the Bass Rock, or the blue line that was the coast of Fife. Best of all was when driving rain or sleet blanketed the sea and people stared stonily from their windows, like Lewis chessmen, as they waited out the storm.

Dunbar harbour and the streets around it felt like another world entirely. The outer harbour water was oily, and slapped heavily against the walls; grey lifeless fish would sometimes float on the swell; the swill of fish guts and the smell of sea urchins and seagulls combined to create an unforgettable stench. Few buildings from the sixteenth century remain, yet the Dunbar of Mary's reign would in many ways be familiar to the town's inhabitants today. On a charity fundraising outing while I was at school, a friend and I rattled tins in over thirty pubs, all within a stone's throw of the boats, and were generously rewarded. In Mary's era, the taverns were almost as numerous. Despite the armies and posses passing through, that trade remained a mainstay.

On a recent return visit, on a clear-blue July afternoon, the scene around the harbour was as alluring as a brochure for Brittany or Cornwall. Brightly coloured fishing boats tugged at their moorings, injecting a splash of Mediterranean cheer beneath the crumbled stumps that are all that remain of the castle. Dunbar boasts of being the sunniest place in Scotland, and that day the tide was in, the sun bright, and children were jumping into the water off the harbour wall, squealing and taunting each other on. Younger kids scampered about, clutching crabs' claws.

When Mary and her supporters arrived early on the morning of Tuesday 12 March, Dunbar Castle was already renowned. Its frontier location had made it a target for centuries, but never more so than in January 1338, when the English laid siege to it. Lady Agnes Randolph, Countess of Dunbar and March, had been left in charge of the castle while her husband went off to fight as the wars of independence gathered pace. The countess, nicknamed Black Agnes supposedly for her Spanish colouring, was fearless. Whenever an English cannon ball ricocheted off the walls, she would dart out onto the ramparts and mockingly dust the spot where it had landed. When the English commander took her brother hostage and threatened to execute him if she did not surrender, she told the commander to go ahead. That way, she'd inherit everything. During all this, provisions were arriving by a secret sea entrance. Eventually, after six months, the English were worn down, and retreated. Since then, it is said that Agnes's ghost walks the castle walls. If that is true, she must tread thin air, because almost nothing is left of this once spectacular building.

Shortly after Mary's abdication in 1567, the castle came under yet another siege, to oust Bothwell's men. Thereafter, at the prompting of Moray, who was by this time Regent, Parliament revived an act from the days of James IV, insisting that Dunbar Castle be 'cast

down utterly to the ground and destroyed in such a way that no
foundation thereof be the occasion to build thereupon in time
coming.' This edict applied also to Inchkeith island, both of them
considered 'unprofitable to the realm and not able to defend the
enemies thereof'.

Cost of repairing the castle had always weighed heavily on the
Treasury. In 1457 it had been partially pulled down, to prevent
an English occupation. Under James IV and the Regent Albany
it was substantially rebuilt, to accommodate 500 soldiers. It was
used to store gunpowder and the king's arsenal. But during Henry
VIII's Rough Wooing, in 1548, when the English sacked or
burned everything in their path, it was set alight. Shortly after
this, Marie de Guise initiated a series of improvements, but much
of its reconstruction was undone as part of the provisions of the
Treaty of Edinburgh. Thus, for a century, its fortunes rose and
fell, much like the royal family's. By the time of Mary's visit with
Darnley, it was among the country's most impregnable strongholds. Within eighteen months, however, it would be toppled,
destined to become the haunt of seabirds rather than statesmen
and royals.

What little remains hints at its former scale and strength. A
sprawling building, it was constructed in two halves. The outermost
citadel was set upon rocks that loom over the harbour mouth, and
enclosed a courtyard. A sheer wall joined this section to the inner
structure, where the outline can still be seen of the imposing block-
house built, by Albany, on a small hill. Although mostly eroded,
what survives is a slim bridge above the sea, part of the original
rampart that connected the landward building with the seaward.
Beneath this fragile-looking arch, waves suck in and out across the
shingle. This might have been the back entrance through which
supplies for the besieged were smuggled in.

The castle, a prime example of medieval defensive architecture,
protected harbour, coast and town alike. It also acted as a watch-
tower for any who malevolently crossed into Scottish waters. How
far it has fallen since then. What was still standing by the nineteenth

century was mostly demolished to make way for a modern harbour. Now, a stump of wall rises above the ruins like a dilapidated chimney stack. It has become an emblem of Dunbar, its Leaning Tower of Pisa. The remnant of a wall beneath this outcrop has been colonised by kittiwakes; each has its own berth among the scalloped stones, where it sits like an ornament in a shadowbox. The gulls' cries are piercing, the smell pungent.

Signs warn the public from clambering up the ruins, where doorways and wind-blasted steps lead nowhere. Gun ports recall its glory days. It is said that a large room, twelve feet square, in the north-west quarter, was where Mary stayed. That visit with Darnley lasted merely a week, but she put it to good use. While resting, she gathered allies to her side, rallied an army of 4,000 Borderers, and ordered more troops to muster at Haddington. Her composure was remarkable given the ordeal she had experienced. Having Darnley by her side would have been both a comfort – he could not get into trouble while under her eye – and a scourge. Whenever she looked at him, she would see not a husband but a treacherous coward.

At this precarious juncture, Mary rose to the challenge. It seems almost to have galvanised her. Perhaps it cleared her head after the almost unreal events of the past few months, in which, against all warnings, she had bound herself to one of the least trustworthy men in Europe, and swiftly realised the mistake she had made.

What went through her mind, in the night-time gloom of Dunbar? Whether she and Darnley shared a room or he slept elsewhere, having him close would have been unnerving, knowing as she now did how dangerous he could be. Was it here that she began to contemplate how to be rid of him? Possibly, but it seems more likely that thoughts of revenge and reprisal were, for the moment, trained on her rebels at court.

After a week in which she recouped her strength, Mary rode out of Dunbar and, heading in procession to Haddington, stopped there for the night. Cupped by the Lammermuir Hills, Haddington was at the heart of a county that was to play a pivotal role throughout Mary's life. Above all others, this region would prove to be the crucible in which Mary Stuart's legacy was shaped. Dunbar lay on its southern edge, framed by the sea, and the rest of East Lothian was studded with castles and tower houses belonging to her enemies. She would have been well aware of this as, the next morning, her party saddled up and left Haddington for the capital, anticipating a showdown.

The fearsome Ruthven, who played such a pivotal part on the evening of Rizzio's murder, had his base at the fabulously grim Dirleton Castle. With drum towers, dungeon and drawbridge, it comes straight from the pages of a medieval romance. Since its thirteenth-century origins and the violent encounters of later centuries, its air of menace has been tamed by the tranquillity of the village green outside its walls, where cottage gardens fill the air with the scent of wisteria and roses. A severe and magnificent fortress that must once have loomed like a miniature Edinburgh Castle, it is the focal point of this idyllic location.

An easy ride from Dirleton lay the Earl of Morton's castle at Whittinghame. This squat red rectangular tower, dating from the late fifteenth or early sixteenth century, was embedded in woodlands, near the Iron Age fort of Traprain Law. It was close to the village of East Linton, and a few miles from Maitland of Lethington's tower house on the outskirts of Haddington. It is said to have been on a visit by Bothwell and Maitland to Whittinghame Castle in 1567 that they and Morton discussed how they might dispose of Darnley.

On the approach to North Berwick, a few miles upcoast from Dunbar, where Mary's son James VI made an example of its regicidal witches, lies Tantallon Castle. Shaped like a sandcastle, and owned by the Douglases, the terracotta-coloured sandstone walls of this fourteenth-century monolith stand out dramatically against the backdrop of the Bass Rock. Both are symbols of solidity and endurance. One of the Earl of Morton's properties, and far more prestigious than Whittinghame,

Tantallon was the crème de la crème of castles. Surrounded on three sides by sea, it had a massively high and thick curtain wall on its landward neck. Fortified against attack by trebuchet and artillery, it looked impregnable. Even so, it came under attack from James IV, and also James V, who captured it. But it was Oliver Cromwell who caused its downfall. In 1651 his army assaulted it so relentlessly that the Douglas family decamped, leaving it to sink gradually into its present picturesquely crumbling state.

East Lothian witnessed the transformation of Mary Stuart in the public opinion from a wise and well-loved ruler to a national liability. Her first escape to Dunbar with Darnley was a clever tactic, neutralising the danger he posed and putting herself beyond harm. When she repeated the visit with Bothwell, the following year, she was beginning to narrow her options. At Carberry Hill, a couple of miles outside Musselburgh, she was to have her first taste of disaster. All this, of course, lay in the future. In the meantime, as she emerged from the nightmare of Rizzio's murder, on 18 March Mary left Haddington and rode through the heart of the Lothians with her 8,000-strong army. As she passed through hamlets and villages, with the sea on one side and rolling hills on the other, the cheers of her people must have lifted her spirits. It is unlikely she could have envisioned coming to grief in such a beguiling landscape.

Upon arrival in Edinburgh, it was quickly clear that the queen's display of force was unnecessary, since her enemies had fled to England. The army disbanded, and a sense of relief but also disappointment and anticlimax must have followed them home. With Darnley denying any involvement, and firmly under Mary's thumb at last, his associates were in disarray. Even Knox, who applauded Rizzio's death while having no part in it, had decamped to Ayrshire, beyond reach of Mary's wrath. Moray, for his part, was in Linlithgow. A gulf now opened between him and the other rebels, as he took advantage of his uneasy reconciliation with the queen. For this, and other instances of ruthless self-advancement, he has made a name for putting his own interests first in every decision and predicament. His ultimate aim was the throne, and at this juncture, when everything was in flux, it must have seemed not entirely beyond his grasp.

Chapter 21

'For that you saved his life . . .'

EDINBURGH CASTLE

With the queen back in Holyrood, the atmosphere at court crackled with tension. Mary was seven months pregnant, and her mind likely to have focused as much on her own and her child's safety as the state of her kingdom. For his part, Darnley was universally reviled, for breaking faith with his co-conspirators and, if not precisely breaking his wife's heart, putting her in terror of her life.

Ten days after returning to Holyrood, Mary appointed Rizzio's eighteen-year-old brother Joseph to his post. It was a very pointed act and suggests either that she had learned nothing from the Italian's murder or she wanted to show her enemies she was not cowed. Despite the companionship of her Maries, it seems she felt the need for further allies. Possibly Joseph's presence was a comforting reminder of her great friend, or perhaps she was keen to show kindness to David's brother for whom Holyrood must have seemed a threatening place. If this were so, stepping into David's shoes cannot have done much to reassure him.

As the factions around her regrouped, Mary's position grew increasingly vulnerable. Fearing the disaffected lords might snatch the infant as soon as it was born, Moray, Argyll and Glencairn urged the queen to put herself beyond danger. Mary had restored this trio to favour and pressed them to reconcile with Bothwell, Huntly and Atholl. They became her inner circle, but she had yet to forgive those directly involved in Rizzio's slaying. Morton, Ruthven and other culprits remained in England, where Ruthven died soon after, having appeared to repent heartily of his sins moments before meeting his maker. Mary knew nothing of Moray's or Maitland of Lethington's involvement behind the scenes.

Two weeks after her return from Dunbar, Mary carefully packed her bags and prepared to take refuge in Edinburgh Castle. She and her maids and midwives compiled lists of what would be required, and carts were drawn up at the doors to carry off the enormous inventory of items essential for a protracted and potentially perilous period of confinement.

In early April, Mary took up residence. She must have shuddered as the portcullis clanged behind her, knowing that she would not leave until she had safely given birth; perhaps never. Although she was not easily frightened, she was threatened on every side, by her impending delivery and by her enemies. There was nothing her courtiers could do to help with the birth, but to guard against ambush, Moray and his associates ordered one or more nobles to keep close to her at all times.

Edinburgh Castle was forbidding, with at least five imposing towers within its walls. A drawing from 1560 shows a citadel reminiscent of the tiny city of San Gimignano in Tuscany, with its profusion of minatory fortresses. It is not a place where most mothers-to-be would choose to have their baby, yet it is possible that Mary agreed to her councillors' advice because she, too, was keen to be protected. Security in and around the clifftop castle was tight.

The great iron portcullis through which she entered – the present one is from the 1570s – led by a twisting cobbled street to the heart of the castle, the Palace Yard, now called Crown Square. In contrast to the military atmosphere of the rest of the surroundings, this is an elegant square, begun by James III and continued by his son James IV, who wanted to evoke the Italian piazzas he so admired. It was into this inner sanctum, protected from assault by the sheer drop beneath its windows, that Mary moved. With her came her four-poster bed, tapestries, carpets and all the comforts necessary to turn a cold and unlived-in set of apartments into a haven and home.

The castle rock was virtually indestructible before the advent of artillery capable of destroying its walls. Mons Meg, which is one such weapon, today overlooks the Argyle battery, where a row of smaller cannons points over the city. A bombard or siege cannon, made in the Belgian town of Mons, it could spit a stone ball bigger than a basketball almost two miles' distance. In its heyday, this monstrous gun was rolled out of the castle, dragged by a team of oxen, for use in various attacks. The sight of it alone would make most sensible mortals surrender, as was the case at Dumbarton Castle in 1489, whose rebels saw the error of their ways before the fuse was lit.

The gullet of Mons Meg is so capacious that the playwright Ben Jonson was told that 'one got a woman with child in it'. By the time Mary married the Dauphin, it had been overtaken by nimbler weapons, but it was fired to mark the occasion. The ball was later found in what is now the Royal Botanic Garden, almost an hour's walk away, in the area then known as Wardie Muir.

Edinburgh Castle has a menacing presence. Rising from black basalt crags, it is dour and glowering, as if frowning down on the city. As the Glasgow train crawls into Waverley Station, you can gaze up at the rugged cliff face, often running with rain, and wonder why anyone without harness and crampons would attempt to breach its defences this way. But it has been done. In March 1314, when the castle was in English hands, Robert the Bruce's nephew, Sir Thomas Randolph, led a party over the top. While others created a disturbance at the main gate, they were able to overpower the guards, and retake it.

This extinct volcanic plug is believed to be the oldest continuously inhabited fortified location in Britain, and archaeological evidence confirms inhabitants from the Bronze Age at least. The Romans also commandeered it. With an eyrie's view over the Firth of Forth and to the Pentlands, it has a peerless position. The rest of Edinburgh spills from its gates, the Royal Mile running straight from its doors downhill towards Holyrood Palace. But to get a sense of the capital's original personality and purpose, you must go inside the castle walls.

Edinburgh Castle is Scotland's most visited heritage location, and
before the pandemic was attracting well over two million visitors a
year. When I queued to get in, it was a day of umbrellas. A broad
esplanade acts as its forecourt, and where it meets the Royal Mile –
Castle Hill – is where so-called witches and criminals were executed.
Today it is the site of concerts and, during the summer season, the
world-famous military tattoo. When I lived six miles away in
Musselburgh, the grand finale's fireworks could be heard every night,
regular as clockwork, as befits the army.

This approach to the castle is dominated by the sheer half-moon
battery, which is unclimbable. A wide stone bridge crosses into the
Victorian gatehouse. This dubious addition was built in 1888 and
was intended to evoke the Middle Ages more impressively than the
obliterated original, which was genuinely medieval. Once inside, its
age and mood become apparent. As the narrow high lane curves
under the portcullis, and into the self-contained precincts, the black-
ened stonework and dark alleyways give a fleeting sense of what in
the sixteenth century was almost a city unto itself.

It is a warren, comprising batteries, kitchens, cellars, former
barracks (now the Scottish National War Memorial), prisons, the
Governor's Georgian house, the Argyle Tower, and more. When
fully garrisoned, Edinburgh Castle would have teemed with activity
as hundreds of men, women and children went about their business.
Like a monastery, it must have been a fully functioning society,
albeit noisier and rougher. It recalls the comedian Billy Connolly's
observation of working in a Clyde shipyard: 'As soon as that gate
shuts, a shipyard becomes a complete wee town. You could buy
shoes, cigarettes, transistor radios, cheap booze. It was an amazing
place.' A large part of the yard's appeal for Connolly and other work-
ers was the camaraderie they found among like-minded men. The
same might have been said of the castle.

Much of what sightseers find today was built long after Mary's last
visit, and the skyline she saw as she approached up the High Street
is largely demolished. Among the towers that loomed over her party
as they drew near was that named for David II, now a ruin. The

oldest, dating from the Norman period, was called St Margaret Tower, in homage to the exceptionally pious and stern Queen Margaret. The oldest building in the castle is the chapel dedicated to her by her son David I. It dates from around 1130, when it was incorporated within a Norman-style keep.

The chapel is narrow, high and steeply roofed, its scorched walls evidence of the many sieges the castle endured. Margaret was made a saint half a century after her death, and every royal wife from the eleventh century to Mary, Queen of Scots wore Margaret's birthing gown to help bring them through their delivery safely. It is said that, to preserve its sanctity, this was not washed between one birth and the next. Knowing how fastidious and fashionable Mary was, it is hard to credit that she allowed this filthy garment to be pulled over her head. More likely, surely, she had it placed beneath her pillow, or draped upon the bedstead, if she tolerated it at all.

The castle held associations closer to home and probably a great deal more meaningful for Mary than a garment encrusted with stains. Her mother Marie de Guise had retreated here during the siege of Leith, when she was mortally ill. She died on 11 June 1560, and her embalmed corpse lay in the castle for nine months before it was safe to transport it to France for burial. It is poignant to think what she must have suffered, realising the end was close. Her young widowed daughter would soon return to a country riven by religious strife. Without her mother to guide her, and with no husband for support, she would be prey to every faction.

Marie de Guise was well aware of how unversed Mary was in Scottish affairs, beyond the broad brushstrokes of political life. What would she make of this unvarnished and peppery people, compared to the unctuous manners of the French court? Doubtless in her last moments, Marie de Guise's mind was turned wholly on her own predicament and the world to come. Despite the presence of her French companions, and the priest performing the last rites, it must have been a lonely passing without her daughter at her side.

The most glamorous and evocative structure still intact from 1566 is the Great Hall, built for James IV in 1512, the year before he died. Soon after her return to Scotland, Mary hosted a banquet here before joining a procession down the High Street to greet her subjects. Now restored to its original state, only the hammer-beam roof, constructed from Norwegian oak, remains untouched since James IV's day. The array of ferocious weaponry displayed around the walls is a reminder of how close most soldiers had to get to the enemy in combat, and what courage that must have taken.

In a low, claustrophobic chamber within the Royal Palace lie the Honours of Scotland. Encased in glass, on a bed of royal blue velvet, they sit glinting and unreachable, like Smaug's treasure. The ornately hilted sword of state, the silver sceptre and the exquisite golden crown, studded with gemstones, pearls and amethyst, were first used together at Mary's infant coronation in 1543. The hushed atmosphere of this crypt-like room adds to their aura. Visitors owe a debt to Sir Walter Scott for tracking down the regalia after they had been missing for over a century. The iron padlock on a forgotten oaken chest in the palace Crown Room was broken at his command. There they lay, wrapped in linen. Hidden away in 1707, they were restored to their dignity after a disappearance of 111 years.

But the room that people most want to see is where Mary gave birth to her son. Tucked off the queen's main apartment, the lying-in chamber is an irregularly shaped closet, dominated by a deep stone fireplace. Not much larger than a dressing room, its window looks out over Old Edinburgh. A bright space, which has since been panelled in oak and painted with the Scottish royal coat of arms, it was just big enough to hold a bed, chair, and Mary's midwife and ladies-in-waiting.

For days and weeks ahead of the confinement, the queen had little or no male company. Shortly before sequestering herself for the birth, she was blessed by a priest. Unless a doctor was required, all subsequent dealings were with her Maries, other close female friends, and the midwife. Bowls of sugared almonds or other treats would be placed in her outer room for visitors, where her 'presentation' bed was draped in magnificent blue velvet and taffeta. But by the time

Mary went into labour, only a handful of companions were allowed into her presence.

When the moment came to retreat to the chamber, a cradle awaited the new arrival. It had been prepared with copious linen drapery, an extravagance itemised in the Treasurer's Accounts. The room was turned into a cocoon, as closely resembling the warmth and darkness of the womb as possible to make the baby feel immediately at home. Daylight was partially blocked by drapes or tapestries, and while the window was open a crack, the fire was also lit. As the hour of delivery approached, drawers and doors in the apartments were perhaps opened, symbolically to ease the baby's passage. Talismans might also be brought to give the queen courage to face the birth. Although Mary was a devout Catholic and there was a crucifix in the room as a focus for her prayers – something ordinary Scots were no longer meant to possess – few women baulked at superstitious aids at this risky and scary time. In an attempt to help, Mary Fleming's sister cast a spell to transfer the pains to Lady Margaret Reres, but this brought no benefit whatsoever.

Women in Stuart times might give birth in bed, or crouching, cradled from behind by the midwife. Or they might use a birthing stool. Not surprisingly, given the secrecy and discretion that surrounded childbirth, little is known about the queen's delivery other than that it was an ordeal. As she bit back her screams, it was little help for Mary to remember that her pain was preordained and necessary. The Church taught that womankind had to suffer for Eve's sinfulness; it's not difficult to imagine what most women made of that.

Of more help were herbal potions, some of which could ease pain. Marie de Guise had been skilled in the use of herbs and attended many births where she helped soothe the mother. It is possible that the ladies of the court had inherited some of Marie's knowledge, yet taking potions could be even more dangerous than the cause of pain. Opium poppy was used as a painkiller but was potentially fatal if overprescribed, especially when mixed with poisonous deadly nightshade and hemlock. This combination was used only for the most excruciating surgical procedures.

Mary was in labour for twenty hours, and the birth was agonising. There were moments when she questioned why she had ever married. If she screamed, there was no-one beyond her companions to hear, the men of court keeping far away. At one point Mary was in such distress she believed she was likely to die. Her first thoughts were for her unborn child, and she prayed for God to save the infant. Before taking to her lying-in chamber, she had drawn up a detailed will, in case she did not survive. In doing this she was not being unduly pessimistic or morbid. Many women in this period died in child-birth, or in the days that followed, although newborn babies were at even greater risk.

Giving birth was a test of physical and mental strength for all but the most robust. Mary had suffered many ailments, some of them serious, but she had undergone nothing to compare with this. Did she find comfort in knowing she was close to her mother's apart-ments, where her spirit might still linger? Or did the thought of Marie de Guise's death make her dread her own? We will never know. Of more practical benefit were the ministrations of her ladies-in-waiting, who removed the pins from her hair and bathed away her sweat with cool water. The midwife knew how to massage her to ease the pains and if necessary to intervene to reposition the baby to make the birth easier.

That night must have seemed never-ending. Even the arrival of daylight and birdsong brought no immediate relief. Mary laboured on until eventually, between the hours of ten and eleven on the morning of 19 June 1566, James, the future king of Scotland, England and Ireland, made his appearance. As described by Mary decades later to her secretary Claude Nau, to whom she related her life while in prison in England, 'The prince came into this world with a large and thin caul, which covered the whole of his face.' This was a rare occurrence. Its peculiar appearance might have alarmed the new mother, since the baby's face appeared from beneath a trans-parent skin, yet it was perfectly natural. Before Mary was able to hold her baby, the caul – the amniotic sac – would have been removed by the midwife.

Giving birth to James, writes Jenny Wormald, was 'the one great success of Mary's queenship'. Exhausted by her suffering, Mary might well have agreed, before sinking back onto her pillows. With the caul removed, the midwife would cut the baby's umbilical cord, at four fingers' length, and take him away to be bathed. Since it was the tradition in medieval France to rub a newborn in salt, and cleanse its gums and tongue with honey, James might well have been thus annointed by Mary's midwife Margaret Asteane. He would then have been swaddled tight in linen, to keep his limbs straight, before being brought back to his mother.

Once Mary was assured that he was healthy, she could rest, while the wet nurse, Lady Margaret Reres, took him for his first feed. After this, he was placed in his mother's arms, possibly smelling of rose oil, with which he might be massaged after each nappy change.

Only at this point could the father be admitted. When Darnley entered, no doubt a little unnerved by the all-female gathering and the almost reverential air that attends any happy birth, Mary pulled back the shawl. She wanted to show him that the child was indeed his own, and not Bothwell's bastard as he feared. Despite having made a public show of reconciliation with Darnley for the past few weeks, Mary's anguish and fury at the way he had treated her were all too plain as she presented James for inspection: 'he is so much your own son', she said, 'that I fear it will be the worse for him hereafter'. How Darnley responded has been lost in time.

That evening, 500 bonfires were lit in and around the city, and the castle fired all its guns. Fireworks were set off at Stirling Castle, and the court gathered at St Giles' Cathedral, not far from the castle, for a service of thanksgiving. In the days that followed, James slept in Mary's room, and although Lady Reres and Margaret Little suckled him and servants rocked the cradle, Mary kept James by her bedside. James's father was not trusted to be alone with him. Indeed, Darnley was reported to be 'vagabondising' every night. His comings and goings throughout the small hours meant the castle gates were forever opening and closing, making Mary's situation less safe than she would have wished. For his part, Darnley was still plotting behind her back, to raise support from Spain, and possibly oust her from the throne. Little wonder she kept her child within her sight. During this time, she bestowed a knighthood on Anthony Standen, the equerry who had helped her escape from Holyrood after Rizzio's murder. While Darnley tapped a sword on his shoulders, the queen indicated the baby's cradle, saying to Standen, 'For that you saved his life . . .' The state of the marriage by this point must have seemed irretrievable.

Mary's advisor Sir James Melville rode hastily to London following the birth and, after making Cecil promise to keep the news secret, had an audience with Elizabeth at Greenwich. He reported that when he arrived

> she was in great merriness and dancing after supper; but as soon as the secretary Cecil whispered the news in her ear of the prince's birth, all merriness was laid aside for that night; every one that was present marvelling what might move so sudden a change; for the Queen sat down with her hand upon her cheek; and bursting out to some of her ladies, how the Queen of Scotland was lighter of a fair son, and that she was but barren stock.

Chapter 22

'If we lose this one we will make another'

TRAQUAIR HOUSE

At the height of summer, on 19 August 1566, Mary, Darnley and their two-month-old baby, set out for Traquair House in the Borderlands for a hunting break. It was the fifth anniversary of Mary's return to Scotland, and if she reflected on what had happened in those years as the miles passed, and considered how her once-bright prospects had been blighted by the man she had married, her mood might understandably have been low.

Since their baby's arrival, tension between the couple had worsened. James, however, was thriving, described by the English ambassador Henry Killigrew – Cecil's brother-in-law – as 'well-proportioned and like to prove a goodly prince'. Mary remained in poor health, having not yet fully recovered from the gruelling birth. In previous weeks, when on holiday in Alloa as a guest of the Earl of Mar, she had been vituperative towards Darnley, swearing in a manner onlookers could scarcely credit. As Traquair drew closer, it was plain that this was no romantic break, nor a moment when the pair hoped to mend their ruinous relationship away from the eyes of the court.

Accompanying them were not only palace servants, and the attendants and wet nurses who looked after the baby, but a party of lords looking forward to the hunt. Among them were Moray, Huntly, Bothwell and Atholl, the key players of Mary's inner court.

Traquair, a medieval tower house, lay in the heart of the Ettrick Forest, one of the finest remnants of the great primeval Caledonian

Forest which had once blanketed the country. It stretched for miles, encompassing Selkirkshire and parts of Edinburgh and Peeblesshire. In its heyday the Ettrick Forest was predominantly treed by oaks, among which deer, boars, wolves and bears flourished. Rivers, such as the Tweed and Teviot, were abundant in salmon, eels, lamprey and trout, and home to beavers and otters. As the royal train swiftly moved to its destination, Mary must have longed for the quietness and seclusion of the forest. Given her condition, it was probably the thrill of hawking she hoped to enjoy rather than the rigours of the chase.

The Ettrick Forest had been a jewel of the Lowlands for centuries. When under the control of Edward I and his successors, its wood raised valuable funds. Robert the Bruce bestowed it on Sir James Douglas in return for his service, but in 1455 it was forfeited by the Douglas family and annexed to the Crown, thereafter becoming a royal hunting ground. A faded mural in one of Traquair's upper rooms, thought to date to around 1530, depicts an eager hound following the scent. From its earliest days, hunting was its *raison d'être*.

Traquair is a fairytale house, nestled among rolling hills and pastureland, but the region was utterly lawless in this period, and was to grow even more so. As the century progressed, it approached a state of near anarchy; keeping it under control was a constant challenge, as all the Stuart monarchs discovered. Traquair acted as the centre of royal power, and early in her reign Mary had appointed John Stewart, Laird of Traquair, to the perilous position of assisting the Warden of the Middle March. His brief was to help keep the area's brutal adventurers and brigands in check. She also put the garrison of soldiers in Hermitage Castle, in the dreaded district of Liddesdale, in his charge. In undertaking his duties, the Laird of Traquair proved so steadfast that in 1565 Mary knighted him, and appointed him captain of her bodyguard. He was one of the devoted band who helped her escape Holyrood earlier in the year, an act she never forgot.

The violent reiver gangs who stole and plundered across the

Borders, and the mafia-like feuds that blighted the region, were
not just a headache for Mary's government. Her father and grandfather before her, and in time her own son, struggled to bring its
warring clans and diehard criminals into line. Mary had no illusions about the scale of the problem: 'crewell murthur becum as it
wer commoun, nocht onelie amangis thame that hes querrell, bot
kynnisfolk unnaturallie slayis utheris, without feir of God, reverence of thair Majesteis, and as thair wer na authoritie abone thair
hedis . . .' ['Cruel murder becomes common, not only among
those that quarrel, but kinsfolk unnaturally slay others, without
fear of God, reverence of their Majesty, and as if there were no
authority above their heads . . . .'] It was an indictment that, in
hindsight, might have been applied equally to some of her inner
circle, and even to the queen herself.

The thugs of the region were a suppurating sore. The chronicler
Robert Lindsay of Pitscottie, who was a close contemporary of Mary,
relates that in 1528, James V 'made proclamation to all lords, barons,
gentlemen, landward-men, and freeholders, that they should
compear at Edinburgh, with a month's victuals, to pass with the
King where he pleased, to danton [daunten, or frighten] the thieves
of Tiviotdale, Annandale, Liddisdale, and other parts of that
country'.

But the king had other pleasures in mind beyond policing. As
Pitscottie relates, he

also warned all gentlemen that had good dogs to bring them, that
he might hunt in the said country as he pleased: the whilk the
Earl of Argyll, the Earl of Huntly, the Earl of Athole, and so all
the rest of the gentlemen of the Highland, did, and brought their
hounds with them in like manner to hunt with the King, as he
pleased.

The second day of June the King past out of Edinburgh to the
hunting, with many of the nobles and gentlemen of Scotland
with him, to the number of twelve thousand men; and then past
to Meggitland, and hounded and hawked all the country and

bounds . . . I heard say, he slew, in these bounds, eighteen score of harts . . .

Traquair lies not far from the Megget Water, which flows into St Mary's Loch. It had been host to noble and royal hunters since its origins, in the twelfth century. Anecdotes of spectacular kills and miraculous catches were the regular fare of dinner parties, daring feats taking on the status of legend as wine and spirits flowed. Understandably, Mary and Darnley arrived expecting good sport as well as an excellent dinner.

But, as Pitscottie recalled, after James V's almost military expedition, when so many of the forest's wild creatures had been slaughtered, the king

> in order to increase his revenues, turned 10,000 sheep into Ettrick Forest, to graze there under the tending of a thrifty keeper, instead of 10,000 bucks that scoured its woodlands during the bounteous age of Edward I; and by this act he led the way to such a conversion of the entire forest into sheep pasture, as occasioned a rapid and almost total destruction of the trees. The last sovereign of Scotland who visited it for the sake of the chase was the beautiful Mary.

It would seem that by 1566, the sheep had wreaked devastation, and the Ettrick Forest was in steep and irreversible decline. Mary's hunting party set out early in the morning, but after a fruitless day's endeavour, the queen was unusually peevish. She complained that 'the deir sa halelie distroyit that oure Soveranis can get na pastyme of hunting', which was especially galling since 'their Hienessis is purposlie repairit in thie cuntre to that effect'. Locals were suspected of ruining their fun, and while standing at the edge of St Mary's Loch, Mary gave orders to remedy the situation. You can picture her, dressed for the hunt but empty-handed, filled with indignation and fury, while her huntsmen and masters of the hound avoided her gaze. In disgust, she ordered that an armed official be dispatched across the county, to 'command and charge all and sundry thair

Majesteis liegis, that nane of thame tak upoun hand in tyme cuming, to schute at deir with culveringis [cannons], half haggis [hagbuts], or bowis . . .'

Yet even though some prey would almost certainly have gone into commoners' pots, despite strict forest laws against poaching, by far the worst culprits were the sheep her father had introduced. Their teeth could work through undergrowth and saplings faster than scythes. While it took acts of Parliament, rebellions, martyrdom and religious revolt to alter the political climate, a flock of sheep could change an age-old landscape in a matter of years.

An unsuccessful outing was soon to prove the least of the troubles that emerged during the queen and king's break. Probably on the night of their arrival, the loathing between them, which had been simmering since Rizzio's murder, erupted over dinner. Traquair was witness to the breaking point in this wretched relationship, beyond which there was no going back.

This dinner most likely took place in the great hall, now known as the High Drawing Room. A long, low-ceilinged room, its windows look onto the courtyard at the front, and towards the River Tweed at the rear. Today, only a small area of restored painted beams and ceiling evokes the high Renaissance, and the status and ambitions of the Stewarts. The beams were covered over in the eighteenth century, and would have lain undetected if the nineteenth laird had not poked his finger through the plasterwork and revealed what lay beneath.

There are few more enchanting tower houses. Approached by a broad avenue of mature trees it has been a Stuart family stronghold since 1491. The longest continuously inhabited house in the country, Traquair is famous for its loyalty to the Scottish Crown. On a blindingly bright autumn afternoon, when I was to be shown around by the present laird, Lady Catherine Maxwell Stuart, it emerged from among the trees like an artist's impression of Renaissance Scotland. The sycamores were turning ochre, and drifts of leaves spilled across the long field of grass that leads up to the courtyard in which the house stands.

The whitewashed walls were almost luminous in the sunshine. Set behind wrought-iron gates, the main house is flanked by low wings, one of which houses a tiny chapel and a brewhouse. That brewery was in operation when Mary was a guest, and its barrels would have been piled high in anticipation of the royal party.

The house itself, the oldest part encompassing an early peel tower, is four storeys high. Stout corbelled turrets and petite dormer windows are set into the steeply pitched roof, the impression they give intensely Scottish and French at the same time. The embodiment of a country house, it is imposing but inviting. Stepping into the stone-flagged entrance, visitors are faced with the memorial arms, commemorating Mary's visit. Beneath is a copy of the death warrant for her execution, signed in Elizabeth I's spiky hand. It is a dreadful reminder of what lay ahead for the queen, an end that in August 1566 would have been unimaginable.

The oldest part of the house sits to the left of the entrance. Dating from the early twelfth century, the original wooden structure was replaced two centuries later by a fully fortified stone peel tower, which in turn was expanded in the sixteenth and early seventeenth centuries, to the present house. Nothing has been added for 300 years.

Rising from the entrance is a flight of stone stairs that narrows with each ascent, leading from the domestic floor to drawing rooms, library (shelved from floor to ceiling) and a series of stately bedrooms, now available for honeymooners and holidaymakers.

Although the Stuarts of Traquair were devout Catholics, they briefly changed their colours. (They also changed the spelling of their name around the same time.) As this coincided with the introduction to Scotland of the reviled Episcopalian prayerbook, which caused riots in Edinburgh and Glasgow, this manoeuvre did the seventh laird no favours. The family's commitment to the Catholic faith was soon restored, and one bedroom is designated the priest's room. Behind false bookshelves is a steep set of stairs, an escape route by which the priest could disappear whenever necessary.

Beyond its windows lies the Well Pool, a remnant of the Tweed's natural course before it was redirected to protect the foundations. When Mary was in residence, the river ran close to her bedchamber. The country air might have given her untroubled sleep, but with her mind turning over all her woes, and feeling far from well, she could lie awake listening as it flowed beneath the windows.

Under glass in the wide, airy galleries on the upper floor are copies of business documents signed at Traquair by Mary and Darnley. There are also items that belonged to the queen – her crucifix and rosary, a pair of shoes, and needlework and tapestry. Another striking remnant is the four-poster bed she slept in, not while at Traquair but when at Terregles Castle, in Dumfriesshire, which was owned by the Maxwells. Because of the Maxwell Stuart lineage, some of Traquair's furniture comes from Terregles, which was demolished after the Second World War. One day the grandfather of the present Lady Traquair peeled away the mourning black that covered the bed. Beneath was a glimpse of its original primrose yellow, which has since been gloriously restored. Ornate and dramatic, it could be a prop for a Mozart opera. At its foot stands the hefty carved wooden cradle, where the infant James was rocked to sleep. Assuming that he was with his parents on this visit. Historians differ on this point, some saying James was at Mary's side, others that he was placed in the care of the Earl of Mar and his wife in Edinburgh Castle. It's a small matter but, like so many aspects of Mary's life, is open to debate.

Stewart of Traquair was honoured by her presence, and his hospitality as generous as he and his servants could devise. On the morning of the hunt, the riders took an early breakfast with them to picnic on in the forest, but dinner was an altogether more splendid and protracted affair. Platters heaped with fish, meat, vegetables, fruits and puddings were carried from the kitchens to be placed before the diners. The waiting staff must have been awed by the queen's presence. Perhaps even more intimidating were her courtiers, the regal Moray, and the brooding Bothwell, whose reputation for violence was well known in these parts. So too was Darnley's, whose fine clothes and haughty air could not disguise his temper as he sat beside his wife, growing more boorish with every goblet he downed.

Wine was poured in quantity, along with beer. Yet the servants who attended the table, before retreating beyond sight to the edges of the room, would have been dismayed. As the meal progressed, the atmosphere turned ugly. Eventually it exploded in an unforgettable scene that surely reached the ears of the cooks and butlers below stairs before anyone at Holyrood ever heard of it.

Claude Nau records Mary's version of what happened:

While at supper the king asked her to attend a stag hunt. Knowing that if she did so she would be required to gallop her horse at a great pace she whispered in his ear that she suspected she was pregnant. The king answered aloud 'Never mind, if we lose this one we will make another' whereupon Traquair rebuked him sharply and told him that he did not speak like a Christian. He answered 'What! Ought not we to work a mare well when she is with foal?'

The evening had been ruined, and even if Mary continued as if all was well, she was in torment. That her visit lasted only two days suggests that she cut short the holiday. It might have been the lack of game that hastened her departure, but Darnley's behaviour is a more likely cause.

His remarks were doubtless fuelled by alcohol, but the words were not merely humiliating but savage. If the couple had attempted a rapprochement – and it is possible that Mary's whisperings were intended to suggest this, even if it was illusory – all hope of their future together expired. Whether Bothwell spoke up is not recorded, but by this time Mary was leaning heavily upon him, as one of her most robust and trustworthy allies. The following year, when Darnley was murdered, it seems likely that Stewart of Traquair, who was a supporter of Bothwell, was also party to the crime. What he had witnessed in his own home might well have persuaded him that this was a man both queen and country could well do without.

Chapter 23

The Queen's Mire

HERMITAGE CASTLE AND JEDBURGH

Despite the turmoil in Mary's personal life, she did not shirk her responsibility for maintaining peace across the realm. It might even have proved a welcome distraction. In October 1566, she set out for Jedburgh, to preside over the annual justice ayres, or circuits, where those who had broken the law were brought before the royal court. The ayres lasted a week, barely long enough, you might have thought, to scratch the surface of the problem, yet they were symbolically important for reinforcing Crown authority. The queen's route took her via Borthwick Castle, Peebles and Melrose, where she had summoned followers to join her. A few miles further south lay Jedburgh, a beautiful abbey town that was already becoming renowned for its orchards of sweet pears. The exquisite twelfth-century Augustinian abbey around which it is built would never recover from the depredations of Henry VIII's armies. Its tracery of ruins must have stood, in Mary's day as in our own, as a reproach to the pugnacity of dynastic and political ambition.

Despite being expected to join Mary at the ayres, Darnley did not accompany her. He made no attempt to hide or heal their rift, but at this point Mary was not aware of the full extent of his perfidy. Unknown to her, he had written to the Pope and to the Spanish and French kings to denounce his wife for failing to advance the Catholic cause. He was also making plans to leave the country. This was an alarming prospect because, as John Guy writes, 'Darnley plotting abroad would be even more dangerous than Darnley plotting at home'. It was evident to everyone, including themselves, that the couple were as good as estranged.

Shortly after Mary set out for Jedburgh, news reached her that Bothwell was dangerously wounded. On a mission to capture the worst offenders ahead of the justice ayres, he had been ambushed by the Elliots, among the fiercest of the Border clans. His injuries were extensive – 'ane in the bodie, ane in the heid, and ane in the hand' – and it was feared he might die. (He bore a scar on his forehead for the rest of his life.) Too gravely hurt to be put on his horse, he had to be dragged on a dray back to Hermitage Castle. His ordeal did not end there. When they reached its gates, it was discovered that the prisoners had risen and captured the castle. They would agree to let Bothwell's men bring the unconscious earl inside only on condition they were released.

Contrary to rumours, Mary did not immediately leap upon a horse and ride to Bothwell's side, although she asked to be kept informed of his condition. The court proceedings continued, during which she irritated Moray by the leniency of her sentences. Where he would have had the handful of criminals brought before them executed – the others had fled from Hermitage and were now beyond reach of the law – she merely fined them. It was almost a week before she and her lords, including Moray, left Jedburgh to see how Bothwell fared. They did so after hearing that the earl was recovering or, as others assert, when it seemed likely he was about to die.

The fifty-mile round trip to Hermitage Castle was arduous, but the queen was a skilled horsewoman, and in normal circumstances it would not have taxed her. Unfortunately, she was still in uncertain health, and on her way to Jedburgh had suffered sharp pains in her side, which did not bode well. Her weakened state must have made the trip to Hermitage more gruelling than anticipated.

Of all the buildings associated with Mary, none is more bleak or unforgiving than the pitiless fortress at Hermitage. The monumental and starkly unrelieved walls, with a few small, once-barred windows, are a chilling response to where and when it was constructed. Hermitage was terrifying because its threatening appearance mirrored the menace of the region in which it lay. Scanning its walls, you feel the need to check over your shoulder.

The domain of the Hepburn family, Hermitage lies in Liddesdale, which in this period was the most lawless and volatile district across these isles. Bothwell had the temperament to keep a lid on the turmoil of what is often referred to as the Debatable Lands, so-called for the coming and going of armies and outlaws who either claimed it for their own, or ravaged it, or used it as a base for their savage activities across the border. Of the various dales that comprise the Borderlands, Tweeddale, Teviotdale and Annandale were all laws unto themselves, but Liddesdale was by far the worst. The heart of the Debatable Lands, on the cusp of the border, it was a small but fearsome district that formed a buffer between Scotland and England.

The ferocity of the Border clans was unparalleled, and struck terror into any who had to enter their territory, and all who lived there. The great 'surnames' who ruled the district with almost psychopathic brutality were coalitions of family groups and associates under the command of, among others, the Armstrongs or Elliots, the Ridleys, Nixons, Grahames and Croziers. Allegiance between them was based on kinship, expedience and self-interest rather than nationality. An outlawed band of Armstrongs, for instance, did filthy work for the English march wardens against their own countryfolk along the border, while the worst of the reivers would kill their own parents or brothers, or set homes alight to burn entire families if it suited their ends. 'Scumfishing' was one way of taking revenge. With the occupants boarded up inside, the gangs would stack wood or straw against the walls and set them on fire, thereby suffocating those indoors. Cattle and sheep were herded off by the light of a full moon and grain stores emptied. Protection money was demanded from villagers and farmsteads to protect them from these raids, in so doing bringing entire communities under the gangs' control. Any who ratted would not survive long, and nor would their kin.

Around Hermitage, the landscape was so treacherous it was possible for outlaws to lure those trying to bring them to justice into bogs and mires, where they could be picked off at ease or left to founder. The reivers' small, agile ponies had learned to navigate their way through the marshes, and to this end often went unshod.

At one point, the Debatable Lands were given carte blanche for murderous mayhem. A parliamentary Act of 1537, repeated in 1551, stated that all Englishmen and Scotsmen were allowed 'to rob, burn, steal, slay, murder and destroy any person or persons, including their bodies, property, goods and livestock in the Debatable Land'. It was like putting ferrets in a sack, in the hope they would eradicate each other and save others the trouble.

Bothwell, despite being a cultivated man in some respects, was essentially a thug, well suited to dealing with the criminals running loose in the district. The Elliots nearly did for him, and it is tempting to speculate that they might perhaps have done the country a favour had they succeeded. But by the time the queen and her coterie reached the castle, he was making a good recovery.

After a five-hour ride over moorland and rugged hills, Mary's party arrived around noon on 15 October, according to the *Diurnal of Occurrents* (an anonymous history of the sixteenth century), although some say it was 16 October. She spent an hour or two at her lieutenant's bedside, most likely discussing the ayres, and then she and her companions left. It was a businesslike appointment, although the queen was clearly relieved to learn that Bothwell was on the mend. Doubtless she missed his protective presence. Even so, whether rumours were spread by those of her entourage who wished her ill, or people drew their own conclusions, that fateful day in Liddesdale helped fuel suspicion that the queen and the earl were in an illicit relationship.

Hermitage is spoken of as if it is cursed. It has been described as the 'guardhouse of the bloodiest valley in Britain', its name originating perhaps in the French word for guardhouse. Sir Walter

Scott, custodian of Borders lore and never one to underplay the romance of any situation, wrote: 'The Castle . . . unable to support the load of iniquity which had long been accumulating within its walls, is supposed to have partly sunk beneath the ground; and its ruins are still regarded by the peasants with peculiar aversion and horror'.

Hermitage Castle's appearance is like a something from a Middle Eastern war zone. Stories abound of the ghostly presences among its ruins. One such is the Sheriff of Teviotdale, who was thrown into its pit prison and left to starve to death. Another is Sir William de Soulis, a necromancer who was said to murder children and use their blood in his spells. Outraged locals set upon him, wrapping him in lead and throwing him into a cauldron of boiling oil. Alternatively, he was executed with relative humanity by the king, for trying to overthrow him. However he met his end, his malevolent figure is said to haunt the building, as do the sobs of his young victims.

To learn of this before visiting might prejudice most people against a place, yet you could reach Hermitage knowing nothing, and still find it chilling. Here, history reaches out to you. The impression of mercilessness was no doubt intentional. In horizontal rain, as on my last visit, it feels menacing. From a distance, the lit-up ticket booth appeared like a pinprick of human warmth in the wilderness. Beyond, the castle loured. No other word will do. Despite a profusion of pink willow herb to soften the approach, it is formidable.

For a start, its walls are sheer. Two of them are cut away into enormous flying arches which look like a giant's doorways but are in fact buttresses. Their purpose was to support the covered wooden walkway that once projected from the roof and on which soldiers would patrol and fight off attack. Incredibly, in its heyday, its barracks could hold 1,000 men and 200 horsemen.

The castle is further protected by gun-loops and an earthen embankment on its weakest side. The raised mound on which it stands is likely to be where an early-fourteenth-century wooden structure stood before being rebuilt in stone for its Cumbrian owner,

Lord Dacre, around 1360. A few years later Dacre was ousted by the Douglas family, who created the grim building that still, partially, stands.

Given the weather, it was no surprise to have it to myself. Ten minutes were spent huddled under a doorway, peering into the roofless interior and waiting for the storm clouds to pass. They hung overhead, dark as an army of Armstrongs. When it was clear they had settled over the valley for the rest of the afternoon, there was no option but to explore in the rain.

Hermitage was built around several towers, including one for the well, one for prisoners, a central block and the Douglas tower, which provided five-star accommodation. It was most probably here that Mary was entertained when she visited Bothwell. Today, it stands open to the sky. Stepping around puddles in the cobbled courtyard that is all that remains of Dacre's finely built stone house, I climbed slippery stairs to the prison tower. The cell for captives lies ten or more feet below floor level, but has a window and latrine. This was luxurious by medieval standards, suggesting its occupants were highborn. Those from the lower orders were thrown into the windowless pit that lay beneath it.

As always, it was a relief to emerge from the castle and drink in the prospect of gentle, unwooded hills and the babbling Hermitage Water, which runs past its walls. Much is made of Liddesdale's ferocity in the sixteenth century, but the castle's barefaced gloom is not reflected in the landscape. Sheep graze on tussocky grass, untroubled by history. The twisting back road on which the castle lies passes fields of black goats, cattle and swathes of dense woodland. It is sobering to think of the misery the reivers and clan feuds brought to those who once occupied this valley, living as best they could off the land.

* * *

With their business concluded, Mary and her attendants set off for Jedburgh. A thick mist had descended, making it a more punishing ride. The queen's party followed a barren and windswept route known as the Thieves Road, which led over the marshes and hills beyond Hermitage. This rough terrain could be a quagmire, and Sir Walter Scott, who described it as a 'pass of danger', reported seeing 'the bones of horses which have been entangled in it'.

As her horse picked its way over the boglands, unable to see further than a few paces ahead, Mary slipped from her saddle. Fortunately, she landed in a marsh, now called the Queen's Mire. A short distance from Hermitage, the mire lay between the Barley and Crib burns, beneath the evocatively named Crossbow Hill. Mary appeared to be unhurt, and after brushing down her skirts, swung herself back onto her horse. The posse continued, reaching Jedburgh by mid evening, when all seemed well. But by the following day Mary had fallen gravely ill and it was soon feared she might die.

Violently sick, she was so weak that there were spells when she could neither talk nor see. She also suffered convulsions. Anticipating the worst, she summoned Moray and the other lords to pass on her last instructions. As they gathered at her bedside, she insisted that Darnley was not to take power, and that her son was to be her successor. Until he was old enough to rule, he was to be well brought up. What her nobles' feelings were on seeing their queen in this condition is not recorded, but the suddenness of her collapse must have been shocking.

Not long after gathering her courtiers, Mary fell into a coma-like state. She became deathly cold and still, and some of her companions, believing she was already gone, opened the windows to release her departing spirit. Meantime, according to secretary Claude Nau, 'The earl of Moray began to lay hands on the most precious articles, such as her silver plate and rings'. On this and a later occasion, it seems he was like a magpie, unable to resist the allure of jewellery. If Nau's account is correct, then this is one of the lowest ethical points in Moray's career, evidence of a man lacking both heart and integrity.

Fortunately, Mary's French physician, Arnault, did not despair as easily as others. Seeing subtle signs of life, with great wisdom he bound her legs and arms as tightly as if she was in swaddling, thereby improving her circulation. He gave her an enema, and, forcing open her mouth, he spilled some wine down her throat. A little later, when she was sufficiently conscious, he give her a medicinal potion, after which she brought up a quantity of blood. Thereafter, she began slowly to recover.

Some later suggested she had been poisoned, but Mary attributed her collapse to the stress of recent events, in particular the behaviour of her husband. In August, after her trip to Traquair, she had sent her infant son for safety to Stirling Castle, with a heavy guard to protect him on the journey. Fears of James's abduction had been heightened by her husband's erratic and hostile behaviour. It was not impossible that he could be kidnapped and a regent installed until he came of age, while Mary was imprisoned or disposed of. Scurilously, George Buchanan saw the source of her near fatal collapse as the result of her 'exertions by day and night' with Bothwell, who, he suggested, was staying in the room below her. He did not allow the fact that Bothwell was not in Jedburgh at the time – and was indeed barely well enough to travel – to spoil a salacious story.

The queen had been under extreme duress at several points since the night of Rizzio's murder, but her health had fluctuated since she was young. Whenever under intense pressure – as on learning of her mother's death – she would suffer a collapse. Some have suggested she was afflicted with porphyria, which ran in the royal line, but modern medics cast doubt on that diagnosis. What ailed her in Jedburgh, and the pains she previously complained of in her side, as well as fainting fits, might have been caused by a gastric ulcer. This might also explain her rapid return to health between episodes.

The town house in Jedburgh where Mary reputedly stayed during the ayres, and where she was to lie, mortally ill for almost two weeks, was a substantial, fortified building. A short step from the high street, and overlooking the A68 as it heads north to Edinburgh and south to Newcastle, it was owned either by the Scotts of Ancrum, or more likely the Kerrs of Ferniehurst. The property on the present site, known as Mary, Queen of Scots' House, is arguably not the 'bastel-house' or fortified tower she knew, but built shortly afterwards, on the same location. If that is the case, unless there was a fire it is not clear why a property fit to receive the nation's most distinguished member fell so quickly into dilapidation that within a few years it had to be rebuilt. Another possibility is that when she was in Jedburgh Mary did not stay here but at another residence owned by the Kerrs.

Nobody seems entirely certain. Alison Weir writes that the queen took up residence in what is currently the Spread Eagle Hotel, which contains evidence of a medieval tower. This three-star inn is in the centre of the high street. Towards the end of Mary's visit, writes Weir, fire ripped through the building and the royal party was obliged to relocate to the town house. She believes the present town house is the original. While she continued to convalesce, Mary paid a rent of £40 to Lady Ferniehurst for a stay of little more than a week. Scotland's architectural bible, *The Buildings of Scotland*, does nothing to clarify matters: 'contemporary record is silent as to the whereabouts of the queen's lodging on that occasion and, to judge from its appearance, the existing house is unlikely to have been erected much before 1600'. It seems most probable that she was a guest in one of the town's several defensive towers – one of which is incorporated within the hotel – which were built after Jedburgh castle was demolished in the fifteenth century.

Whether or not Mary stayed in this particular bastle-house, be it for weeks, a few days, or not at all, it nevertheless manages to offer a glimpse of her era. A most attractive tall, crow-step gabled building, with one wing a storey higher than the other, it is constructed from pink and yellow local sandstone. In the seventeenth century it would have been harled, with a thatched roof. Within the slim central tower is a turnpike stair that grows more like a corkscrew as the building rises. By the time visitors reach the first floor, they must duck their heads. Two blocked-up doorways high in the walls and visible from outside suggest that initially the upper floors were accessed by outdoor stairs.

The room in which it is said Mary lay close to death looks out of two tiny casement windows onto the gardens and its pear trees that enfold the house. Above Mary's room is another low-ceilinged chamber, called the Maries' Room, which was for her ladies-in-waiting. With recently painted wooden beams and modern murals, the house has been a museum since 1930. Two years earlier, in 1928, during a fundraising campaign to preserve the house, J.M. Barrie told an audience in Jedburgh that the previous night, Mary had appeared to him in a dream and told him the Casket Letters were forgeries.

Throughout its various rooms, and in the attic gallery, the queen's story is told in artefacts, paintings, letters, documents and photos. There is a shoe she left behind, because its heel was broken, whose stylish elegance evokes a woman of glamour and confidence. There is a silver communion set, and a lock of Mary's auburn hair. A snippet from the gown she wore on the day of her execution comes from Sir Walter Scott's extensive and not always authentic collection of memorabilia. There are coins minted in her reign, and a small French cannon she gave to the Kerrs during this visit. A watch discovered in 1817 in the mire where she fell came to light thanks to a tunnelling mole. It is thought to be hers, as is a French enamelled thimble case, dropped on her Hermitage day trip during a halt to mend her dress.

These are mere fragments from her life. Nevertheless, they bring the queen close, filling in the sepia images we have of her with honest colour. They refute the idea that she was from a different world than ours and are a reminder that the decorative items she owned are just as pleasing to us, and still far above most people's means.

In the weeks, months and years that followed Mary's time in Jedburgh, as her troubles mounted, she was to express the wish that she had died here. It is sobering to reflect that this frontier town, on the edge of the border, might have been where her story ended.

Much of the Jedburgh museum is devoted to Mary, but by far its grisliest memento is of her third husband, Bothwell. After fleeing Scotland in 1567 he fell foul of the Danish family with whose daughter he had had an affair. Taken prisoner by the king, as a potentially useful political pawn, the earl spent the rest of his days in a series of increasingly abject prisons, ending in a castle dungeon, where he was kept in unspeakable conditions. He died, allegedly insane, in 1578, and the Jedburgh collection contains a startling nineteenth-century photograph of what is said to be Bothwell's mummified head. Seemingly preserved by the conditions of its burial, it looks disconcertingly newly dead, complete with hair, eyes, eyebrows, mouth, teeth and broken nose. His remains lie in a coffin in the plain whitewashed church of Faarevejle, near Dragsholm in Denmark, despite attempts to have his body repatriated to Scotland.

During Mary's illness her husband attended her once, when she was convalescing. Bothwell also visited, although still recovering from his assault. He had to be carried by litter, and arrived a week earlier than Darnley. In his defence, it seems Darnley was belatedly informed of her collapse, and came as soon as he could, by which time she was greatly improved. That he spent a single night in the town suggests either a considerable difference between his and the earl's concern for the invalid, or in the warmth of the welcome they received. The earl stayed in Jedburgh for several days, during which time he regained his health. He was also able to be present at meetings with and about the queen. This was of utmost importance to him, so that he could not be outmanoeuvred by Moray, whom he did not trust.

Both men were opportunists, who put their own interests first. Bothwell's enduring devotion to the Crown, first to Marie de Guise and then to her daughter, was not merely the action of a loyal and decent servant, but of one who knew on which side his bread was buttered. And one who would, if at all possible, demand marmalade. Moray was inscrutable, but there was never any doubt about his ambitions.

It was while Mary was recuperating, and still in despair at her marriage, that Darnley's future began to take shape. Unburdening herself to Maitland, Mary revealed how wretched she felt. Maitland reported to Archbishop Beaton:

the occasion of the Queen's sickness, so far as I understand, is thought and displeasure, and I trow, by what I could wring further of her own declaration to me, the root of it is the King. For she has done him so great honour, contrary to the advice of her subjects, and he, on the other part, has recompensed her with such ingratitude and misuses himself so far towards her that it is a heartbreak for her to think he should be her husband, and how to be free of him she sees no outgait.

This was the opportunity her nobles had been waiting for to find a way of putting an end to the problem he posed.

Chapter 24

'Unless she was free of him she had no pleasure to live'

CRAIGMILLAR CASTLE

Craigmillar Castle, on the outskirts of Edinburgh, is the epitome of a picturesque ruin. Although dilapidated, with its imposing curtain wall and broken-down silhouette of battlements and towers, enough remains to imagine how it must have looked four or five hundred years ago. The Great Hall at its heart, with its enormous stone fireplace and deeply set windows, reeks of Mary's time, as do its vaulted kitchens and cellars, where you can almost hear the sizzling of bygone roasting pigs.

Carried by litter, and accompanied by Moray, Maitland and Bothwell, Mary slowly made her way back to the capital after the justice ayres. Her royal progress took her through Berwickshire and East Lothian, and as she approached Edinburgh, her court congregated at Craigmillar.

Mary was still in Jedburgh when she learned how doggedly Darnley was undermining her, claiming she had betrayed her faith. She grew so distressed it was feared she was about to suffer a relapse. Confiding her feelings to Moray and Maitland, she told them that 'unless she was free of him in some way she had no pleasure to live, and if she could find no other remedy, she would slay herself'.

Still not fully recovered, and attended closely by her physicians, the queen reached Craigmillar on 20 November 1566. Plans were in train for an ostentatious baptism for James in Stirling Castle the following month, and she intended to stay here until she was ready to head north. Organising this event offered some relief from her otherwise black thoughts.

When Mary made her momentous visit, the name Craigmillar was illustrious. Taken from the Gaelic *Creag Maol Ard*, meaning high bare rock, the earliest part of the castle had been built in the late fourteenth century. It was one of the first examples of tower house design in Scotland, containing the Great Hall, and a warren of bedchambers and rooms. Its parkland stretched to Holyrood Palace. From 1374 to the seventeenth century it was owned by the Prestons, whose coat of arms is prominently displayed throughout the castle. One of the city's most influential medieval families, they held the distinction of having donated the arm bone of St Giles to the parish church named after him, in the fifteenth century.

The old tower sits at the core of the castle, with walls almost three metres thick. It is vertiginously high, and the view from the battlements looks out across the city, over the Firth of Forth to Fife. In style it is modelled on the David Tower at Edinburgh Castle, which could be seen from its walls. Many additions were made in the following centuries, and by the time of Mary's residence, the sense of security this extensive fortress offered would have been especially welcome.

She arrived in a very low mood. According to Philibert du Croc, the French ambassador, she spoke often of wishing to be dead. Sir Simon Preston, who was on the Privy Council, and was Provost of Edinburgh, had failed to help Mary after Rizzio's murder, but because of his previous record of loyalty she chose to forgive him. Doing so allowed her to live in a more congenial place than Holyrood Palace, with its raw memories and bloodstains. For the present, Preston appeared to be her friend. She could not foresee that within a few months he would become her jailer.

The issue of Mary's entitlement to the English crown continued to be thrashed out during these weeks, but she had already scored a real dynastic and diplomatic victory. When in Jedburgh, believing she would die, Mary had sent a message to Elizabeth to ask that, in the event of her death, she would act as James's protector, treating him as if he were her own child. Elizabeth agreed. This was a far-sighted request, flattering the Queen of England, securing James's safety, yet neither threatening the Scottish lords' independence nor compromising Elizabeth's position.

The issue now facing Mary was whether she should divorce Darnley or have their union dissolved. The marriage could not be annulled on the usual grounds of consanguinity, since Mary had asked for a papal dispensation to marry her cousin, albeit recklessly holding the ceremony before such permission arrived, on the assumption it was on its way. Furthermore, if it were dissolved, James would be rendered illegitimate, as her courtiers were quick to point out. A divorce could be gained if Darnley's infidelity could be proved, but if they divorced, Mary could not remarry while remaining in the Catholic faith.

These were the matters that absorbed the court's attention as November turned to December. After a serious relapse, during which she vomited a copious amount of blood and briefly looked once more as if she might perish, Mary swiftly recovered her health. The most dramatic period of illness in her life was finally over.

Foremost among her advisors at Craigmillar was Moray, along with Maitland, Argyll, Huntly and Bothwell. The only missing figures were those still in disgrace and exiled in England, chief among them the remorseless Morton. The gathering of such disputatious and undependable individuals under one roof would, in ordinary circumstances, have been a recipe for friction. Indeed, Bothwell's mistrust of Moray was such that he did not want to let him out of his sight. It was reported that the Lieutenant of the Borders had planned to kill Moray while he was at Jedburgh but was thwarted by his own brush with death. Maitland had, in the meantime, been restored to his position as Mary's secretary and was once more purring in a position of power. In the potentially heated atmosphere of the cloistered court, perhaps he hoped to act as peacemaker.

Living in such close quarters must have been like boarding school, the stage set for quarrels and intrigue. But the situation was so grave, it seems they had finally found a cause around which they could rally. Now, as never before, their interests coalesced behind a single aim: to deal with Darnley.

The elderly Simon Preston would have had less time for plotting than the others, being more concerned with ensuring the castle's domestic machinery was running smoothly. A prolonged royal visit was a mark of distinction for the host, but it put such a strain on the castle's finances, and on the stamina of its servants, it was an honour better enjoyed in memory. Preston was more fortunate than some, since with James's baptism scheduled for mid December, this visit was relatively short. Sometimes a royal train could descend on a household and outstay their welcome by weeks if not months; only when the midden outwith the walls grew so high and noisome it could no longer be ignored did they pack up and move on, leaving their hosts to clear away their mess. Yet even the hard-pressed Preston could not have missed the atmosphere of foreboding that enveloped the castle. With the winter nights growing longer, and the darkness deeper, his guests sensed a gathering storm. Some, perhaps, looked forward to it.

For the moment, the lords humoured their queen by endlessly debating the pros and cons of each move, even suggesting that Darnley might be charged with treason, which was a capital offence. Behind her back, very different talks were taking place, during which they agreed to dispose of Darnley in one fashion or another. Not only was Moray probably well aware of the plan to kill Darnley, but from the outset he might also have been intending to frame Bothwell for the deed. Whatever his involvement, he left little trace of it.

It was during these weeks that the infamous Craigmillar Bond was drawn up. Never since produced as evidence, and presumably destroyed, its contents were in part memorised by those involved, and were later revealed. Before his execution in 1573, one of Bothwell's men, James Ormiston, recalled the wording of the document, which was signed – at the very least – by Maitland, Huntly, Argyll, Bothwell and the lawyer Sir James Balfour, who is believed most likely to have composed it:

> It was thought expedient and most profitable for the Commonwealth, by the whole nobility and Lords underscribed, that such a young fool and proud tyrant should not reign or bear rule over them; and that, for divers causes therefore, that these all had concluded that he should be put off by one way or another; and whosoever should take the deed in hand, or do it, they should defend and fortify themselves.

Claude Nau's memoir of the queen claimed that this bond was handed to Mary by Bothwell on the field of Carberry Hill, before he fled and she was taken captive. It seems likely that, if true, it was removed from her by her captors before they could stand accused of being accessories to murder.

If the most obvious and brutal solution to her problem was voiced plainly in Mary's presence, there is no evidence of it. At the very least, sinister solutions were probably hinted at, or suspected, since she went out of her way to stress that she would not endorse violence. When Maitland told her that the lords were keen to put an end to the marriage and her difficulties, without damaging James's status, he effectively alluded to drastic measures by saying that, whatever route they took, Moray would 'look through his fingers thereto, and behold our doings, saying nothing to the same'.

Alarmed, Mary insisted that their actions must not harm her son's position: 'I will that you do nothing by which any spot may be laid to my honour or conscience, and therefore I pray you rather let the matter be in the estate as it is, abiding till God of his goodness put remedy thereto, than you, believing to do me service, may possibly turn to my hurt and displeasure.'

The castle has an atmosphere conducive to plotting. Perhaps its best view is from the air. In its roofless state, it is like a hive with the lid removed, its chambers, towers and courtyard laid out for inspection. The old tower contains a small chamber where it is said the queen stayed during her visit, but it is more likely that Mary's apartments were in the more modern eastern range of the castle. Nor is there any evidence that she took refuge in the castle's old kitchen after Rizzio's murder, as some accounts suggest. It is, of course, possible that she found comfort here during her visit, when initially she feared her nobles might be again conspiring against her, but in common with many aspects of Mary's story, there is as much legend as hard evidence, leaving the imagination in limbo.

By the end of her visit, and her deliberations with the lords, Mary was left to decide whether to reconcile with her husband or divorce him. It seemed obvious a rapprochement did not appeal. In the early part of her visit to Craigmillar, Darnley had arrived, seeking a resumption of married life. Mary refused outright. It was a miserable encounter, with the queen saying she would not reimburse Darnley's expenses for travelling unless he promised to return to Stirling forthwith. His mortified response is easy to imagine. Resuming some form of marital stability at a future date was not entirely out of the question, but, as this fractious encounter suggests, the augurs were not good.

While Mary wavered, the lords, it seems, had already decided. The queen's reputation, then as now, hangs on whether we believe she knew nothing of the plot to kill her husband, suspected their plans but turned a blind eye or was unwittingly overruled by her nobles, who saw the king's death as the only way to ensure stability for the country. Whatever the case, to see the nobility supporting her, rather than conniving with Darnley as they had over Rizzio's murder, must have been welcome for Mary. It is possible that she tacitly accepted that assassination was inevitable, even if she could never explicitly endorse it. However, some historians take a different view and are convinced that while at Craigmillar, Mary decided to ask for an annulment and end her troubles in this way.

Whether or not she knew of the nobles' bond to murder Darnley, it was at Craigmillar that Mary's fortunes began to slide through her fingers. When she left, on 7 December, it was for a short stay at

Holyrood, before heading to Stirling Castle, and her son's baptism. This spectacular event can almost be viewed as an attempt to reset her reign and silence any who doubted her Catholic credentials or her authority to rule. The choreography of the baptismal events was put largely into the hands of Bothwell, thereby excluding Darnley and emphasising Bothwell's position in the queen's esteem.

Anxious and miserable, Mary issued orders forbidding anyone from bringing firearms into the court. She also confided her fears in Sir James Melville. He wisely urged her to put aside any thoughts of revenge and focus on winning over her own subjects, and the people of England. Meanwhile Darnley, feared to be likely to collude with foreign ambassadors during the proceedings, was kept under strict surveillance and effectively grounded.

Queen Elizabeth's good favour was evident in the bejewelled golden font she sent as a gift. It was so enormous that the infant could have been bathed in it. Even more encouraging was news, conveyed by Elizabeth's representative, the Earl of Bedford, that she wanted to arrange a meeting to discuss Mary's claim to the English throne.

The baptism took place on 17 December. The King of France was one of James's three godparents – the child was christened Charles James in his honour – and was represented by the Comte de Brienne, who carried the infant to the chapel. The count and the rest of the royal party made their way in a grand procession from the royal apartments to the door of the chapel royal, first passing through an aisle of courtiers, their way lit by flaming torches. The Archbishop of St Andrews conducted the ceremony, and various Catholic nobles bore the accoutrements of a medieval Catholic christening – including the ceremonial candle, or cierge, the salt and basin – like so many good fairies around the cradle.

Acting on behalf of the Duke of Savoy as godparent was the ambassador Philibert du Croc, while the prince's aunt, Jean, Countess of Argyll, took the infant from the arms of the Comte de Brienne. Standing proxy for Elizabeth as godmother, she held James throughout the ceremony. The English queen rewarded her generously for this act, although it greatly displeased the Protestant clergy.

Court and chapel guests were splendidly dressed, since Mary personally paid for lavish outfits for her nobles. According to an inventory, they wore cloth of gold, and silver, and were dressed 'rather above than under' their status. For the occasion, Bothwell was resplendent in blue, Moray in green and Argyll in red. This triumvirate, and Bedford, stood outside the chapel as the ceremony took place, along with others, and doubtless were beautiful to behold.

The christening was conducted with full Catholic rites, and on only one point did Mary baulk. It was common for the priest to spit into the baby's mouth during the ceremony, but she forbade this. The archbishop was believed to have syphilis: in Mary's words he was a 'poxy priest'. Other than this, the event matched Elizabeth's font, being sumptuously extravagant and stylish. Three days of dancing and feasting, theatre and song followed, with a bull hunt among the entertainments. Inspired by a similar event Mary had witnessed in France organised by Catherine de' Medici, these elaborate festivities included a mock siege in a fantastical turreted fortress, which had been constructed in the valley between the castle esplanade and the town. The storyline portrayed Prince James as the hero, successfully fighting off attack by Moors and Highlanders. This was followed by a display of fireworks so spectacular it had taken forty days to prepare. The cost of these proceedings obliged Mary to borrow money from the merchants of Edinburgh, and also to raise taxes.

Darnley's non-attendance at the ceremony, or at any time during the celebrations, was seen as a mark of his ill temper and fury with his wife for making Queen Elizabeth a godparent to his son and confining him to his quarters. His behaviour was also intended to cast doubt on the child's paternity. Some onlookers, however, suggested that Mary expressly forbade him to attend. That casts a different light on proceedings. If true, then a wiser and less arrogant man might have read the runes and taken flight that night.

By now, the constant presence of Bothwell at the queen's side was beginning to grate. It was he who welcomed ambassadors at the door of the chapel before the christening. This mark of high distinction was surely a sign, it was whispered, of his intimacy with the queen.

On Christmas Eve, Mary made the momentous move of pardoning those who had been involved in Rizzio's killing. It was a dramatic volte-face, and she did not undertake it with any enthusiasm. Among others, it brought Morton and the Douglas clan back into the fold, who a few months earlier had come close to killing her as well as her secretary. Only Ker of Fawdonside, who had held the pistol to her stomach, and his sidekick George Douglas, were excluded. That Morton remained under suspicion was clear, since for some months following his pardon he was under curfew. Like the others allowed home from exile, he was prohibited from approaching the queen or getting within seven miles of Holyrood.

Mary's feelings on issuing the pardons must have been complicated. Later that day, perhaps keen to put all thought of what her erstwhile enemies might now be plotting out of her mind, she left Stirling to spend the festive season at Drummond Castle. Bothwell was one of the party. Her husband, meanwhile, left for Glasgow, to be with his family. He was not merely geographically distant from his wife but, with his fellow conspirators restored to her favour, he was politically isolated too. His situation was now perilous. He would have been as aware as the queen that, by pardoning Morton and his cronies, Mary had allowed his worst foes to return. It was little less than a death sentence.

Chapter 25

'Intolerable stink'

KIRK O' FIELD

For a brief period, after two embittered months, it seemed as if the rancour between Mary and Darnley had abated. At Christmas, Mary was still contemplating divorce, and while this suggests no softening towards her husband, it is hardly the attitude of one conspiring towards his death. Then in January, she heard that he had fallen seriously ill at the family home in Glasgow. It was assumed to be smallpox, but medical conjecture suggests it was very probably a recurrence of the syphilis he had been suffering before he and Mary married. If the enormous strain of the past few months had all but broken Mary's health, it seems he had been similarly afflicted.

Shortly after leaving Stirling on Christmas Eve, Darnley became so unwell he was widely thought to have been poisoned. His hair fell out in clumps, and, according to George Buchanan, who relished the scene, he suffered 'black pimples all over his body, grievous sweat in all his limbs, and intolerable stink'. His syphilis, it would seem, had returned with full force, and he was to spend the next few weeks on the brink of death. Plans to sail overseas to safety were put on hold.

Mary waited a couple of weeks before making for Glasgow. She spent that period reconsidering her position. An outcry from Europe at the prospect of her divorcing perhaps made her pause. On learning that Darnley was actively plotting to snatch and imprison James, she seems to have adopted the principle of keeping her friends close and her enemies closer. Reconciliation was the wiser move.

With the air of a loving wife rather than one who has been cruelly wronged, Mary visited her husband in the Lennox Stuart family's Glasgow stronghold. Nothing of this remains except a venerable plane tree under which, allegedly, Mary nursed him. Since her visit was in the depths of a Scottish winter, that seems far-fetched.

Finding her husband in such a weakened state, wearing a taffeta mask to hide the foul, weeping pustules and to diminish the stench of his breath, Mary must have been shaken. It is not hard to imagine the queen quickly adopting her bedside manner, showing genuine concern and kindness. Indeed, Darnley later wrote to his father Lennox of 'my love the queen, which I assure you hath all this while and yet doth use herself like a natural and loving wife'. Perhaps memories of caring for Darnley at Stirling Castle softened her heart. It would have been understandable if, as she sat by him, she allowed herself to wonder if they might ever rekindle their old affection. But any daydreaming would have been short-lived. The sight of her husband brought so low might have inspired pity, but Mary no longer had any illusions about what sort of a man he was. She may indeed have wondered if it would be best if he succumbed to his disease.

Mary played the good wife to perfection, perhaps even convincing herself. Her visit was prompted by her wish for him to return to Edinburgh, where she would look after him and he would have access to the best medical advice. Obviously, she pointed out, he could not return to Holyrood, for the danger smallpox posed to young James, but he could convalesce in the comfort and security of Craigmillar Castle. It offered the seclusion he required and a vast parkland in which he could stroll once he was feeling stronger. It was also well defended from unwanted visitors. Here he could recuperate until he was fully fit.

When inquiries began into Darnley's murder, his servant Thomas Crawford gave a statement in which he alleged he overheard Mary and Darnley's conversation in Glasgow, during which she cajoled him to relocate to Edinburgh:

He said he would go, if they might be at bed and board as husband and wife, and she to leave him no more: and if she promised this on her word, he would go where she pleased – without this, he would not go. She said if she had not been so minded, she would not have come so far, and gave him her hand and faith of her body, that she would love and use him as her husband. But before they could come together 'he must be purged and clensed of hys sicknesse . . . For she minded to give him the bathe at Craigmiller.'

He then asked me what I thought of his voyage? I said I liked it not, for if she had desired his company, instead of to Craigmiller, she would have taken him to his own house in Edinburgh, rather than a gentleman's house 2 miles out of town – therefore my opinion was she took him more like a prisoner than her husband. He answered he thought little less himself: save the confidence he had in her promise only. Yet he would put himself in her hands, 'thowghe she showlde cutte hys throate'.

Darnley was venal, vain and amoral, but he was not entirely dim. He still greatly and rightly feared the enemies he had made at court, above all Moray and the remorseless Earl of Morton, who had returned to Edinburgh after his pardon. Mary had put her litter at his disposal for the journey, and as he approached Edinburgh, Darnley had a sudden apprehension of danger and insisted on being taken to the palace instead of Craigmillar. He was reminded that this was not possible, but seeing his terror, Mary suggested he could lodge in the Old Provost's Lodging in Edinburgh, at Kirk o' Field, on the city walls, which was much closer to Holyrood. A few weeks earlier, she had granted it to Robert Balfour, brother of Sir James Balfour, who is thought to have drawn up the Craigmillar Bond. Was this mere coincidence or evidence of a carefully orchestrated conspiracy? We will never know for sure.

Unable to argue, and no doubt longing for the uncomfortable journey to reach its end, when he could climb into bed to rest, Darnley agreed. On 1 February the royal train clattered into the courtyard containing the lodgings, which were beside the medieval church of St Mary's in the Field. Darnley was helped to his room, where the hearth blazed to banish the February chill.

At the change of plan, Mary had sent orders ahead to Holyrood, and things were quickly organised to make him comfortable. His bedchamber, on the first floor, was furnished with a richly draped four-poster bed, a chair and a velvet-topped table, most of which had been confiscated from the Earl of Huntly's magnificent palace. There was a profusion of tapestries, velvet cushions and a Turkish rug, and beside his bed stood a large tin bath. Treatment for his illness included medicinal baths, possibly containing sulphur. These would have smelled marginally worse than his breath, if, as seems probable, he was being treated with mercury. His veil would also have hidden the copious drooling this cure provoked, by which the patient was effectively poisoned. For some, mercury was more lethal than the disease itself.

The gable of the Old Provost's Lodging, also known as the Prebendaries' Chamber, was built into the city wall which encircled the oldest part of town. Robert Chambers describes it vividly in his vignettes of the city: 'It consisted of two stories, with a turnpike or spiral staircase behind. The gable adjoined to the town-wall, which there ran in a line east and west, and the cellar had a postern [door] opening through that wall. In the upper floor were a chamber and closet, with a little gallery having a window also through the town-wall.'

It was agreed that once he was fully recovered Darnley would return to Holyrood and the couple could resume married life. Whatever her true feelings, Mary made a good show of putting the past behind her. She visited him regularly, often staying until late at night. In the days before her husband's murder, she twice spent the night in the room beneath his to help calm his nerves. Although his valet, Taylor, slept on a mattress on the floor of his room, this did not feel sufficient protection. Knowing his enemies were now roaming loose, Darnley lived in fear of being assassinated. While he was at Kirk o' Field, Mary's half-brother Robert Stewart had in fact warned him to flee while he could, but when questioned by his sister as to what he meant, denied saying any such thing.

On Sunday 9 February 1567, Mary attended the wedding of one of her favourite valets, Bastien Pages. A mischievous Frenchman, he was one of the organisers of James's baptismal events, and had staged a raunchy ballet that grossly insulted Mary's English guests and almost caused a diplomatic incident. This Sunday marked the last day before Lent, and Mary's presence was also required at a formal and hearty banquet in the Canongate. Finally, as the day drew to a close, she made for Kirk o' Field with a host of companions, including Argyll, Huntly, and other courtiers and ladies.

Whatever discomforts Darnley endured at Kirk o' Field, loneliness was not one of them. Every day, he was kept company by a variety of court members, who not only kept him entertained but ensured he had little opportunity to hatch any plots. His little chamber would be filled with card players, gossip and music, and as Darnley's strength returned he picked up his lute and strummed. A love of music was one of his few unchanging passions, and perhaps the best that can be said of him. That Sunday night the atmosphere was particularly convivial, since by now Darnley was almost recovered. He was so well, it was arranged that he would return to Holyrood the following day. So eager was he to be there that Darnley ordered horses to collect him before daybreak. He was like a child barely able to sleep on Christmas Eve.

If Mary knew of the plot to murder her husband, she put herself in grave danger that evening. While her court gathered, the cellar of the house beneath them was packed with gunpowder. It needed only a flint to be struck. Intending to stay at Kirk o' Field for that last night, she was persuaded, possibly by Maitland, to leave instead for the wedding masque. Darnley was upset, and to mollify him Mary slipped a ring off her finger and gave it to him as a gesture of love and commitment. As she was leaving, she saw Bothwell's servant Paris, and while she remarked on how grubby he looked, she thought nothing more of it as she took her horse's reins. Upstairs, Darnley sang a 'merry song' with his valet, and retired to bed. The thought of the last song is poignant. It is a reminder that at twenty he was not so far from childhood.

The *Calendar of State Papers* believed Mary was in league with the murderers and having an affair with Bothwell, the chief assassin. It describes the scene at Kirk o' Field in the hours before the slaying:

> the powder being laid wherat Boithvile was present, he came to the kingis chamber and played at dice with the lords attending the Queen. Then Paris came and gave a sign that all was prepared . . . the queen departit towards Halyrudehous, Boithvile being in hir company, then on the way and after her arrival her sole talk was with Boithvile until 12 o'clock when the Laird of Traquair captain of the Guard went to his bed, leaving them alone together – then Boithvile departing as if to his bed in Lord Ruthven's house, changed his hose and doublet and went to the murder, returning thereafter to his said chamber through her 'watche'.

The implication was clear; Traquair was in on the plot.

At two in the morning, Mary was woken by a tremendous explosion. The noise was so great it was heard across the city, with one witness reporting it sounded like a volley from twenty-five or thirty cannons. Half a mile from Holyrood, the house in which Darnley was staying had been blown to smithereens. The king's unmarked body and that of his servant were found in the gardens. They had either been strangled or more probably asphyxiated.

The townsfolk would have been appalled, and frightened. House fires were common, explosions almost unheard of. They might have recognised it as a symbol of the dangerous times they were living in, a physical emblem of moral turpitude. But who was corrupt, and who blameless?

One of the most famous murders in history remains as tantalising today as ever. Muriel Spark, who spent much of her life in Italy, speculated whether Mary's secretary Joseph Rizzio might have been involved, since Darnley had been instrumental in murdering his brother. Some historians are adamant that Mary was complicit, others that she knew nothing of what was afoot. If she was indeed party to the plans, then she was as cold-blooded as Lady Macbeth. Yet two days earlier, Mary had agreed the terms of her succession to the English throne with Elizabeth. If she were indeed privy to this assassination, then the timing is at best curious, at worst perverse.

Sadly, the site of Kirk o' Field no longer exists. Built on a slight hill, above the fug of the city, this once quaintly medieval corner of Edinburgh comprised a spired thirteenth-century church and grave-yard. Around a square courtyard were several small gabled houses, and the grander residence of the Archbishop Hamilton. This had been built on the razed remains of a medieval hospital, burned by Henry VIII's army. Today, the turbulence of the sixteenth century has been swept away, replaced with the neoclassical brilliance of the University of Edinburgh's Old College.

On the spot where the entourage bearing Darnley arrived, there soars Robert Adam's masterpiece. A magnificent columned and domed edifice, Old College is the heart of the University of Edinburgh, a monument to erudition and enlightenment. William Henry Playfair continued the work when Adam died, but the origi-nal conception was all his. It shows the exalted light in which the university saw itself, and a desire to put darker times behind it. Yet while all trace of the house where Darnley died is lost, it is not forgotten. When the broadcaster and historian Magnus Magnusson sought out the site of Darnley's murder, he found to his surprise that when he was rector of the university, he had been sitting almost directly above it during Senate meetings.

South Bridge, on which Old College sits, is a dreary location, in contrast to the quad's grandeur. Hewn from massive blocks of Craigleith stone, Old College stands opposite a bookshop haunted by students, on the corner of a dog-legged road. This remnant of an older city leads downwards to the lower streets of the Cowgate and Grassmarket, above which the traffic crawls across vaulting bridges. The claustrophobic narrowness of the Cowgate and the dark vennels off both these districts are redolent of the distant past.

To walk through the high cast-iron gates of Old College is to enter another domain. An archaeological dig in 2010 undertaken before re-landscaping the quadrangle held out the promise of unearthing clues as to Darnley's fate. But although fragments of artefacts and bones were discovered, and a number of medieval graves, by far the most exciting discovery was a cache of bottles, bowls and test tubes, some still containing toxic chemicals. These were from the laboratory of the renowned eighteenth-century chemist Professor Joseph Black, and had been stored beneath the old library. There is a certain symmetry in one of the world's finest scientists experimenting in precisely the same location as that where early pyrotechnics irreparably damaged the fortunes of Mary, Queen of Scots and her country.

A contemporary drawing of the scene of the explosion peels back the nineteenth-century overlay of the city to reveal the Edinburgh Mary inhabited. This childlike depiction, sent to William Cecil, offers a crystal-clear layout and message. Alongside the crenellated city walls is the house reduced to dust; within and beyond the walls are orchards, and plentiful trees. On all sides are city guards in helmets and armed with muskets, either on foot or horseback. Various well-dressed individuals in tunics, half-cloaks, hats and wraps stand around in bemused conversation. Beside the half-naked body of Darnley, found dead in his nightclothes beneath a tree, lies his valet, discarded garments, a chair and a dagger. It would seem that, hearing intruders in the house, Darnley was lowered into the garden on the chair by Taylor. This pitiful picture was a humiliating last glimpse of the king, who was drawn with his nightgown lifted above his waist. Nor did the image allow any room for doubt about foul play.

While Moray made sure to be out of town at the time of the explosion – he claimed he had to return home because his wife had miscarried – Bothwell was all too visible and immediately became the prime suspect. According to John Guy, it was Morton who turned two of the Craigmillar conspirators – Bothwell and Maitland of Lethington – into assassins when they met at Morton's castle at Whittinghame. Yet as the Craigmillar Bond appears to suggest, murder had also been contemplated earlier, during the weeks of discussions there, before Morton's return from England. Quite what had been agreed between the leading figures at Craigmillar is unknown. If Morton was indeed the instigator of the plot, then he was acting, if not on Cecil's direct orders, then as this arch schemer hoped he would. Guy believes a reference in 1587, which refers to Darnley's death as being in part the responsibility of 'great persons still living', is shorthand for Cecil. It sounds plausible, since he was focused on keeping the Queen of Scotland far from the English throne. Thus, while Elizabeth and Mary had seemed to be reaching an accord, dealing directly with each other rather than through their diplomats and advisors, Cecil was determined to destabilise the country and cause such havoc that any understanding between them would be killed stone dead. As word of the murder, and suspicion of Mary's involvement, spread, this is precisely what happened.

Chapter 26

'How begrimed you are!'

THE FALLOUT FROM THE MURDER

The aftermath of events at Kirk o' Field was almost as dramatic and destructive as the explosion. It was Bothwell who brought the news to Mary, insisting that he was innocent of any part in it. She believed him. It seems most likely that, in collaboration with several others, he had arranged for the explosion, and lit the fuse. But it was Morton's Douglas relatives who, catching sight of Darnley fleeing in his white nightshirt, murdered him and his valet. Neighbours reported hearing Darnley crying: 'Pity me, kinsmen, for the sake of Jesus Christ who pitied all the world,' before silence fell. This points clearly to the Douglases.

Mary was profoundly shaken, not least because initially she believed she had been an intended victim along with her husband. Her Holyrood apartment was quickly draped in black, and she sent to Florence for the finest black cloth for mourning clothes for herself and her court. A swift post-mortem showed that Darnley had suffered a broken rib and internal injuries. This suggested either that he had been catapulted from the house by gunpowder yet remained miraculously externally unscathed, or had fallen in his haste to escape the room and, with his valet, had been suffocated when the Douglases realised he had not been killed in the blast. They had had the foresight, it would appear, to be nearby at the time of the explosion to make sure Darnley did not thwart his fate.

The king's corpse was put on a board and carried to Holyrood, where he was embalmed and prepared for public view. Mary stood looking down at his body, in the Chapel Royal, with an expression-less face. A few days later, he was buried in the chapel vaults.

The Tuesday following the murder, Mary attended the wedding of a close attendant – to onlookers this looked like callousness – but thereafter she was expected, by custom, to remain cloistered in a blacked-out room for forty days. Her doctors, seeing her distraught, and complaining of the dreaded pain in her side, suggested she should depart for Seton Palace, where she could find peace.

Leaving her child in the care of Bothwell and Huntly – another black mark against her – she retreated to Seton Palace. Doubtless she mourned, but she also brooded on her fear and rage. Learning that Kirk o'Field had been primed with gunpowder and was but a tinder spark from destruction must have been terrifying. Yet, as the finger of blame began to point towards Bothwell, she stood by him: publicly, rashly, stubbornly. In a further sign of how greatly she relied upon his support, she gifted him some of her mother's furs and Darnley's best horses and clothes. Bothwell being short and stocky where Darnley was a reed, the clothes had to be taken to a tailor. With extraordinary courage, given Bothwell's pugnac-ity, the tailor remarked sarcastically on the appropriateness of the dead man's clothes being given to the executioner. The insensitiv-ity of Mary's actions suggests either delusion or ruthless pragma-tism on the queen's part.

By now, she saw Bothwell as her most faithful and unswerving supporter. In this she was not wrong, even though much of his loyalty was coloured by self-interest. Already he was positioning himself, in his own mind, as her next spouse.

Appalled at Darnley's murder, and perhaps feeling guilty and remorseful at the failure of their marriage, the queen proclaimed her intention of finding and punishing the culprits. A farcical trial was held. Darnley's father, the Earl of Lennox, was due to attend and accuse Bothwell, but he was so fearful of reprisals against him from Bothwell's henchmen that, on being told he could not arrive with his army but with six men, he rode back to Glasgow. Meanwhile the city teemed with Bothwell's thugs.

Witnesses were silenced, to protect the conspirators, and others offered evidence distorted to protect the guilty. Some gave testimony elicited under torture. As Antonia Fraser writes, 'There is thus a veil of unreality over the depositions of these minor figures, as in the trial of criminals in some twentieth-century totalitarian state, since their words had to be carefully tailored not to incriminate the men then in power in Scotland.'

Predictably, Bothwell was acquitted. The *Diurnal of Occurrents* notes that he was 'made clean of the said slaughter, albeit that it was heavily murmured that he was guilty thereof'.

It is no wonder the populace was growing disenchanted with its ruler. Posters and placards had already been plastered on the city walls, denouncing the queen and her putative lover, along with her foreign staff (including Joseph Rizzio). The most infamous showed a hare and a mermaid. The hare was a component of the Hepburn crest, but lest the implication was lost, Bothwell's initials were added, as was a phallic circle of drawn swords. Around the mermaid, a symbol of prostitution, were Mary's initials. Incensed by the slur, Bothwell put up his own posters, and after his acquittal challenged anyone brave enough to denounce him openly to settle the matter in hand-to-hand combat.

The courts found culprits for the deed to quell public unrest. Sixty-two suspects were rounded up for Darnley's murder, but in the first months and years after his death only a handful of sorry individuals were executed for the crime while the instigators went free. Nicholas Hubert, known as 'French Paris', who was a former servant of Bothwell, told of how he had been kicked by Bothwell until he agreed to help him bring gunpowder into the Old Provost's Lodging. On the night of the explosion, Mary caught sight of him and remarked 'Jesu Paris, how begrimed you are!', unaware that he had been mining the building with her closest ally. Paris was an unwilling accomplice, but some of the others who were indicted may well have been entirely blameless. On their execution, some made last-minute denunciations of those who were truly guilty, foremost among them Balfour, Maitland,

Morton, Huntly and Argyll. Sensing corruption and a cover-up, the public grew increasingly sceptical. They believed, as Alison Weir remarks, that 'servants were being made scapegoats for the masters'.

Bothwell walked free on 12 April 1567. A few days later, as Lord Admiral, he led the queen's procession into Parliament. During these proceedings Mary took the Kirk formally under the Crown's protection, giving it the security it had wanted since 1560. She also ratified grants to Bothwell and to Morton. Since one was widely believed to be instrumental in the king's murder, as were the other's relatives, it is not surprising that Jenny Wormald writes, 'It did look suspiciously like the pay-off for the deed.'

A week or so later, one of the more infamous bonds in a long line of dodgy alliances during Mary's reign was agreed. The so-called Ainslie's Tavern Bond was a pact between Bothwell and the lords in which they agreed he had played no part in Darnley's murder and promised to support him in his wish to marry the queen. That he was already married to Lady Jean Gordon, sister of the Earl of Huntly, was deemed barely worth mentioning. Nor that by marrying him Mary would be ruining her reputation. Both factors were irrelevant to the lords' ambitions and would not be allowed to impede them.

Ainslie's Tavern sounds like the sort of low dive common on the High Street in these times. Its location has never been identified, and it has been suggested that rather than a fixed abode it refers to some sort of catering business that provided a feast for Bothwell, either in a tavern or in his Holyrood apartments. Whatever the venue, the bond was a serious matter, because it joined Bothwell with an astonishing array of leading figures who sound like something from 'The Twelve Days of Christmas'. It was signed by nine earls, eight bishops and seven barons, among them Morton, Maitland, Argyll, Huntly, Seton and Glencairn. Moray, as was his wont, was nowhere to be seen, although he was ever-present behind the scenes.

It was at Seton Palace that Bothwell first proposed to Mary. She rejected him without hesitation. A mere earl was beneath her, and this one would have sullied her name beyond repair. Since it was at Seton Palace that Mary had seen Bothwell assault a pauper so badly he died, she can have had no illusions about his character. Yet when he told her that the proposal was approved by all these powerful signatories to the bond, she must have paused. Rosalind Marshall is not alone in suggesting that at this point the queen probably conceived or agreed to a means by which she could marry without opprobrium, as if she had no alternative.

Two weeks after Bothwell's acquittal, Mary visited her son in Stirling Castle, planning to bring him back to Holyrood with her. But the Earl of Mar, in whose care James had been placed, refused to let her take him and allowed her access only with two of her attendants. He could not countenance Bothwell gaining control of the boy and holding the court to ransom. Thus, what was to have been a happy occasion, intended to lift the queen's spirits, was troubling. Mary spent two days with James, who would soon celebrate his first birthday, before leaving for Edinburgh.

On her return, she and her party spent the night at Linlithgow Palace. The next morning, on 24 April, they set out for the capital, but within a few miles of their destination they were intercepted by Bothwell and his men. For those taken wholly by surprise – and this might not have included the queen – it would have been an alarming incident. Mary was seized, along with Maitland, Huntly and Melville, and they were hurried off to Dunbar Castle.

It is said that once they were at Dunbar, Bothwell raped Mary. Her previously staunch ally Melville, who was one of the group accompanying the queen throughout her time in Dunbar, wrote that the so-called rape of a monarch, which was a treasonable act, must have been consensual. It seems he could not imagine anyone behaving so brutally with a queen, rather than that he had any evidence of Mary's willingness. One of Bothwell's servants said it happened 'with the Queen's own consent', and John Guy believes Mary would never have married him had he forced himself on her. They had separate rooms in the castle, although much was made of their proximity. Yet, suggests Guy, if Bothwell had tried to get into her room without her consent, she could have bolted the door or screamed for help.

Perhaps so. But since Mary's spirits were low, and Bothwell aggressive, it is also possible that she was overpowered and overwhelmed, by him and by her predicament. Rape victims are sometimes rendered speechless, freezing rather than fighting back. That Mary then spent almost two weeks at Dunbar, without attempting to escape, suggests less that she was contented than that she knew she was cornered. She later sarcastically commented on the lack of action on the part of her courtiers, who might have been expected to come to her aid.

No matter how it is interpreted, the abduction and seduction or rape were unedifying. They all but destroyed what was left of Mary's tattered reputation; Bothwell had none to lose. Dunbar Castle became a site of scandal, a subject of local gossip, but also of national disgrace. Compared with her arrival in 1566 as a courageous queen, pregnant and in danger of her life, Mary's visit the following year might have been seen to bring shame on the town.

If she had colluded in the abduction, then she did so with an eye to the future, to explain her capitulation to the idea of marrying Bothwell who was, in every respect, a dire candidate. From his perspective, he had to ensure she did not renege on their deal. Given the queen's miserable mood in following weeks, rape seems probable, regret certain. Melville and others overheard Mary, when in private with Bothwell, call for a knife so she could kill herself. If it was not forthcoming, she would drown herself.

Quickly – perhaps eagerly? – Bothwell was granted his divorce by Lady Jean Gordon, on the grounds of adultery with her maid. She had only recently recovered from a life-threatening illness, and perhaps saw this as her chance to embark on a happier future. Whatever her reasons, the divorce left Bothwell free to marry for the second time in little more than a year. On their return to Edinburgh, the couple's banns were proclaimed, although not without resistance. John Craig, John Knox's assistant at St Giles', had obviously heard rumours of what had gone on in Dunbar and was unwilling to allow this. He insisted, astonishingly, that before doing so he needed written proof from the queen that she had been neither raped nor abducted against her will. Mary provided this, but when Craig reluctantly announced the banns from the pulpit of St Giles', he vigorously denounced the couple's behaviour. When Bothwell then summoned him before the Privy Council to account for his insolence, which amounted to treason, Craig showed why Knox had chosen him as his sidekick. Instead of recanting, he delivered a sermon and castigated Bothwell: 'I laid to his charge the law of adultery, the ordinance of the Kirk, the law of ravishing, the suspicion of collusion between him and his wife the sudden divorcement, and proclaiming within the space of four days, and last, the suspicion of the King's death, which her marriage would confirm.'

Few clerics today, let alone then, would have the courage to speak truth to power so fearlessly. It can be seen as one of the early Scottish Protestants' finest moments. Bothwell responded in typical manner, by threatening to string Craig up. Nevertheless, the couple were married in a Protestant ceremony in the Great Hall at Holyrood. Some days earlier, Mary had elevated Bothwell to Duke of Orkney, since a duke was a fitting spouse for a queen. On the day of the wedding, 15 May 1567, it was the Bishop of Orkney who presided over the rites. Mary's Italianate black wedding gown, embroidered in gold and silver, was magnificent. Later she changed into a dress of golden yellow, though the suggestion of joy and sunburst this conveyed was far from her mood. Shortly after the ceremony, she was found in tears, telling her friend Bishop Leslie that she regretted agreeing to Protestant rites, and probably much else besides. It was said by Melville that during her short marriage to Bothwell, he was so cruel and controlling he frequently made her weep.

In a letter to the Bishop of Dunblane, Mary tried to explain why she had married him, and in such haste:

This realme . . . cannot be contained in order, unless our authority be assisted and forthset by the fortification of a man who must take upon his person in the execution of justice ... the travail therof we may no longer sustain in our own person, being already wearied, and almost broken with the frequent uproars and rebellions raised against us since we came in Scotland.

This is Mary's *j'accuse*, laying the blame on court and country, which she found impossible to govern, rather than taking responsibility herself. With hindsight, it is hard to imagine the swiftness of events that led to this miserable alliance, and its aftermath. Bothwell had been divorced twelve days when he became Mary's consort. Mary had been widowed twelve weeks. Exactly four weeks after their sombre wedding day, the unlikely couple were on the battlefield at the head of an army, about to fight for her inheritance.

Chapter 27

'Dressed in men's clothes, booted and spurred'

BORTHWICK CASTLE

The international community reeled at news of the Protestant marriage between a devout Catholic queen and a brutish Protestant lord who was not merely unworthy of her in status but widely believed responsible for the assassination of her previous husband. In Catholic Europe, Mary was seen to have betrayed the faith and, in so doing, had destroyed any hope of reigniting the Pope's cause within Scotland, let alone rallying English believers. At home, as abroad, she was deemed no better than a murderer who had colluded with her lover to kill her unwanted husband. That was not in itself the worst of crimes she could have committed, since monarchs had always ruthlessly rid themselves of troublemakers, and taking lovers was nothing new. Both could be forgiven and forgotten. Marrying Bothwell, however, was beyond the pale.

The rebels had by this time begun making moves against Bothwell and the queen. They presented their disaffection as resentment at seeing the duke raised above them, but this was window dressing, since it was they who had encouraged him to marry Mary. Their bond with the earl, which he had used to press his suit with the monarch, was quickly revealed as an expeditious tactic aimed at bringing down the queen, and him with her. In abducting Mary, Bothwell had crossed a line, and they ended all pretence of being his allies. Even before the marriage banns were called, the lords made a new bond among themselves promising to free the queen from Bothwell's clutches and take care and control of young James. They did not bother to ask if she wanted to be freed, because for them it was imperative to be seen to be acting in support of Mary's best interests, despite the fact they were likely to destroy her in the process.

Well aware of the trouble brewing, Mary summoned a muster of troops at Melrose in the Borders for the middle of June. Shortly before this, on 6 June 1567, she and Bothwell rode to Borthwick Castle, twelve miles south of Edinburgh. On the same day, the newly formed Confederate Lords, as they were called – twelve earls and fourteen lords – publicly announced their intention to liberate Mary from captivity. This declaration framed their actions as loyal, not rebellious.

Borthwick Castle was one of the places to which Mary retreated when she needed pampering and relaxation. She once confided to the Archbishop of St Andrews that the luxuriously appointed castle was 'the only place I felt truly happy and safe'. Nevertheless, on her final visit, the strain and dread she had endured since the murder of Rizzio and her husband spilled out in a shocking spectacle.

From the outside, Borthwick Castle looks impregnable, its walls fifteen-foot thick in some places, a mere eight in others. Built as a keep in the early fifteenth century for Sir William de Borthwick, as reward for offering to take James I's place as a hostage with the English, it has two massive tower blocks and a high surrounding wall. There used also to be defensive ditches. The ninety-foot-high towers are its distinguishing feature. Prisoners were sometimes taunted with the promise of being set free if they could leap between them. In the gloomy recess below, the dauntless or desperate would doubtless have broken their backs.

The Waverley railway line from Edinburgh to the Borders runs past Borthwick Castle, a picture-book fortress which, as dusk approaches, is lit by fairy lights strung along its lush avenue of trees. An altering whine in the train's engine alerts passengers to the castle's approach. At this point, the Borderlands are drawing close, the scenery growing wilder and more beautiful.

From the carriage it is possible to see the eastern flank of the walls, which were battered by Oliver Cromwell's cannons, and the steep outside staircase leading to its small, defensible door. A Saltire flag flies from the rooftop, whose battlements could have been drawn by a six-year-old. Across the aisle you can also catch a glimpse of Crichton Castle, Bothwell's seat, a crow's flight away.

On the January day when I arrived, a sprinkling of snow lay on the steep descent to the castle. Thick frost coated the hills and fields of the valley, above which it rises on a knoll. A private property, used for corporate entertaining, the castle has occasional open days when the public is admitted. Early for the appointed hour, I sat in the car under the trees leading to the castle gates. It was a Sunday morning, and nothing much stirred. Woodsmoke rose in the still air over the valley, and crows cawed in the bare branches overhead.

When Mary and Bothwell arrived for what might, at a stretch, be called their honeymoon, it was far from quiet. Bothwell soon departed to raise support for the anticipated attack. He was not long returned when, on 9 or 10 June, the Confederate Lords presented themselves at the castle walls with an army of 700 or more. Led by Morton, Home and Mar, this intimidating force included Atholl, Glencairn, Lindsay, William Ruthven (Patrick Ruthven's son) and the loathed Ker of Fawdonside, whom Darnley had pardoned without Mary's knowledge on Christmas Eve. Firing their guns to show they meant business, they then stated their intention of taking the queen into safekeeping and demanded that Bothwell come out and face them.

What followed was a telling moment in Mary's career. She and Bothwell's party could not resist opposition of this size. Nor could the castle withstand sustained siege. It seems strange they had relocated themselves here, when Dunbar or Hermitage castles would have offered better protection.

Late that evening, to allow Bothwell to escape from the postern gate to try to raise further support, Mary took to the battlements. From here she addressed the lords in a vigorous dialogue that soon descended into mudslinging on both sides. Since her marriage to Bothwell, members of the court had noted how much coarser the queen's language had grown. If nothing else, it seems Mary had learned from her famously profane husband. His 'filthy language' when talking about women the night before his wedding was so offensive that Sir James Melville left the table.

Sir William Drury, who was present at the Borthwick encounter, recorded that the queen traded insults with the army, her only means of defence. He then crossed this passage out, from embarrassment at the unseemliness of a woman he greatly admired thus demeaning herself.

It was an astonishing scene. For a monarch to sink so low, to lose all majesty, in full view of her foes, is hard to fathom. If those like Knox who believed women were not fit to rule had witnessed this, they would have considered themselves vindicated. Never before had Mary lost control of herself, and of a situation, in this way. As she leaned over the parapet, shouting to be heard, she unwittingly revealed how far she had come from the serene, confident and tolerant queen of better times. Where was the woman who after Rizzio's savage murder dried her tears and, intent on revenge, outwitted her captors and escaped with her life and her crown intact? She was long gone, leaving a much reduced woman in her wake.

After the slanging match, Mary retreated and awaited back-up. It was to be a long and fruitless wait. The following night, on hearing that the rebels had entered Edinburgh and had been applauded by crowds, she realised she had no option but to escape. Disguising herself as a page, 'dressed in men's clothes, booted and spurred' she was lowered by servants by rope from a window in the Great Hall onto a horse. This was no small feat, given the height of the window and terror of being observed. Then, in darkness, she rode a mile over the valley to Black Castle, at Cakemuir, where she was met by Bothwell. From there they made for Dunbar Castle, to remuster.

Originally reached by a portcullis and ramp, the entrance to Borthwick Castle would have been so narrow as to restrict access to one person at a time. Today there is no such squeeze, and the arched doorway into the wholly renovated castle is inviting rather than inimical. Inside, near to where the ancient door once stood, are the remains of a stone niche in which a piscina filled with water awaited visitors. Its purpose was less for hygiene than security. As guests washed their hands, it would have been possible to spot any weapons hidden up their sleeves.

The Great Hall is dominated by a medieval-sized hearth, in which a blazing log fire was leaping the morning of my visit. Close by is the window from which Mary clambered. One of several deep window recesses, it looks down onto the area beneath the walls. It is a long drop.

The hall is lit by a double corona of lights that hang above an enormous dining table. Once a year, the castle holds a celebratory banquet in honour of Mary, Queen of Scots, offering medieval dishes such as soup à la reine and tronçon of wild turbot with braised snails, pearl barley and garlic.

Staring down upon diners from the arrow-slit embrasures high on either side of the chimney are two sets of armour clutching swords. Their boots are so pointed they could shuck oysters. A minstrel's gallery, where musicians played for Mary, offers a vantage point over the room and its partially vaulted ceiling; the remnants of a medieval fresco are faintly discernible on the higher walls.

The top floor of the castle is reached by a twisting stone stairway scratched with masons' marks. The garrison lay beneath the roof, and in Mary's era 200 soldiers were permanently in residence. From there, a small door leads onto the roof, through which Mary made her way to the battlements.

Directly above the Great Hall lies the State Room, which the queen occupied. The fireplace is as capacious as that downstairs. Mary's bedchamber, off this grand hall, overlooks the gardens and the river valley beyond. Bothwell's apartment, as furnished today, is more sombre and imposing, with a claw-foot bathtub occupying a recess hidden by a velvet curtain. Most people in his era were lucky to have a bed, let alone sheets, but the queen insisted on fresh bed linen every day. Few Border lords would have taken a bath on a regular basis, if ever. But, if he wished to please a woman as sophisticated as Mary, it is just possible that Bothwell became an exception to that rule.

Putting Borthwick's comforts behind her, Mary rode swiftly for the safety of Dunbar. While she planned her next move, the Confederate Lords dealt her a further blow, which she discovered too late. They had turned James Balfour of Pittendreich, Keeper of Edinburgh Castle, to their side. Not that this would have been difficult. Although he was one of Bothwell's supporters, Balfour was a wily, treacherous individual whose own survival was uppermost in his thoughts.

A high-profile lawyer and judge, he had been a friend of Darnley and was taken into Mary's council not many weeks before his murder. A devout convert to Protestantism, he had been implicated as a young man, along with one of his brothers, in the murder of Cardinal Beaton at St Andrews. For his part in this he was imprisoned as a galley slave in the same French fleet as John Knox. When he negotiated his release by reverting to Catholicism, Knox reviled him. This would become a pattern. Throughout Balfour's self-serving and ruthless career he flip-flopped whenever it was to his advantage.

Balfour was widely believed to have been involved in Darnley's killing. It was at his brother Robert's house, at Kirk o' Field, that Darnley had been staying when the assassins came for him. Possibly the gunpowder for the deed was stored in his nearby house. After his name was publicly linked to the scandal, Balfour kept a heavy guard at his door, and avoided venturing out after dark, fearing the wrath of Edinburgh's citizens. When one of his servants threatened to reveal all, hoping to claim the reward and pardon that Mary offered for information about Darnley's death, Balfour murdered him.

After the Confederate Lords made their pact to free Mary from Bothwell, they signed Balfour up to their cause. Consequently, when the newly married couple were mustering their forces in Dunbar, Balfour lured her out earlier than she had intended by suggesting she should ride on Edinburgh and defeat the insurgents. He assured her the artillery of Edinburgh Castle would be used to aid her. Instead, as Mary and her men left Dunbar, he surrendered the castle to the Confederate Lords. His conditions were clear: he wanted assurance that his claim to its keepership would be upheld, and that he would be pardoned for his role in Darnley's murder and protected from reprisals by Mary's loyal lords. It was a devastating betrayal. Had Balfour held out against the Confederates, they could not have taken Edinburgh. Now, with the castle in their hands, the capital was theirs.

Chapter 28

'Burn the whore'

CARBERRY HILL

The morning of 15 June 1567 was gloriously bright and warm. Before dawn, the Confederate Lords, under Morton and Atholl's leadership, had left Edinburgh and taken the road to Musselburgh, six miles away. As the army wound out of the city, the sea would have glittered like turquoise under the morning sun. With Home and Morton's cavalry in front, the main troops marched under Mar, Glencairn, Lindsay and Ruthven. They carried a banner showing the body of Darnley at Kirk o' Field, beside which his fatherless son knelt, beseeching 'Judge and revenge my cause O Lord'. The message could not have been clearer.

Mary and Bothwell had spent the night at Seton Palace, a few miles further down the coast. This was the last moment of relative ease the queen would ever know, although her feelings the night before battle could hardly have been comfortable. Rising shortly after daybreak, they departed at five o'clock. The queen's army, encamped near Prestonpans, followed them onto Carberry Hill, a wooded knoll a couple of miles south-east of Musselburgh.

When Mary's troops met those of the Confederate Lords, the outcome was hard to predict. The rebels had raised a great deal of support, with their claim to be liberating the queen. They had a force of around 3,000, and while the queen's army was probably only marginally smaller, it was to shrink fast as the day progressed.

As so often on the trail of Mary, places that witnessed the dramatic high points of her story are almost eerily quiet. It takes an act of

determined concentration to visualise the scene, as the queen and
Bothwell arrayed their troops at the crest of what is now thick
woodland and received the first of several messengers. This was the
French ambassador du Croc, who was appalled at the behaviour of
the Confederate Lords towards their sovereign. A self-appointed
arbitrator, given permission by Maitland to parlay, he pleaded with
the queen to surrender. If she did, Bothwell would be given a safe
passage to leave the country, and she would be restored to the
throne. Mary's answer was unequivocal: the lords arrayed against
her had actively encouraged her to marry Bothwell, and she would
stand by him. In despair at her response and the lords' intransi-
gence, du Croc rode back to Edinburgh, leaving them to settle it
themselves.

The site of this encounter was again bathed in sunshine the day I
followed a well-trodden path into the woods. A canopy of trees
closed overhead, the leafy undergrowth criss-crossed by trails beaten
by legions of dog walkers. Birds were in full song, and the light
arrived filtered by the juicy green of summer leaves. A buzzard
wheeled lazily overhead.

The depth and age of the woods felt like a sanctuary rather than a
scene of battle. There was a shiver of leaves, and a roe deer was staring at me, its head and shoulders framed by bushes, as if hanging on
a wall. After a moment it stepped carefully out onto the path,
continuing to stare, before bounding off into the trees. High in the
treetops came the sound of something cracking nuts or seeds. One
tree trunk, either lightning-struck or diseased, rose lifeless into the
sky. Woodpeckers appeared to have been working on it, creating
their own Apprentice Pillar.

Noticeboards at various points tell the story of Mary's showdown
with the rebels. At the edge of the trees, by a meadow-like field, the
vista beyond opened up. Framed by foxgloves, it was intensely peaceful. Under brilliant sunshine, Carberry Hill overlooked the Firth of
Forth, blue as the summer Mediterranean. On the horizon was a
white cruise ship. Within what felt like touching distance were the
crags of Arthur's Seat and Holyrood Park, the fringe of the capital's

tenements, Leith Docks and the Pentland Hills. Across the sea lay the Ochil and Lomond hills and the rolling fields of Fife.

Not far off is the plain, near the hamlet of Cousland, where the Confederate Lords made camp. As Mary surveyed the prospect from horseback – towards the city, across the Forth and down coast deep into East Lothian – her kingdom was spread at her feet like a carpet. It is a poignant image, because within a few hours of reaching Carberry Hill, Mary would enter the closing chapters of her Scottish years. Come evening, her inheritance would be lost forever.

Heading deeper and higher into the woods the trail skirts the remains of an Iron Age fort behind which Mary's army probably positioned itself. Another sign points towards Queen Mary's Mount, but it is something of an anticlimax. Close to the back road to Tranent, on the edge of farmland, stands a tall memorial stone. It reads: 'At this spot, after the escape of Bothwell, Mary, Queen of Scots mounted her horse and surrendered herself to the Confederate Lords 15 June 1567'. The clearing in which it stands is small and scruffy, but originally it was open land until a copse was planted at the end of the eighteenth century. Behind the memorial is a slack electric fence around a meadow. Old beech trees stand guard over the memory of Mary's defeat. One is carved with names, initials and dates, a different historical record, written by penknife.

By evening, when Mary mounted her horse and followed William Kirkcaldy of Grange off the field, the day that had begun so hopefully had slipped beyond her control. For hours, messages had been relayed between both sides. Armed combat was suggested, between Bothwell and one of the Confederate Lords, but he insisted it must be Morton who met him. Ducking almost certain death, the aged and stout Morton nominated the more youthful Patrick Lindsay for this ordeal. He was more than willing, and in preparation took off his armour in order to gather his strength. But as the heat intensified, languor gripped both sides. In their suits of steel, they must have stewed. Before advancing, Mary's army awaited the arrival of Hamilton and his forces, but they never materialised. Nor did water, since the scouts sent out in search of it were taken captive. All the royal army had to drink was wine, with predictable results. The lords' army, by contrast, was camped close to a stream.

Gradually, disheartened and exhausted, Mary's side began to slip away. At the last moment, realising battle was futile, she vetoed Bothwell fighting Lindsay. As their numbers dwindled and it became clear that they were on the back foot, even her ebullient and pugnacious husband realised that marching against the Confederate Lords was no longer an option. There was nothing to be done but accept their terms, by which a proper inquiry into Darnley's murder would be made by Parliament and Bothwell given a safe passage to leave.

Naively, Mary believed the rebels would keep their word to treat her well and restore her to power; Bothwell, better versed in treachery, suspected otherwise. As the sun began to go down, they embraced publicly for the last time. As her secretary Claude Nau reported, Bothwell slipped her the bond from Craigmillar, which showed Morton and Maitland's hand in Darnley's death, and told her to keep it safe. He then galloped for Dunbar, where he intended to raise support. Only after he was beyond reach of enemy pursuit did Mary graciously allow her horse to be led away through the rebels' army, towards Edinburgh. On a pony behind her rode the faithful Mary Seton.

It would be interesting to know at what point Mary realised her predicament. Wearing borrowed clothes from Dunbar, where she had fled from Borthwick Castle without any of her belongings, she was dressed in a borrowed red petticoat that reached her knees, her sleeves tied back with ribbons, and a velvet hat. Although she was filthy from the dust and heat of the day, her demeanour, initially at least, would have been regal. Perhaps the sight of the two well-known young thugs who rode close by her side, as if guarding a prisoner, was her first apprehension of the trouble ahead. When soldiers began to jeer her, calling her a murderess and shouting 'burn the whore' and 'drown her', she would finally have grasped her situation. As she rode into Edinburgh, townsfolk, many of them women, came out to hurl insults at the queen who had so disappointed them. Tears of rage and shock ran down her face.

But while Mary was stunned at her reception, she was not cowed. On this nightmarish journey, she spoke ceaselessly of 'hanging and crucifying' the lords who had betrayed her. John Guy describes how she later summoned Lindsay, and told him, 'I will have your head for this'. None of this boded well.

For one night only, Mary was lodged in the house of Simon Preston, owner of Craigmillar Castle, Provost of Edinburgh, and until recently one of her adherents. His fortified residence, known as the Black Turnpike, was directly opposite the Tron Kirk. (An inscribed door lintel, believed to have been saved when it was demolished in 1788, is held at Sir Walter Scott's house at Abbotsford.) She was shown into a spartan room upstairs, where guards remained with her through the night. She was not allowed her maids, and her captors stood close by, even when she used the privy. Lest she forget what had brought her low, within view of her window was displayed the banner of the murdered Darnley and the beseeching child.

The night she passed is the stuff of fiction. By this point, Mary was several weeks pregnant, a fact that was widely known. This has generally been assumed as the reason why she stuck so faithfully to Bothwell. By now, it was obvious theirs was not a romance but a marriage of convenience. Mary must have feared that to betray Bothwell was to ruin the prospects of her unborn child.

At some point during these miserable few hours, she saw Maitland of Lethington passing on the street. Leaning out of the window, Mary called to him several times but, Judas-like, he ignored her, pulling his hat over his ears and pretending he heard nothing. Later, they did speak. Throughout their heated conversation, as Mary told her secretary Nau, Maitland could not meet her eye. He advised her to reject Bothwell and said that if she would acquiesce, he would be able to protect her from those who wanted her dead. She in turn told him that she would publish the Craigmillar Bond, showing who was responsible for the murder. As Nau relates: 'She told him that she feared that he, Morton and Balfour, more than any others, hindered the inquiry into the murder to which they were the consenting and guilty parties. Bothwell had told her so, who swore, when he was leaving her, that he had acted entirely by their persuasion and advice, and showed her their signatures.' In light of the threat the bond posed to the conspirators, it is likely that during Mary's stay in Preston's house, it was forcibly removed from her possession.

By morning, Mary was even more distraught. In a forlorn, ragged state, her bodice unlaced and her hair tumbling around her face, she leaned out of the window and appealed to the townsfolk to rescue her. An unruly crowd gathered, but nobody came to her aid. It is an astonishing vignette. In a few hours, Mary had lost her dignity, her crown and her people. All that was left was her life, and that hung in the balance.

Chapter 29

'Great, gloomy tower'

LOCHLEVEN CASTLE

The manner in which Morton treated the queen after her capture shows a bully enjoying his power. Since Mary would not renounce her husband, and with Bothwell on the loose, the lords were rightly worried that a vengeful rescue party might be raised to free her. As public anger against her mounted, it also became obvious that the queen would have to be moved somewhere more secure.

On the evening of 16 June, twenty-four hours after her surrender at Carberry Hill, Mary was walked by Morton and Atholl down the High Street to Holyrood Palace. Ahead of her strode 200 soldiers carrying the wretched accusatory Darnley banner. Bringing up the rear were the Confederate Lords, with 1,000 of their armed supporters. Historian Kate Williams writes, 'she was the single woman in the midst of over 1,200 men, the power imbalance never more evident'. No doubt the lords feared an ambush, but even onlookers must have felt this display of force around an unarmed captive was excessive. As crowds shouted and spat, Mary cried out that she was innocent of any crime and was being unlawfully held. The contrast between this and her first public procession through the same street in 1561 does not need to be underlined. The narrowness of the street, leading to the gates of the palace, was a gauntlet to be run. As one who had so enjoyed riding with the hounds, Mary was now like the hunt's prey, seeing all exits blocked.

Reaching Holyrood, she was attended by Mary Seton and Mary Livingston. Their feelings at seeing their mistress in utter disarray and distress can be imagined. Offering comfort, they were also able to dress the queen in her own clothes, a luxury she had not enjoyed for days. Nor had she eaten since being escorted from Carberry Hill, for fear of poisoning. Yet as she was sitting at dinner, midway through the meal, Morton, who stood threateningly behind her chair, abruptly told her she must leave at once. There was no time even to pack essential belongings, and she was hurried out in her nightgown – a substantial garment compared to those of today – and a cloak.

Vaguely hinting that she was being taken to see her son, Morton, along with Lindsay, Ruthven and an escort of soldiers, rode with Mary to Leith. There they made the crossing by boat to Fife and then continued on horseback through the night for Perthshire and Loch Leven. The loch is a short distance from Kinross, and the queen was rowed across the water to Lochleven Castle. The creaking of oars as they drew closer, in the grey early hours of the morning, must have been a melancholy sound. With every stroke Mary was being carried further from hope of rescue.

Under these frightening conditions, Mary was possibly too dazed to gather her thoughts. Later, perhaps, the many layers of significance of the lords choosing Lochleven for her jail would have become clear. This solid fortress had been built in the 1300s as a royal castle and state prison. It was owned by Sir William Douglas, Moray's half-brother by Margaret Erskine, former mistress of King James V. Old Lady Douglas's daughter Euphemia Douglas was married to Sir Patrick Lindsay, who had threatened to cut Mary into collops.

To be housed in a state prison was bad enough; to be guarded by Moray's brother and mother was surely testimony to his hand in bringing about Mary's disgrace. Moray had been clever enough never to be in the country during the most dramatic events, and yet his fingerprints were, and would continue to be, found on almost every action that destroyed her. At present, Moray was in France, but in due course he would visit Mary at Lochleven, an encounter that neither would forget.

Today, Lochleven Castle is an alluring ruin, reached by motor-boat, but its charms were evident long before our own time. Indeed, it was deemed so picturesque that in the late seventeenth century the Jacobite architect Sir William Bruce – who remodelled Holyrood Palace – designed his family home on the banks of Loch Leven so that it showcased the castle. When the front and rear doors of Kinross House stood open, the castle could be seen as the captivating focal point of a graceful, Renaissance vista. During the building of that magnificent country house, which would fit perfectly in the heart of Florence, Bruce and his wife stayed in the castle. Predictably enough, it is said to contain Mary's restless spirit.

Other than walls that would put off most attackers, the most prominent feature of the castle is the square tower, or keep, in which the Douglas family lived in considerable comfort. When Mary was helped from the boat, sometime after daybreak on 17 June, she was taken across the drawbridge and into a ground-floor room in the 'great, gloomy tower' that still dominates the island. Claude Nau records that 'the queen's bed was not there, nor was there any article proper for her rank'. Soon after she was given rooms in the Glassin Tower. This romantic-looking conical building stood across the courtyard from the keep. The queen's chambers, on the second and third floors, were more suitable for her needs.

From her windows, where she must have spent many hours scanning the horizon, Mary watched the waters lapping the castle walls. In 1567, the island was much smaller than today. A massive drainage scheme in 1830 made the loch's level drop, in the process enlarging the castle grounds and adding three new islands to the loch's previous four.

Weeks or months after her arrival Mary was again relocated, to the impregnable keep. This was entered by an outdoor wooden staircase that opened into the second-floor hall, where she was to spend most of her imprisonment. Her rooms occupied the fourth and fifth floors, above cellars, kitchen and hall. Her main living area was on the fourth floor, and overhead lived her physician, who did not want for work. These private apartments were reached by spiral staircase.

To make way for Mary, the Douglases moved their quarters to the hall in the inner courtyard, although Sir William's young wife,

Lady Agnes Douglas, usually slept in the same bedroom as Mary. The guard around her was strict, and Lady Douglas became a human limpet, sticking to her at all times. So too did the laird's daughter and niece who, aged about fourteen and fifteen, were infatuated with their reluctant guest. While there is no evidence that the Douglases were in any way cruel, Sir William was under orders from Morton to kill Mary if she tried to escape, and would not have hesitated.

After her gruelling overnight journey and the shock of recent days, Mary scarcely ate or spoke for two weeks. Her fears were in no way allayed when Morton, on his departure, consigned her to the care of Lindsay and Ruthven.

This tiny outcrop, a mile from shore, was to be Mary's jail for the next ten and a half months. During that period, the pieces on the political board continued to shift, in and out of her favour, both at home, in England and on the Continent. Unthinkable though it was on the day she arrived at Lochleven, by early summer the following year the tide appeared to be swimming with her.

Even before she arrived at Lochleven, the ruling lords' council had issued a warrant for her indefinite incarceration. It cited as cause the fact that she had actively helped Bothwell and hindered the apprehension of Darnley's murderers, all of which conspired 'to the final confusion and extermination of the entire realm'. This document was signed by Morton, Atholl, Mar, Home, Glencairn, Lindsay, Ruthven and others. That the ringleaders of the rebels were willing to commit high treason shows their confidence. From this day onwards, the Confederate Lords revealed the depths of their venality, self-interest and conviction. Individually, many of them were gifted and even – up to a point – moral and decent men. What drove them to such lengths was in some instances as much religious or constitutional conscience as expediency and power. Regardless of their individual positions, collectively they posed a potential threat to the Crown itself.

That was the view of Elizabeth I when she heard that Mary had been imprisoned. Far from siding with the Confederate Lords, as they had anticipated, she spoke of sending her army to free the queen. This was not a sign of affection for her cousin, for whom she now felt little warmth, but outrage that any monarch could be so treated. Persuaded not to go to war but instead to use diplomatic channels, Elizabeth sent her envoy Sir Nicholas Throckmorton to negotiate Mary's release and reinstatement. It was a deadly mission, as well he knew. Throckmorton was a seasoned ambassador. He understood how it felt to be imprisoned by enemies, having once come close to execution by the French. He was a kindly advisor to Mary, but his heart was with the Protestants, as a result of which neither side wholly trusted him. Cecil, however, thought highly of him.

Scotland at this moment was synonymous with violent death, even of the highest ranking. Throckmorton was refused permission to visit Mary and was politely warned by Maitland not to interfere, for his sake as well as the queen's. Even so, he persisted because Mary's life was plainly in danger. Various of the Confederate Lords had been behind the murders of Rizzio and Darnley, and it would have been simple to dispose of the queen in such a remote location and pass it off as an accident or suicide. This was a fact of which Mary would have been all too aware.

Profoundly alarmed, Throckmorton smuggled a message to her, carried in the scabbard of Sir Robert Melville's sword – the brother of Mary's aide Sir James Melville – pleading with her to break all ties with Bothwell. She refused, because 'taking herself seven weeks gone with child, she should acknowledge herself to be with child of a bastard and to have forfeited her honour'. At this response, Throckmorton was uncertain what more he could do. News of the pregnancy, meanwhile, shocked Elizabeth, who, heeding scuttlebutt rather than knowing the facts, assumed Mary had conceived out of wedlock. Hearing that the lords planned to make her abdicate, Throckmorton smuggled another letter to Mary in the same manner. In it, he urged her to agree to this step, solely in order to save her life. A forced abdication was not legal, as he told her, and could later be revoked.

In early July, during which this unfolded, Mary appeared to be in better spirits. She was eating and dancing and 'getting fat', according to one observer, evidence possibly of her pregnancy. But, perhaps on learning of the plan to force her to abdicate, or simply because of the strain of her incarceration, Mary suffered a miscarriage sometime in the third week of July. During this distressing episode, she was found to be carrying twins – midwives would as a matter of course check the afterbirth for any abnormalities. That fact could not have been established unless she was at least eight weeks pregnant, and probably considerably further gone than that. This therefore places the conception either around the date of her wedding, or at some point before she and Bothwell were married in May, maybe in Dunbar Castle after her abduction and alleged rape. It was not so early that it confirmed she had been unfaithful to Darnley, as some alleged. Not that they could have proved who the father was either way.

The miscarriage caused Mary to haemorrhage, and she became exceedingly ill. Added to physical pain was the anguish of such a loss. The twins were buried in the castle grounds, although their resting place has not been discovered. So far from help and any prospect of rescue, Mary's misery can only be guessed. Since she had never fully recovered from the birth of her son and her collapse at Jedburgh, her physician must have been anxious about the effect of this new blow on her strength and mental state.

The Confederate Lords' regime was no more heartless than many that were to follow. Nevertheless, it is disturbing that, seeing how low she had been brought, the lords took advantage of this moment to press their case for abdication. While she was bed-bound, Sir Robert Melville arrived on the island, with two notaries, and privately encouraged her to sign, for her own safety. It was the intimidating Lindsay, along with Ruthven, who presented her with the deeds of abdication. When the queen refused, Lindsay roughly handled her, saying he would cut her throat if she did not agree. The echo of the night in her supper room at Holyrood Palace after Rizzio's murder is unmistakable.

With utmost reluctance, Mary signed her abdication, all the while, as Claude Nau writes, stressing it was done against her will. A few days later, at the crowning of James VI in Stirling, Lindsay and Ruthven swore an oath in church, before the Bishop of Orkney and John Knox, that the prince's mother had abdicated entirely of her own will. Few lies were more blatant.

In the same meeting with Robert Melville, Mary conceded to Moray becoming Regent, and to a council of lords, with Morton at its head, taking charge of the country until his return from France. Moray was by now heading home to assume this role. Mary might already have known that, early in July, he had been urged to return to take up the Regency. Passing through London, Moray spoke with Elizabeth and the Spanish ambassador, Guzman de Silva. He professed grief and anger at his sister's forced abdication, and his determination to help her in any way he could, but nobody was fooled.

Compounding Mary's troubles was the Pope's declaration that, on hearing of her marriage to Bothwell, he had broken with her. Added to this, Bothwell was outlawed by the Confederate Lords. This shrewd move prevented him from trying to raise support for the queen, and forced him to flee, first to Spynie Palace, and thence to Orkney. He set sail for the north with his army in four men-of-war he had in his charge as Lord Admiral. His time in Scotland was nearing its end.

By the middle of July, the first whispers of the so-called Casket Letters were circulating, boding ill for the queen. These were a stash of letters, purportedly between Mary and Bothwell, that were found in a silver casket under the bed of Bothwell's Edinburgh tailor, George Dalgleish. Their wording seemed to prove her foreknowledge of Darnley's murder. The contents of this box changed in subsequent months, suggesting the inclusion of at least one forgery that was later removed. That so-called proof of her guilt was not produced at an earlier stage to justify her imprisonment is baffling, if they were indeed genuine. The authenticity of this collection of supposedly incriminating documents would be debated – and allegedly proved

– by her foes while Mary was imprisoned in England, and used to condemn her, in her absence, in an English court. Long before then, however, they tarnished her name and her prospects.

The cache that was presented as evidence against her was written in French. It contains eight letters, two marriage contracts and twelve supposedly adulterous sonnets, from Mary to Bothwell. None of the letters has an addressee. Each ends suddenly, with no signature. Only one is dated. The originals have disappeared, leaving contemporary translations. At face value, some of the contents are damning, suggesting collusion between lovers in a plot: 'You make me dissemble so much that I am afraid thereof with horror, and you make me almost to play the part of a traitor. Remember that if it were not for obeying you I had rather be dead.' And: 'Think also if you will not find some invention more secret by physick, for he is to take physick at Craigmillar and the baths also. And shall not come forth of long time.' When unpicked, however, discrepancies of dates and events, as well as their tone, cast doubt on the letters being anything more than fragments or first drafts of genuine correspondence from Mary to unknown recipients. These were interspersed with other material, possibly forged, or from someone else's letters. That Cecil dismissed the sonnets and marriage contracts as irrelevant speaks for their negligible significance.

Given that this material was initially overlooked by Mary's accusers, yet later produced as proof of her guilt, it is tempting to view the Casket Letters in the same light as the notorious Zinoviev letter that saw Ramsay MacDonald ousted as Labour prime minister in 1924. That missive, purportedly from a senior member of the Communist Party in Moscow to its British counterpart, urging seditious activity a few days before the British general election, led to a Conservative landslide. It has since been widely accepted as a forgery.

Debate continues to this day over the provenance and authenticity of the Casket Letters. Jenny Wormald believes they incriminate Mary, and makes a persuasive case, but many historians, including Antonia Fraser, remain either sceptical or convinced this was a brazen attempt to frame the queen. Whatever the truth, rumours of evidence proving the queen's murderous intentions began to spread, and soon reached Elizabeth I.

Five days after abdicating, Mary heard the castle guns being fired and saw bonfires blazing in the courtyard at Lochleven. The laird was having a party, and when Mary asked what this signified, she was told it was a celebration for her young son becoming king. Her captor indicated that she too should be in celebratory mood, but unsurprisingly, the queen retreated indoors, in tears.

James, who had recently turned one, had been crowned in the Protestant church near Stirling Castle, with Morton and Home saying his vows on his behalf. How his mother must have felt envisaging the scene, with her most loathed enemy at its heart, we can only speculate. But amongst feelings of betrayal, rage and sorrow she must surely also have felt concern for James. If his guardians and keepers could treat her like this, how would one so young and unprotected fare under their control? Uppermost in her mind was the fact that, at the age of twenty-four, after less than six years' rule, she had been robbed of her crown.

Chapter 30

'He who does not keep faith . . .'

ESCAPE FROM LOCHLEVEN

In the middle of August, the newly returned Moray stepped into a boat and was rowed across Loch Leven to meet his half-sister. It was a tempestuous and unpleasant episode. Entering Mary's chamber, where she had no option but to receive him – gone were the days of giving or refusing an audience – Moray began by railing against her ill-judged marriage to Bothwell. When he had calmed down, he asked her advice on whether he should take up the offer of the Regency, even though he had already accepted. Her response was hardly that of a woman whose spirit has been crushed. Reminding him that he was her father's bastard son, she continued, 'He who does not keep faith where it is due will hardly keep it where it is not due.' Stung, Moray told her that he had in fact agreed to become Regent. They parted acrimoniously. Antonia Fraser believes that Moray almost certainly threatened Mary with execution, leaving her to spend the rest of that evening in panic.

Moray returned the following day. As John Guy writes, 'he used every technique of psychological intimidation to induce a sense of gratitude in her, alternately threatening and comforting her, and promising to mitigate the worst plans of Lindsay and his friends if she cooperated, even though they were really acting on his behalf'. During that conversation, she embraced him and gave him her blessing as Regent. It was typical of Mary, to be one day all but estranged from someone, the next showing affection and gratitude. Whether she really believed Moray would honour his promises, of course, is unlikely. As with Darnley, the point had been reached when she understood exactly the sort of man she was dealing with.

A week later, on 22 August 1567, Moray was appointed Regent. In his relatively short tenure of the role he had long hoped for, he proved a sensible, competent ruler. Nobody can doubt his political nous. But that he was lacking in integrity – at the very time when his sister was being castigated for her 'moral turpitude' – is also indisputable. When Mary lay, presumed dying, in Jedburgh, Moray had begun purloining her possessions. Now, as Regent, he had the right to all her jewellery, or so he told himself. At Holyrood, he appropriated everything, even items that could not be considered the property of the state, such as gifts to Mary from her husband Francis and Henri II. Her priceless collection included rings and necklaces, brooches and ornaments. Moray gave some to his wife but held onto the prize: a magnificent many-stringed necklace of black pearls, each as fat as a grape, which Mary had worn when Queen of France. The year after her abdication, he offered them for sale to Catherine de' Medici and the covetous Elizabeth I. In the end, they passed into Elizabeth's hands, at a bargain price. She is wearing them in a portrait celebrating the defeat of the Spanish Armada. Despite Elizabeth's rage at the lords forcing Mary off the throne, and her refusal either to acknowledge Moray as Regent or James VI as monarch, the Queen of England seems not to have been squeamish about appropriating her cousin's belongings. Moray was probably correct when he implied to Cecil that for all her protestations, Elizabeth did not entirely dislike the situation in Scotland.

In her will, Mary had bequeathed certain of her private jewels to relatives but had asked that others were to become the property of the Scottish Crown estate. Moray honoured none of that. Showing how deeply his behaviour grieved her, on hearing of Moray's assassination, in 1570, Mary arranged for a pension to be paid to his killer. She knew how to nurse a grudge. His murderer was a member of the Hamilton family, which had long suspected Moray of intending to win the throne for himself; Mary shared that belief.

But while Moray had only a few years ahead of him, the end of her own days in Scotland was fast approaching. Buoyed by the contents of the Casket Letters, and by public support for their regime, the Confederate Lords issued an Act against Mary in early December, charging her with the murder of Darnley and with intent to murder her son. Shamelessly backdating their justification for high treason, they claimed these charges were the reason for locking her up. In this telling, their actions were recast as legal.

For his part, Bothwell had evaded the dogged Kirkcaldy of Grange and had sailed for safety to Norway. There, on disembarking, he had the sort of bad luck more usually found in soap operas. He was recognised by kinsmen of Anna Throndsen, the Norwegian mistress he had promised to marry, who notified the King of Norway and Denmark of his presence. Immediately, Bothwell was imprisoned as a political hostage. Much like his wife, he was to spend the rest of his life behind bars. Unlike Mary, his prisons grew increasingly grim. It was said that by the final stages of his life, his cell was too low for him to stand, and that he died insane.

With prospects fading of bringing Bothwell to account for Darnley's death, the lords made Mary their target. The timing was wily. She was charged on 4 December, four days before her twenty-fifth birthday. In Scottish custom, any monarch on reaching the age of twenty-five could revoke land grants and preferments given to the nobility during their minority. Even though Mary was technically no longer queen, and knowing that her abdication was illegal they appeared to be taking no chances when safeguarding their assets. Yet even as they retrospectively shored up their arguments for imprison-ing her, Mary's allies were rallying. The Hamiltons, who saw them-selves as next in line to the throne, were eager to topple Moray and began to plot his overthrow. They and the Setons openly announced their support for the queen. Mary was secretly sent a ring represent-ing Aesop's fable of the mouse and the lion, in which the mouse gnaws through the lion's ropes. Presumed to be a present from Mary Fleming, who was married to Maitland of Lethington, Mary inter-preted it as Maitland promising to help her.

Closer to home, some of the queen's captors were falling under
her spell. Ruthven had already been dismissed for begging her to
marry him if he helped her flee, although this was more likely oppor-
tunism than love. Soon, George Douglas, the youthful and good-
looking brother of Sir William, the laird, grew increasingly close to
her, and it appears that Mary was far from reluctant in encouraging
his hopes. Knowing as we do what the future held for her, it is easy
to skip over this part of the drama, which was growing more convoluted with every month she spent on the island. George Douglas is
usually represented as besotted and faintly risible in his affection for
the beleaguered Mary. Sir Walter Scott is more generous. In his
novel *The Abbot* he depicts Douglas as a noble, brave and courtly
gentleman, devoted to the queen and her liberty. Less kindly, he kills
him off on the battlefield, many years before his real-life counterpart
died.

From Mary's perspective, Douglas was a better prospect as a
spouse than Bothwell had ever been. At this messy juncture in her
saga, with the pregnancy ended and Bothwell as good as gone, speculation was beginning to mount over whom she might next marry.
Even Morton was suggested as a candidate, although the lords knew
he would be a hard sell. Had Mary married George Douglas, who
knows how events might have unfolded. The delicacy of her situation in Lochleven was as finely calibrated as a goldsmith's scales. In
hindsight, her flight and the tragedy that followed seem inevitable.
But in the spring and early summer of 1568, things might have gone
another and better way.

Whatever Mary's true feelings or intentions, George Douglas
represented her chance of breaking free. Also in thrall to her was a
page known as Willy Douglas or 'the orphan', who was either one of
the laird's young cousins or illegitimate children. Both men were to
remain intensely loyal to Mary. Douglas was a member of her retinue in England for some time, and Willy was her servant for the rest
of her life; he is remembered in Mary's last will and testament.

It was Willy, rather than the swashbuckling George, who proved
dauntless in liberating the queen from her tower. His first audacious

bid to free her failed, and the method he devised – of disguising the queen as a washerwoman – was later comically employed by Kenneth Grahame in *The Wind in the Willows*, as Toad is sprung from jail. For the participants, it was anything but amusing, since the boatman recognised Mary and returned to the castle. After that misfire, which fortunately for Mary never came to the ears of Sir William, George quarrelled ferociously with his hot-headed brother and was banished from the island. This enabled him to gather support, and some time later Willy arranged Mary's exit.

Conveniently for their plans, Lady Douglas had just given birth. While she recovered, she was unable to maintain her surveillance of the queen. Taking advantage of this opportunity, Willy and Mary plotted an escape which drew on Mary's love of dressing up and disguise. As the start of May was approaching, they arranged a series of boisterous May Day festivities, in which Willy played the fool with Mary in tow. A notoriously rowdy and spirited occasion, in which the principle of misrule permitted normal conventions to be overturned for a short spell, May Day allowed commoners as well as aristocrats a well-deserved break from formality. The games and play-acting orchestrated by Willy and the queen were a cleverly calculated distraction, creating an air of chaos in which their actions might go undetected. That Mary was prepared to risk such a venture shows the depths of her despair. Letters she had previously smuggled out begging her relatives in France, as well as Elizabeth I, to save her, had brought no rescue.

Dressing up, not as a man as so often before but as one of her own attendants, Mary managed, with considerable difficulty, to elude her teenage admirers. There were many scares during the process, obliging her to call upon her acting skills and Willy to summon nerves of steel. When old Lady Douglas noticed horsemen gathering on the far shore of the loch, Mary distracted her by castigating her perfidious son Moray. Soon after, the laird spotted Willy tampering with the boats, which he intended to scupper, obliging Mary to pretend to faint.

After dinner, Willy slipped the laird's keys into his pocket while serving him wine – it was surely not his first glass – and Mary, in maid's disguise, walked coolly across the busy courtyard and out of the castle gates. When it was clear nobody was following, Willy threw the keys to the gate into the mouth of a cannon and hurried her to the boat. There, she hid beneath the boatman's bench. Even when the queen was recognised by washerwomen on the loch side, she was not betrayed. It must have been a heartening moment, showing that not all her subjects were against her. Might her fortunes be on the turn?

Waiting on the mainland were George Douglas and her servant John Beaton, who galloped with her to where Lord Seton and others awaited. That night Mary crossed the Firth of Forth in quite different spirits from her last trepidatious crossing. By midnight on 2 May, she was safely ensconced in Niddry Castle, surrounded by supporters. Against all expectations, she was free.

Chapter 31

'By battle let us try it!'

As in previous moments of political crisis, Mary seems to have been energised by the prospect of a fight. Leaving Niddry Castle with Lord Seton a day later, she rode west for Cadzow Castle. This was an ancient Hamilton retreat, a former royal hunting lodge, whose ruins sprawl on the edge of the Avon gorge. The castle might still be standing had the Hamiltons not supported the queen, thereby bringing the wrath and the cannons of the Confederate Lords upon them.

On Mary's liberation, a strongly worded proclamation was drawn up, though never made public. It denounced the lords as traitors, declared Mary's abdication invalid and named the Hamiltons as heirs to the throne after her and James. Many rallied to her, including an impressive number of earls, bishops and lairds. Not all the west was for her, but with the powerful Earl of Argyll switching back to her side, along with the ever-faithful Huntly and the likes of John Maxwell, Lord Herries, she hoped to bring the country under her control once more. Her aim was to reach Dumbarton Castle, which had held out for her during Moray's Regency, and await back-up from the Highlands and Islands, and possibly France. Yet even while a guest at Cadzow, Mary recognised the dangerous fault lines within her own side. The Hamiltons were like cuckoos, hoping that Mary would fall from the nest and leave them with the roost to themselves. They did not hide their ambitions. That might explain why the proclamation that named them as heirs was never published, and why Mary seemed, in principle at least, open to the improbable idea of marrying Châtelherault's mentally ill son.

Keen to leave Cadzow, Mary's plan was to give Glasgow a wide berth, since this was where Moray was staying. Outraged at her escape, he had refused to negotiate with her. But while she hoped to reach Dumbarton Castle without engaging, she declared herself prepared to face him if necessary: 'By battle let us try it!' she said, reminding her entourage of her martial lineage. The Hamiltons, who saw an opportunity to crush the Regent, were eager to encourage rather than avoid conflict. As the royal army skirted the city, Moray's hastily mustered men – around a third smaller in number than the Royalists – quick-marched the three miles from their meeting place in today's Gallowgate. Ahead of them raced 200 cavalry under Kirkcaldy of Grange. Riding pillion behind the horsemen were soldiers carrying hagbuts, heavy, muzzle-loaded firearms. When they reached the village of Langside, the hagbutters concealed themselves in the thick hedges along the main street, guns at the ready. Moray's army was in place on the hilltop, now Queen's Park, even before the Royalists took up their position to the west.

Queen's Park, the Southside's 'heart and lungs', is a lushly-treed, open public space with magnificent views. Towards its crest there is a cobbled enclosure, with a vantage point that looks over the rooftops of Glasgow in the valley below, with its cathedral, universities and spired churches. Beyond, to the north, you can see as far as the Campsie Fells and Ben Lomond. The park was quiet when I visited, the children's play area empty. On a woodland path that descends the hill, it was possible briefly to imagine this was countryside, miles from concrete and traffic. Among the trees at the park's highest point, in a clearing, a circle of low boulders around the ashes of a bonfire are thought to be the remains of a military post during the Battle of Langside. But the hill's history stretches much further back. Two and a half thousand years ago there was an Iron Age fort that was later used by the Romans as a camp. More recently, it was a popular Sunday walk for Victorian Glaswegians, who would leave the sooty city and cross the river to eat apples and gooseberries with cream in the park, supplied by local fruit growers. These days the park has allotments, whose holders can grow their own fruit.

Few places have been better named than the district of Battlefield, where Mary's army faced Moray's. Where Battlefield Road meets the park, men in armour and horses in breastplates assembled. Musketeers and pikemen marched alongside them, with carts bearing provisions and medical supplies at the rear. A towering pencil monument marks the moment when the two sides rushed upon each other on 13 May 1568. A lion tops the monolith, a fitting symbol for the queen who was starting to roar, facing the position the queen's army took, at Clintcart Hill, now Mount Florida. The memorial is built where the Regent's right flank stood, at the foot of the park.

Langside became a flourishing weaving community in the eighteenth century, and its terracotta tenements and villas embedded in gardens hint at its Victorian and Edwardian swagger. In Mary's era, it was a strung-out rural settlement amidst open land. Taking advantage of his smaller army's advantageous position, Moray attempted to outmanoeuvre a formidable enemy. That he succeeded was in large part because of the military acumen of Morton and Kirkcaldy of Grange.

After an unproductive exchange of artillery from the armies' respective hills, Hamilton led the vanguard with his mass of infantry. As his men charged up Langside's narrow main street, Moray's hagbutters picked them off from behind the hedges. Battlefield Road, narrower than today, was where the fighting was fiercest. For infantry and cavalry, it was a death trap.

Lord Herries's Borders cavalry were ferocious in attack, and while the Hamilton infantry were being destroyed, they managed to press the Regent's cavalry back. When it seemed Moray's cavalrymen were faltering and Herries' attack might succeed, Kirkcaldy of Grange – destined to be Mary's nemesis – summoned reinforcements and shored up their line. All might still have gone the queen's way had the soldiers under the command of the Earl of Argyll not been thrown into disarray by their leader's sudden indisposition. Argyll was Moray's brother-in-law, and whether he was genuinely unwell, or was secretly working on Moray's behalf, remains unknown. Rosalind Marshall writes, 'there were plenty of people ready to decide that his illness was more diplomatic than real'.

Without Argyll, the Highlanders fell apart. Seeing this, from her observation post at Cathcart Castle to the south (now demolished), Mary rode headlong down among them, hoping to spur them into action, and prepared to lead the attack. But almost unbelievably, she found her men keener to fight each other than the enemy. Quickly it became clear that all was lost. Her courage failing her, she realised she must flee.

The Battle of Langside was a mere skirmish compared to many conflicts, and yet it was utterly decisive. Estimates vary between 100 and 300 dead on Mary's side – including many Hamiltons – whereas Moray's troops were barely scathed. More of the queen's supporters might have perished if the Regent had not called back the pursuit of those abandoning the field. In his memoirs, Melville recorded that the Regent ordered his men to 'seize and not slay' the escapees, and added that 'Grange was never crewell'. The worst casualties occurred in the first encounter, in Battlefield Road, he noted, 'be [by] the schot of the soldiours that Grange had planted . . . behind some dykis'.

In less than an hour, the fight was over. The queen, who had been crowned on the thirtieth anniversary of Flodden lost her throne on the battlefield. She appears to have been oblivious to the fatal precedent her grandfather and father set.

Chapter 32

'Three nights living like the owls'

DUNDRENNAN ABBEY AND EXILE

In abject panic at the thought of being captured by Moray, Mary fled from Langside. She was no longer the assured monarch, intent on regaining her throne, but a fugitive whose only thought was escape. On the battlefield, some of her closest supporters had been taken prisoner, among them the stalwart Lord Seton. He would not be released until the Regent Moray was assassinated eighteen months later. In the harrowing days to come, the Borderer Lord Herries was to be Mary's devoted aide. Since the road to Dumbarton was blocked by Moray's men, and certain he would be giving chase, they rode by night for Herries' lands in the south-west. They may have stopped at his castle at Corra and then made for the Maxwell family seat, Terregles Castle, near Dumfries. It was a hellish journey for the queen, who had lost her nerve and dreaded to hear her half-brother closing in on her. Such was the party's alarm, they destroyed a wooden bridge at Tongland to delay those on their trail. A rare moment of respite for Mary was found when a cottager offered her sour milk and oatmeal.

In his memoirs, Nau's record of this episode is given simply as a list, as if, even years later, the queen could barely speak of it: 'How she drank some sour milk in the house of a poor man. How she borrowed some linen. How she caused her head to be shaved. How she was twenty-four hours without eating or drinking. How the Laird of Lochinvar gave her some clothes and a hood.'

Nothing remains of Terregles Castle, which was demolished after the present Terregles House was built, yet it represents a keystone in

Scotland's history. The four-poster bed in which Mary might have slept that night now lies in Traquair, silent witness to the queen's final hours in her homeland. For it was here, at Terregles, that Mary announced she was going to England, to seek Elizabeth's help. Her lords and associates were astounded, appalled, but she dismissed their protests. There would have been an air of unreality about the scene, as the queen, almost unrecognisable with her shorn hair, and wearing hand-me-downs, refused to listen to their concerns. It was as if the trauma of the battle had paralysed her powers of reason. In her mind, the only safe option was to throw herself upon the mercy of her cousin in England, a relative who – as her advisors would point out – had so far resisted all attempts to meet, and had done nothing to free her from Lochleven.

At present, she was in the south-west of Scotland, a Catholic heartland. Soon she would be in the north of England, where Catholic interests also remained powerful. It was a dangerous environment in which to operate, given the threat she posed to the English queen. Yet despite her supporters' dogged attempts to make her see sense, she was hell-bent on crossing the border. Few in her entourage can have slept much that day, as they awaited dusk, when they could embark on the final stages of their journey.

In darkness, Mary and her companions left Terregles and rode nearly thirty miles to Dundrennan Abbey on the Solway Firth, from where she planned to sail to England. Days later, when recording that flight in a letter to her uncle Charles, the Cardinal of Lorraine, she spoke of spending three nights 'living like the owls'. Their calls would have filled the Galloway dark as the party slept on the cold earth, with no fire for cooking or comfort for fear of woodsmoke giving away their presence.

When finally they reached the abbey, it was to be a refuge for her last night in the country. Here she was a guest of the Cistercian monks who surreptitiously kept the old faith alive in this remote outpost, far from the eyes of the Protestant regime. Begun in the later twelfth century, Dundrennan had been one of the most prestigious Cistercian abbeys in Scotland, second only to Melrose. It answered to its mother house of Rievaulx in Yorkshire, but even before the Reformation it was falling into disrepair. When Mary arrived, it was run by a commendator, not an abbot. This was an administrative rather than a spiritual placement intended to stamp out the corruption with which this order, like all others, had been increasingly afflicted. Since this unordained official was Lord Herries' son Edward Maxwell, their welcome was warm. Edward was a devout Catholic and had defied orders to destroy the abbey. The arrival of Mary was bittersweet: an honour he would remember for the rest of his life, but tainted by the queen's miserable circumstances. Meanwhile, knowing that the Regent could be in pursuit, the abbey inmates must have quaked, wishing the queen would be on her way.

Today, Dundrennan village, which acts as gateway to the abbey, is a hamlet of whitewashed cottages strung along the roadside. Something in the quality of light hints at the sea, which lies hidden down a sandy track a mile or so away. The abbey is spread on the plain directly below the village, close by the Abbey Burn. It is startling to find a ruin of this scale in such a remote location. Its gaunt, broken walls tower over the trees and the Hockney-green fields of cattle in which it sits. On my arrival, on a summer morning of torrential rain and fitful sun, a gusty wind washed through the trees around the walls. The sense of seclusion was profound. By contrast, when the royal party arrived, horses were lathered and travellers exhausted, their nerves and tempers frayed.

Modern visitors step through a door in the outer wall and find themselves on an immaculate lawn, in what would have been the western nave. The foundations of the long-gone nave, chapel, chapter house and living quarters rise out of the green sward, in low stone walls and stumps. The soaring façades of the eastern transept and presbytery, and their rounded Romanesque and pointed Gothic windows, are but a hint of the abbey's former grandeur. In its heyday it could boast of the earliest Gothic design in the country.

Beyond the cloister is the chapter house, with its intricately carved entrance and flanking windows, and flagged floor with pillar stumps.

Surrounding the main abbey are the remains of monastic buildings –
a 'warming room', where frozen monks could huddle by the one fire
allowed to them, a refectory, novices' room and latrines. At the eastern
edge of the grounds is a graveyard, its headstones reaching as far as the
abbey ruins. There can be few more tranquil resting places.

In the main abbey, the remnants of the quarters where Mary spent
her last night in Scotland are on the western range. They sat above a
row of barrel-vaulted cellars that had formerly been cells for lay
brothers. The commendator's apartments, where Mary slept, stand
open to the sky, overhung by trees. Here, Mary wrote a letter that
represented the point of no return. She put it into the hands of John
Beaton, her devoted servant, along with a diamond in the shape of a
heart. Elizabeth had once sent this jewel to Mary, 'as a pledge of
amity and good will'. Mary instructed Beaton to take it to Elizabeth
himself. She inscribed the letter, 'From Dundrenan', and its tone of
lament and anger is still resonant.

> You are not ignorant, my dearest sister, of great part of my misfor-
> tunes, but these which induce me to write at present, have
> happened too recently yet to have reached your ear. I must there-
> fore acquaint you briefly as I can, that some of my subjects whom
> I most confided in, and had raised to the highest pitch of honour,
> have taken up arms against me, and treated me with the utmost
> indignity.
>
> By unexpected means, the Almighty Disposer of all things
> delivered me from the cruel imprisonment I underwent; but I
> have since lost a battle, in which most of those who preserved
> their loyal integrity fell before my eyes.
>
> I am now forced out of my kingdom, and driven to such straits
> that, next to God, I have no hope but in your goodness. I beseech
> you, therefore, my dearest sister, that I may be conducted to your
> presence, that I may acquaint you with all my affairs.
>
> In the meantime, I beseech God to grant you all heavenly bene-
> dictions, and to me patience and consolation, which last I hope
> and pray to obtain by your means.

To remind you of the reasons I have to depend on England, I send back to its queen this token [the jewel] of her promised friendship and assistance.

Your affectionate sister,

M.R.

Meanwhile, Herries had sent a note to the Deputy Governor of Carlisle, requesting permission for his queen to land in England and take refuge there. Alarmed that Moray would catch up with her, Mary did not wait for an answer to either missive.

And so to the coast. On the afternoon of 16 May 1568, where the Abbey Burnfoot meets the sea, known as Port Mary Cove, a fishing boat awaited the queen, her companions and the tide. The track to Burnfoot is narrow and rutted. The final stretch runs through a Ministry of Defence firing range, where a sign advises visitors to keep out when flags are flying or lights displayed. The road ends in sand dunes and marram grass, and beyond their shelter is a beach of fat, sea-smoothed pebbles. In the distance, the Solway Firth stretches flat and grey to Cumbria. To the west is a line of wind turbines.

The river mouth has cut a deep defile as it enters the sea, and at high tide the gully can be twelve feet deep. This was more than sufficient for a boat big enough to carry a queen and her twenty or so attendants. These included Livingston, Fleming, George and Willy Douglas, and Herries.

Clattering over the pebbles towards the woodland that fringes the beach, I looked for the rocks on which it is said Mary's followers knelt as they pleaded with her not to leave for England. They knew – as should she – that Elizabeth would not, and could not, be her saviour. As they pointed out, and probably not for the first time, the history of Scottish kings on English soil did not end happily: James I had been taken prisoner, and her own father had baulked at meeting Henry VIII at York for fear of capture.

Later, Mary was honest enough to admit that her 'best friends' and allies, Lord Herries in particular, had begged her to reconsider.

They urged that at the very least she change course for France, where she had friends, relatives and an income as dowager queen. If she headed for England, even though she was to spend her first night at a house of one of Herries' friends in Workington in Cumberland, she would be viewed as the enemy. By contrast, if she stayed in Scotland, she could rally support and once again challenge her usurper. The same was possible among her French Catholic relatives. England, on the other hand, represented a dead end.

For Mary, though, the fatal decision had already been taken, and no-one could persuade her otherwise. Not even a dramatic final dash by Archbishop Hamilton could sway her. As she rode into the water for the boat, he plunged into the river, grabbing the bridle of her horse and imploring her 'not to trust her person in England'. It made no difference. As she embarked, she was confident that she would be back in Scotland in a matter of weeks at the head of a French or English army.

It has been said that during the four-hour crossing Mary suddenly asked the skipper to sail instead for France, but the tide by then was against them. If true, the consequences of her swithering were to be dismal. It might have been better if she had no last-minute intimation of the terrible error she was making.

For those, like me, who wish she had heeded the good counsel of her advisors, Port Mary Cove is a mournful place, haunted by 'what ifs'. At the moment of departure, Mary rashly ignored those who had her best interests at heart, her judgement yet again deserting her. Only she can be blamed for this dreadful miscalculation, and the years of captivity that followed.

Chapter 33

'No luck ever blessed him who hated Mary Stuart'

How many verdicts have been delivered on Mary, Queen of Scots? Was she personally responsible for the calamities that made her reign, and her country, so dangerously unstable? Was her return blighted even before her homecoming? Did she court disaster by never learning enough about Scotland to understand how to rule it?

In her own time, and in the centuries since, she has been variously viewed as entirely innocent of blame in her misfortunes, or guilty, not merely as accessory to murder but of terrible judgement and miscalculations. Some who doubt her part in murder nevertheless believe she failed in her primary role as a queen, to govern wisely and maintain stability. Many see her as a hapless victim of misogyny and the ruthless machinations of deadly opportunists. Others think she floats somewhere between all of this, neither blameless nor culpable, inhabiting the legal limbo known in Scotland as Not Proven.

Historians and writers have usually formed their views about her before they set pen to paper. At the outset I was far from certain, and even now am baffled by her sometimes erratic and inexplicable acts. Yet I found that following closely in her footsteps across Scotland, standing in the great halls, chambers and grounds of the castles and palaces where she lived adds a dimension to her story that, if not precisely tangible, offers a raw, three-dimensional glimpse of what her world was like that goes beyond the documentary evidence. The reminders of warfare and the scale of fortifications and security which surrounded her at every step – not to mention the hundreds of armed guards who accompanied her on the road – are the kitchen-sink realism of her day. The ostentatious splendour of aristocratic and royal residences was merely a political *trompe l'oeil*, a flimsy veil over the stark truth that these were intensely dangerous times, when every guest might be an assassin.

The question of Mary's reign and its failures is so closely bound up with the country's ruling class that it is almost impossible to make a positive case for one side without damning the other. One party, be it the queen or the Earl of Moray or her mercurial supporters, cannot emerge from analysis with their image entirely intact except at the expense of others.

Stefan Zweig wrote: 'No luck ever blessed him who hated Mary Stuart, and those who loved her were consigned to an even more terrible end.' This operatic summation shows how much myth has grown around her. Zweig's conclusion is fatalistic, as if laws greater than those by which humans are usually governed created a pattern around Mary that damned all in her train. It is a sweeping state-ment, spoiled simply by being untrue. Arguably the most pernicious enemy she faced – often without knowing it – was Sir William Cecil, and no bad luck befell him. From his position behind the English throne, even before Mary's homecoming, he was pulling strings among Scottish lords while pouring poison into the ear of his monarch; latterly he ensnared the captive Scottish queen into a fatal conspiracy that sealed her fate. His sole motivation regarding Scotland was to bring about Mary's destruction, thereby protecting Elizabeth and the Protestant order. The question is to what extent he would have succeeded without the enthusiastic support of her disaf-fected court. Cross-border alliances between the nobles and the English during Mary's reign created a network of tunnels beneath her feet, which would one day bring her crashing down.

Mary's personal flaws are commonly seen as her Achilles' heel. She could be enchanting, but also headstrong. She was a poor judge of character, and a bad picker of men. When she married Darnley, it seemed as if she was driven more by lust and resentment at Elizabeth's quixotic demands than by cool calculation. When low, as she frequently was in the latter years of her reign, the depth of her misery is reminiscent of clinical depression. Yet she could also be dauntless; timid she was not. It does appear, however, that she had moments of panic and irrationality. Quite probably the terror of events that began with Rizzio's murder shook her to the core. Allied with episodes of life-threatening illness, which left her weak and anxious, she found herself assailed on all sides, including by her own health. In this state, she was desperate for someone on whom she could lean. That she chose the Earl of Bothwell says as much about the nature of the factions at court as it does about her lack of judgement. If he was her best chance of prevailing against her foes, how intimidating must they have seemed?

It is tempting to see Mary as fatally undermined by Darnley's self-aggrandising behaviour, from which the rest of her misfortunes flowed. Yet she willingly chose him as her husband, and her mishandling of his introduction to court, her heedlessness of the impact on her lords of having a young man like him set above them, was nobody's doing but hers. The damage Darnley did to her, and the country, contradicts the assumption – which Mary held – that a female ruler needs a spouse to assist in upholding her authority. In this Elizabeth was more astute. And in Mary's blatant favouritism towards David Rizzio, which froze out her inner circle, she was also found wanting in personal dignity and political perception. Indeed, in many aspects of her rule, even before it began to crumble, Mary lacked judiciousness. It is hard to avoid the conclusion that even at the high point of her career, before her secretary's killing, she was still capable of behaving like a spoilt child who believes she can do no wrong.

Among the gaps in her armour was someone on whose advice she could rely, a person who would insist on being heard, even when she wanted rashly to follow her instincts. Instead she was surrounded by many who were waiting to pounce. Her position was extraordinarily isolated. Had Marie de Guise been alive to guide her, tragedy might have been averted. The same could be said had she married into a family versed in Scottish affairs yet not consumed by personal ambition.

This is not to exonerate her nobles. There were moments when the violent infighting around Mary, the jostling for supremacy, the lying, deceit and treachery, and of course the killing, are breathtaking. At almost every turn, Mary was betrayed and conned, undermined and traduced. In certain cases, the motives of her foes are understandable. The Earl of Huntly, as King of the North, was outraged that she made no move to reverse the Reformation. He could scarcely credit that she rejected his support even though between them they might swiftly have restored the old order. The Earl of Moray often behaved reprehensibly, yet in his pursuit of power he was also honouring the country's deeply held beliefs as well as his own. His Protestant credentials, unlike those of the venal Morton and other expeditious converts, arose from genuine conviction. And while there was much faith and hope about his methods, though very little charity, he was a true believer. He was also steely, rational and consistent.

Mary, it seems, greatly underestimated the country she was born to rule. Worse, she appears not to have tried to understand it. Her homecoming promised so much, and yet on her arrival she was already a misfit. Jenny Wormald's contention that she never wanted to return at all, and had no interest in running the country, is persuasive. Raised in the hothouse of the French court, she had absorbed the tone and entitlement of her autocratic Guise relatives. The absolute rule of the French monarchy was foreign to the more nuanced situation in Scotland, where the monarch's position was less imperial and, ostensibly at least, more consensual.

This much Mary seemed to appreciate, as demonstrated by her reluctance to challenge the religious status quo, even though it had no legal foundation. Was Mary's apparently relaxed attitude the result of deliberate restraint and respect for a decision taken before her return? Or was it the assurance that, so long as she could continue to practise her own faith, to which she felt entitled, it did not matter that she would stand out as an anomaly amid a nation of Calvinists?

If that is the case, then in this respect she was like her mother, who, for all her foresight, also misjudged the feelings of the Scots. When Marie de Guise flooded the country and her household with the French, as a bulwark against the religious reformers, she appeared untroubled by the friction this would cause.

The people of Scotland welcomed Mary with open arms on her return, and her story need not have descended into mayhem and murder. Yet perhaps even the Scots themselves, with their swiftly changing attitudes, did not fully know what they expected or wanted of her. Compared to the royal circles in which Mary moved in France, it was a threadbare country. The French peasantry were also poor, but the ruling elite was fabulously rich. In Scotland, some nobles had abundant wealth, and others clung on by their finger-nails, living on credit, favours and expectations. Hence their suscep-tibility to the offer of lucrative rewards from other nations, notably France and England.

There were many Catholics in Scotland throughout Mary's reign, but by its end all hope of a religious U-turn had faded. The Mary who stepped onto the quayside at Leith in 1561 might have been an emissary from another world. She represented old Europe, with its Catholic powerhouses, under the watchful eye of the ever-vigilant Pope. More importantly, and more worryingly, she also represented old Scotland.

The castles, palaces and tower houses in which she lived were built and updated in the image of her great-grandfather James III, her grandfather James IV and her father James V. The presence of all three was pervasive, but their era was gone. Since Mary had no intention, initially at least, of overthrowing Protestantism, her refusal to renounce her Catholic faith put her at odds with the shifting mood of the populace. Increasingly, she was a relic of another age. The Protestant reformers represented the future and modernity. They had thrown off the medieval chains of the Catholic church, which had grown increasingly cumbersome and corrupt by her father's day.

There was a clearer, sharper air in the country, but it had a cutting

edge. Like many converts, the reformers were exceptionally protective of their position, and passionately devout. Writing in the twen-
tieth century, Nicolas Bouvier, from Geneva, the heartland of
Protestant revolution, reflected that Knox 'was more of a patriot and
a Scot than a fanatic'. That is highly debatable. Less easy to counter
is Bouvier's notion that things could perhaps have gone in a different
direction if Mary had been wiser. His opinion of her intellectual
capabilities is low: she was 'muddled, somewhat naive and limited,
and . . . only occasionally able to understand what was really at
stake . . .' More interesting is his certainty that 'with a slightly more
politic head screwed on, she would have been able to conclude a sort
of "edict of Nantes" with John Knox'. The Edict of Nantes, which
was the work of Henri IV of France in 1598, allowed Protestants
their rights within a largely Catholic country. Conceivably, Mary
might have negotiated a similar arrangement on her arrival, thereby
returning Scotland to the Catholic fold. But this does not take into
account the general mood of the country. There were substantial
swathes of Catholic supporters, but just as many, and arguably even
more, had turned their faces towards Luther, Calvin and their
followers.

It was Mary's misfortune, if that is the right word, to come home
to a country immeasurably altered from the one she left as a child.
The religious ferment and fervour of these decades make it hard to
assess with any certainty who is most at fault. Could anyone in her
position have held back the remorseless progress of Protestantism?
This was a Europe-wide revolution beyond any single monarch's
control. Yet were the Lords of the Congregation wrong in following
their consciences and embracing this more egalitarian, democratic
and potentially republican doctrine?

That Mary recognised the pivotal role of religion is seen in the
way that, once captive in England, she reframed her image as that of
a Catholic martyr. In her dealings with her Scottish subjects, Mary
might have behaved peerlessly, and the outcome remained the same.
She was caught between the rock of religious reform and her claim
to the English throne. Ultimately she died because that claim was

solid. That she never allowed Elizabeth to forget it made her a perpetual threat. For her homeland, so long as Elizabeth remained on the throne this was of secondary importance. Scotland needed a ruler with the guile and gravitas to pull its competing and warring factions together, and to resist pressure from the forces beyond, foremost England and France. It needed someone with qualities of leadership, political courage and integrity at the helm. While she possessed elements of each, which in less tumultuous times would have sufficed, Mary was too easily thrown off course or wrong-footed. In that sense she was like a tree that was planted in the wrong season, whose roots remain shallow and loose. After the joyous early years of her reign, she began to be tossed this way and that by events beyond her control. Eventually she would be toppled.

To paraphrase the novelist Ford Madox Ford, Mary's is one of the saddest stories ever heard. There have been far less capable and considerably more malign kings and queens who kept their crowns and their heads. She had some remarkable qualities, but they were barely allowed expression in the cauldron of the Reformation, whose forces were ultimately too strong for her. From the start, she was out of her depth. On balance, the disastrous events of her time on the throne can be traced back to poor decisions she made, including those allies she chose blindly to trust. Had she been brought up in Scotland, she might have known enough of how its people thought and lived to stay a step ahead of events; as it was, she was always one behind. Facing down men who had brought about a revolution required equal if not greater strength, and this she did not possess. Mary's homecoming was the definition of tragedy.

Further Reading

There have been countless – some might say too many – books about Mary, Queen of Scots, and the sources to draw on are extensive. Every few years new biographies appear, and more will doubtless follow. Some, however, are essential reading, for their erudition and their literary style. Foremost for me are Antonia Fraser's evergreen *Mary Queen of Scots* and John Guy's superb *My Heart is My Own*. Jenny Wormald's political critique, *Mary Queen of Scots: A Study in Failure*, is unmatched for insight and bite, while Rosalind Marshall's economical and elegant *Queen of Scots* is a succinct but scholarly guide to the key moments and locations in Mary's career. An essential tool has been the peerless *Buildings of Scotland* series, with its precise but readable descriptions of the country's most venerable and interesting properties. Many of the histories and records I have consulted are cited below, but this list is intended more as a guide to books and essays readers might find interesting than an exhaustive bibliography.

Stephen I. Boardman and Julian Goodare, eds, *Kings, Lords and Men in Scotland and Britain, 1300–1625* (Edinburgh: Edinburgh University Press, 2014)

Nicolas Bouvier, *So It Goes: Travel in the Aran Isles, Xian, and places in between*, trans Robyn Marsack (London: Eland, 2019)

Fernand Braudel, *Civilisation and Capitalism, 15th–18th century*, in 3 vols, trans. Siân Reynolds (London: Collins, 1981)

David J Breeze and Gordon Donaldson, *A Queen's Progress* (Edinburgh: HMSO, 1987)

Keith M. Brown, *Noble Society in Scotland: Wealth, Family and Culture, from Reformation to Revolution* (Edinburgh: Edinburgh University Press, 2000)

George Buchanan, *The Tyrannous Reign of Mary Stewart*, trans. and ed. W.A. Gatherer (Edinburgh: EUP, 1958)

Calendar of State Papers relating to Scotland and Mary, Queen of Scots, ed. J Bain et al. (Edinburgh: 1898)

Annie Cameron, *The Correspondence of Mary of Lorraine* (Edinburgh: Scottish History Society, 1927)

Jamie Cameron, *James V: The Personal Rule, 1528–1542* (Edinburgh: John Donald, 2011)

Robert Crawford, *Scotland's Books: The Penguin History of Scottish Literature* (London: Penguin, 2007)

T.M. Devine and Jenny Wormald, eds, *The Oxford Handbook of Modern Scottish History* (Oxford: Oxford University Press, 2012)

Elizabeth Ewan, "'Hamperit in ane hony came": Sights, sounds and smells in the medieval town', in Edward J. Cowan and Lizanne Henderson, eds, *A History of Everyday Life in Medieval Scotland 1000–1600* (Edinburgh: Edinburgh University Press, 2011)

Antonia Fraser, *Mary Queen of Scots* (London: Folio Society, 2004)

Frances and Joseph Gies, *Scenes of Medieval Life: Life in a Medieval Castle, Life in a Medieval City, Life in a Medieval Village*, 3 vols (London: Folio Society, 2002)

John M. Gilbert, *Hunting and Hunting Reserves in Medieval Scotland* (Edinburgh: John Donald, 1979)

Julian Goodare, *Queen Mary's Catholic Interlude* (Edinburgh: Edinburgh University Press, Innes Review, 1987)

John Guy, *My Heart Is My Own: The Life of Mary Queen of Scots* (London: Fourth Estate, 2004)

John Harrison, *History of the Monastery of the Holy-Rood* (Edinburgh: 1919)

R. A. Houston and W.W. J Knox, eds, *The History of Scotland from the Earliest Times to the Present Day*, Vol. 1 (London: Folio Society, 2006)

L.A.J.R. Houwen, A.A. MacDonald and S.L. Mapstone, eds, *A Palace in the Wild: Essays on Vernacular Culture and Humanism in Late-Medieval and Renaissance Scotland* (Leuven: Peeters, 2000)

Deborah Howard, *Scottish Architecture from the Reformation to the Restoration, 1569–1660* (Edinburgh: Edinburgh University Press, 1995)

Clare Hunter, *Threads of Life* (London: Sceptre, 2019)

Sir Arthur Keith, 'The Skull of Lord Darnley', in *British Medical Journal*, vol. 2, 8 September 1928

John Knox, *The History of the Reformation in Scotland*, trans. and ed. W. Croft Dickinson (Edinburgh, 1949)

Michael Lynch, *The Oxford Companion to Scottish History* (Oxford: Oxford University Press, 2001)

Michael Lynch, *Scotland: A New History* (London: Pimlico, 1992)

Norman MacDougall, *James IV* (East Linton: John Tuckwell, 2001)

Clare McManus, 'Marriage and the Performance of the Romance Quest' in L.A.J.R. Houwen et al., *A Palace in the Wild* (2000)

Neil Millar, 'Mary Queen of Scots, Golf and the Seton Necklace', in *Through the Green*, the magazine of the British Golf Collectors' Society, June 2015

Rosalind K. Marshall, *Queen of Scots* (Edinburgh: Mercat Press, 1986)

Rosalind K. Marshall, *Virgins and Viragos: A History of Women in Scotland from 1080 to 1980* (London: Collins, 1983)

Maureen M. Meikle, *The Scottish People, 1490–1625* (Great Britain, Lulu.com, 2013)

James Melville of Halhill, *Memoirs of His Own Life* (Edinburgh, 1827)

Sue Mowat, *The Port of Leith: Its History and Its People* (Edinburgh: Forth Ports PLC, in association with John Donald, 2001)

Claude Nau, *Memorials of the Reign of Mary Stewart*, ed. J Stevenson (Edinburgh, 1883)

David Parkinson, ' "A Lamentable Storie": Mary Queen of Scots and the Inescapable *Querelle des Femmes*', in L.A.J.R. Houwen et al., *A Palace in the Wild* (Leuven: Peeters, 2000)

Records of the Parliaments of Scotland to 1707, Keith M. Brown, Alastair J. Mann and Roland J. Tanner, eds (University of St Andrews, https://www.rps.ac.uk)

Graham Robb, *The Debatable Land: The Lost World Between Scotland and England* (London: Picador, 2018)

Joseph Robertson, *Inventaires de la Royne d'Ecosse, Douairiere de France, 1556–1569: Catalogues of the Jewels, Dresses, Furniture, Books and Paintings of Mary Queen of Scots, 1556–1569* (Edinburgh: Bannatyne Club, 49, 1863)

William Robertson, *The History of Scotland during the Reigns of Queen Mary and King James VI till his Succession to the Crown of England* (London: 1759)

Margaret Sanderson, *Mary Stewart's People* (Edinburgh: Mercat Press, 1987)

Walter Scott, *Chronicles of the Canongate* (London: Penguin Classics, 2003)

Walter Scott, *The Abbot* (Edinburgh: Edinburgh University Press, 2000)

Robert Stedall, *The Challenge to the Crown: The Struggle for Influence in the Reign of Mary Queen of Scots 1542–1567* (Leicester: Book Guild Ltd, 2012)

Agnes Strickland, *Letters of Mary Queen of Scots and Documents Connected with her Personal History*, 2 vols. (London: 1842–43)

Alice Taylor, *The Shape of the State in Medieval Scotland, 1124–1290* (Oxford: Oxford University Press, 2016)

Alison Weir, *Elizabeth, the Queen* (London: Pimlico, 1998)

Alison Weir, *Mary, Queen of Scots and the Murder of Lord Darnley* (London: Jonathan Cape, 2003)

Kate Williams, *Rival Queens: The Betrayal of Mary, Queen of Scots* (London: Hutchinson, 2018)

Jenny Wormald, *Mary Queen of Scots* (Edinburgh: Birlinn, 2018)

Jenny Wormald, *Lords and Men in Scotland: Bonds of Manrent 1442–1603* (Edinburgh: John Donald, 1985)

Stefan Zweig, *The Queen of Scots* (London: Cassell, 1987)

Index